Teaching Creative Writing in Canada

Teaching Creative Writing in Canada maps the landscape of Creative Writing programmes across Canada. Canada's position, both culturally and physically, as a midpoint between the two major Anglophone influences on Creative Writing pedagogy—the UK and the USA—makes it a unique and relevant vantage for the study of contemporary Creative Writing pedagogy.

Showcasing writer-professors from Canada's major Creative Writing programmes, this collection considers the climate-crisis, contemporary workshop scepticism, curriculum design, programme management, prize culture, grants and interdisciplinarity. Each chapter concludes with field-tested writing advice from many of Canada's most influential professors of fiction, poetry, creative nonfiction and drama.

This authoritative volume offers an important national perspective on contemporary and timeless issues in Creative Writing pedagogy and their varied treatment in Canada. It will be valuable to other creative teachers and practitioners, those with an interest in teaching and learning a creative art and anyone working on cultural and educational landscapes.

Darryl Whetter is Professor of English Literature and Creative Writing at Université Sainte-Anne, Canada. He is the author of four books of fiction and three poetry collections, including the climate-crisis novel *Our Sands* (2020). He is also the editor of *The Best Asian Short Stories 2022* (2023) and *Teaching Creative Writing in Asia* (2021).

Routledge Studies in Creative Writing
Series Editors: Graeme Harper (Oakland University, USA) and Dianne Donnelly (University of South Florida, USA)

Strategies of Silence
Reflections on the Practice and Pedagogy of Creative Writing
Edited by Moy McCrory and Simon Heywood

Theories and Strategies for Teaching Creative Writing Online
Edited by Tamara Girardi and Abigail G. Scheg

Creative Writing Scholars on the Publishing Trade
Practice, Praxis, Print
Edited by Sam Meekings and Marshall Moore

Teaching Creative Writing in Asia
Edited by Darryl Whetter

Depersonalization and Creative Writing
Unreal City
By Matthew Francis

Digital Storytelling and Ethics
Collaborative Creation and Facilitation
By Amanda Hill

Teaching Creative Writing in Canada
Edited by Darryl Whetter

For more information about this series, please visit: https://www.routledge.com/Routledge-Studies-in-Creative-Writing/book-series/RSCW

Teaching Creative Writing in Canada

Edited by
Darryl Whetter

LONDON AND NEW YORK

First published 2025
by Routledge
4 Park Square, Milton Park, Abingdon, Oxon OX14 4RN

and by Routledge
605 Third Avenue, New York, NY 10158

Routledge is an imprint of the Taylor & Francis Group, an informa business

British Library Cataloguing-in-Publication Data
A catalogue record for this book is available from the British Library

ISBN: 978-1-032-61410-6 (hbk)
ISBN: 978-1-032-61412-0 (pbk)
ISBN: 978-1-032-61414-4 (ebk)

DOI: 10.4324/9781032614144

Typeset in Sabon
by codeMantra

For our students, our teachers

"In a sense, we haven't got an identity until somebody tells our story. The fiction makes us real."

—Robert Kroetsch

Contents

Contributors

Angie Abdou has published seven books and co-edited *Writing the Body in Motion* and *Not Hockey*, collections of critical essays on Canadian Sport Literature. Her sport novel *The Bone Cage* was a Canadian Broadcasting Corporation Canada Reads finalist. Her two memoirs on youth sport hit the Canadian best-seller list. Dr. Abdou is Professor of Creative Writing at Athabasca University and a nationally certified swim coach. Dr. Abdou was recently awarded the Swim BC Volunteer of the Year.

Gregory Betts is a poet and Professor at Brock University. He is the author of 11 books of poetry, including recent titles such as *Foundry* (Ireland 2021), *The Fabulous Op* (Ireland 2021, with Gary Barwin) and *Sweet Forme* (Australia 2020). His poems have been selected by the SETI Institute to be implanted into the surface of the moon, and he performed at the Vancouver 2010 Olympics, as part of the Cultural Olympiad. He is the author of the award-winning scholarly monographs *Finding Nothing: the VanGardes 1959–1975* and *Avant-Garde Canadian Literature*.

Catherine Black is an Associate Professor at OCAD University in Toronto, where she is the Chair and co-founder of the Creative Writing BFA programme. She has published two collections of prose poetry: *Lessons of Chaos and Disaster* and the Pat Lowther Award-nominated *Bewilderness*. Her lyric nonfiction novella, *A Hard Gold Thread*, was nominated for the ReLit Award, and her first novel, *Blessed Nowhere*, was awarded the Guernica Literary Fiction Prize.

Stephanie Bolster's fifth book of poetry, *Long Exposure*, is forthcoming in 2025. Her first book, *White Stone: The Alice Poems*, won the Governor General's Award. Editor of *The Best Canadian Poetry in English 2008* and *The Ishtar Gate: Last and Selected Poems* by Diana Brebner, and co-editor of *Penned: Zoo Poems*, Prof. Bolster has taught Creative Writing at Concordia University since 2000.

Catherine Bush is the author of the forthcoming story collection *Danger Due To* and the climate-themed novel *Blaze Island* (2020) among other novels.

She is the inaugural Writer-in-Residence at the Rachel Carson Center for Environment and Society in Munich (2024) and was a 2019 Fiction Meets Science fellow at the HWK in Delmenhorst, Germany. An Associate Professor of Creative Writing at the University of Guelph, she was the long-time Coordinator of the Guelph Creative Writing MFA.

Stephen Kimber, ONS, is an award-winning writer, editor, broadcaster and educator. A journalist for more than 50 years, he is the author of 13 books, including two novels and 11 works of nonfiction. He currently writes a weekly column for the *Halifax Examiner* and is a contributing editor for *Atlantic Business Magazine*. Kimber was a professor in the School of Journalism at the University of King's College in Halifax for more than 40 years, serving as its Director for close to a decade. In 2013, he co-founded the King's MFA in Creative Nonfiction programme, and he is currently the Cohort Director of its new MFA in Fiction programme.

David Leach is a Professor of creative nonfiction in the Department of Writing, Faculty of Fine Arts, at the University of Victoria. He has been Department Chair, graduate advisor and Director of the Professional Writing Minor in Journalism & Publishing, and is now the Director of the Digital Storytelling & Social Simulation Lab. He is the author of *Fatal Tide: When the Race of a Lifetime Goes Wrong* (Penguin Canada) and *Chasing Utopia: The Future of the Kibbutz in a Divided Israel* (ECW Press).

Jeanette Lynes directs the MFA in Writing at the University of Saskatchewan, where she is also a Professor of English. Her fourth novel is forthcoming from HarperCollins Canada. Dr. Lynes's third novel, *The Apothecary's Garden* (HarperCollins, 2022), was a finalist for a High Plains Book Award and two Saskatchewan Book Awards. She is also the author of seven collections of poetry, most recently, *Bedlam Cowslip: The John Clare Poems*, winner of the 2016 Saskatchewan Arts Board Poetry Award.

Clem Martini is an award-winning playwright, novelist and screenwriter with over 30 plays and 13 books of fiction and nonfiction to his credit, including the W.O. Mitchell Award-winning *Bitter Medicine: A Graphic Memoir of Mental Illness, The Unravelling* and *The Comedian*. His recently premiered play, *Cantata (Rumours of My Crazy, Useless Life)*, was the 2021 winner of Theatre BC's National Playwriting Competition. He is a Fellow of the Royal Society of Canada and Graduate Program Director for the School of Creative and Performing Arts at the University of Calgary, where he also teaches playwriting.

Robert McGill teaches at the University of Toronto, where he has directed the MA programme in English in the field of Creative Writing. His novels include *The Mysteries*, *Once We Had a Country* and *A Suitable Companion for the End of Your Life*. He has also published two nonfiction books, *The Treacherous Imagination: Intimacy, Ethics, and Autobiographical*

Fiction and *War Is Here: The Vietnam War and Canadian Literature*. In 2018, he was named a winner of the Robert Kroetsch Teaching Award by Canadian Creative Writers and Writing Programs.

Natalie Meisner is an LGBTAIQ2S+ playwright and poet who was born and raised in Mi'kma'ki/the South Shore of Nova Scotia and began her work in the indie theatre and spoken word poetry scenes of Halifax. In addition to studying at the National Theatre School, she holds an MFA in Creative Writing from UBC and a PhD from the University of Calgary. She has published seven full-length books in various genres and was Calgary/Mohkinstsis's fifth Poet Laureate. Dr. Meisner is a full Professor of Creative Writing at Mount Royal University. Her books include *Legislating Love: The Everett Klippert Story* and *Double Pregnant: Two Lesbians Make a Family*.

Olga Stein earned a PhD in English from York University and is a university and college instructor. Before embarking on a PhD, Stein served as the chief editor of the literary review magazine, *Books in Canada*. She contributed some 150 reviews and essays, 60 editorials and numerous interviews to the magazine. Her first collection of poems, tentatively titled *Love Songs: Prayers to Gods, Not Men*, will be published in 2025.

Timothy Taylor is an award-winning and bestselling novelist, journalist and Professor at the University of British Columbia School of Creative Writing. He's the author of five novels, three nonfiction titles and a collection of short stories. His journalism appears regularly in *The New York Times, Walrus, enRoute* and numerous other publications. His latest novel is *The Rise and Fall of Magic Wolf* (Rare Machines 2024). He lives in Vancouver.

Andy Weaver teaches contemporary poetry, poetics and Creative Writing at York University, where he is currently the Chair of the Department of English. He has also served as the Creative Writing Coordinator and the Graduate Creative Writing Diploma Coordinator. In addition to publishing academic articles on contemporary Canadian and American poetry, he has published three books of poetry. His fourth book, *The Loom*, is forthcoming from the University of Calgary Press.

Darryl Whetter was the inaugural Director of the first Creative Writing master's degree in Singapore. He is the author of four books of fiction and three poetry collections, including the climate-crisis novel *Our Sands*, from Penguin Random-House. His essays on contemporary literature and Creative Writing pedagogy have been published by Routledge, Oxford University Press, the National Poetry Foundation (US), *Presses Sorbonne Nouvelle*, etc. He is also the editor of *Teaching Creative Writing in Asia*, from Routledge, and *The Best Asian Short Stories 2022*.

Introduction

On Teaching Creative Writing in Canada without Teaching "How to Make Love in a Canoe"

Darryl Whetter

Like all countries, Canada is both unique and not. Yes, both our country and, subsequently, our literature and teaching are informed by seemingly distinct geographic and cultural influences. Physically, aquatically, Canada has more oceanic coastline than any other country ("Countries"), what with our Atlantic, Pacific *and* Arctic coasts, as well as the highest number of lakes per country ("Which"). Canada's pockets of urbanity and population density are sprinkled throughout the second largest country in the world (Saunders), giving us one of the lowest national population densities (O'Neill), a fact learned quickly by any writer attempting a national tour. In one of its many valuable if not commiserative how-to articles, the publicly funded Ontario book site *Open Book* counsels authors, "You can't hit every city on your book tour (and that's okay)" (Bandukwala). What stories, songs and language, the 16 Canadian writer-professors gathered here wonder, does this landscape coax and/or require?

Prolific Canadian writer Pierre Berton appears to have liked, deservedly or not, taking credit for the line, "A Canadian is somebody who knows how to make love in a canoe" (McKillop 151). The writer-professors here, predominantly from Canadian master's Creative Writing[1] programs and from major cities like Toronto, Montréal, Vancouver, Calgary and Halifax, may feel no more connected to canoes than our international readers, yet we novelists, playwrights, memoirists and poets might appreciate, but maybe also resent, that prolific historian and journalist Berton accepted credit for a line, including in the *Oxford Dictionary of Quotations* (Francis), which his biographer Brian McKillop (et al.) suggests wasn't fully deserved (McKillop 151). The Canadian writer-professors gathered here—not quite for the first time (see Dunlop et al.) but certainly most definitively and thoroughly—clearly aren't going to offer students or fellow writers or instructors advice on canoeing (or lovemaking), but this collection is, in addition to addressing contemporary concerns about workshop efficacy and timeless issues in pedagogy for the creative arts, I hope, refreshingly pragmatic. Gone, blessedly, are the days Stephanie Vanderslice's *Rethinking Creative Writing* laments when "professors who believe that showing up for a vigorous three-hour workshop and an hour at the bar afterward is enough" (Chapter 1).

DOI: 10.4324/9781032614144-1

To forgive a nearly 30-year-old television reference with a 130-year-old one from theatre, this volume is in part pitched for fellow CW learners, instructors, scholars and practitioners who, like George Bernard Shaw's Captain Bluntschli, keep an eye on efficacy: "You can always tell an old soldier by the inside of his holsters and cartridge boxes. The young ones carry pistols and cartridges; the old ones, grub" (I.i). More recently, if still distantly, the 1997 *Seinfeld* episode "The English Patient," provides Elaine's relevant critique, "Those sex scenes?! Please. Give me something I can use" (*Seinfeld*). Here, fellow writers, instructors and program leaders is plenty "you can use" on:

How To	*Author(s) and Chapter(s)*
• Fund Your Writing as Nationally Granted University Research	• Whetter, Chapter 2
• Direct an Evolving CW Department or Entire Program	• Leach, Chapter 3 • Lynes, Chapter 4 • Kimber, Chapter 5 • Black, Chapter 9
• Start a New CW MFA Program	• Lynes, Chapter 4 • Kimber, Chapter 5
• Think about the Impact of Literary Prizes on CW Educations, Development and National Literatures	• Stein, Chapter 6
• Replace the Tiny Undergraduate Workshops of Yore with 100+ 'Stadium-Rock' CW Lecture Courses with Several TAs	• Leach, Chapter 3 • McGill, Chapter 7
• Teach Poetry to CW Students Who Think They Aren't Poets	• Weaver, Chapter 8
• Dialogue with Visual and Other Arts and/or Science	• Weaver, Chapter 8 • Black, Chapter 9 • Bolster, Chapter 10 • Taylor, Chapter 13
• Write Better Dialogue (and, Therefore, Characters)	• Martini, Chapter 11
• Embrace the Avant-Garde (Even or Especially If It Might Hurt Your Chances of Publication)	• Betts, Chapter 12
• Write, and Think, across Disciplines	• Weaver, Chapter 8 • Black, Chapter 9 • Bolster, Chapter 10 • Taylor, Chapter 13 • Bush, Chapter 15
• Recognize Writing as Coaching and Learn Writing Instruction from Athletic Coaching	• Abdou, Chapter 14
• Teach Writing the Climate Crisis While Managing Student Despair	• Taylor, Chapter 13 • Bush, Chapter 15
• Transpose Margins and Centres, Especially for LGTBQ+ Writers	• Lynes, Chapter 4 • Meisner, Chapter 16
• Attend to Student Wellness	• Leach, Chapter 3 • McGill, Chapter 7 • Abdou, Chapter 14 • Bush, Chapter 15 • Meisner, Chapter 16

More than 25 years ago, as a graduate student at the University of New Brunswick (incidentally the only major Canadian CW program here without a chapter), I recorded interviews with Indigenous elders for an early (late 1990s) Web publication we entitled "Teachings from the Medicine Wheel." I'm still struck by a comment then from Wolastoqi Elder Imelda Perley, who claimed that of the two major Maritime Indigenous languages my team and I were trying to record, Wolastoqiyik and Mi'kmawi'simk, Wolastoqiyik sounds more riparian, for the more river-dwelling people in what is now the province of New Brunswick, while the Mi'kmawi'simk language sounds more oceanic, originating as it did in what is now the extremely coastal province of Nova Scotia (Whetter, "Teachings"). Like the flow of water, the flow of language can be directed, with good teaching, and directed into literature.

Landscape and language influenced the evolution of a Canada that, shamefully, forcibly replaced its Indigenous culture and development with colonization, first by France then by England. Rather uniquely, Canada retained both those founding colonial strains, beginning—if that's not a naïve or collusive verb ignoring the 8,000ish years prior to European contact—as a bilingual country ("History"). The United States of America, so often our comparator, did not, linguistically at least, found itself on a blended influence of its Spanish, Dutch, French and English colonizers.

Large, officially bilingual and famously multicultural, Canada is a unique landscape for Creative Writing pedagogy, including growing suspicions of the Iowa workshop model. With English monarchs still dominating Canadian currency and, in legal ways like when an elected Canadian Prime Minister can ask the unelected Governor-General to prorogue (i.e., suspend) our democratically elected Parliament, as our two most recent Prime Ministers have done (Harris and Wherry), Canada is far from an English colony but still not completely divorced from England. The other country where I have been a Creative Writing professor, the Republic of Singapore (University of the Arts), is a completely independent country that ended all dependence on the UK, as the newly independent Barbados recently did (McBride).

Canada's status as a midpoint between the USA and the United Kingdom, geographically and, arguably, culturally, marks one of Canada's rare contributions to the global examination of Creative Writing [CW] pedagogy. Risking nationalism and/or armchair sociology, I've always loved the oft-repeated theory that so many Canadian comedians thrive in the US, from Catherine O'Hara to Martin Short to Seth Rogen, because we're geographically and culturally between (and/but not of) the world's two Anglophone colonial powerhouses (Hill). For better or worse, university CW pedagogy remains a predominantly English-language phenomenon. My 2022 Routledge anthology *Teaching Creative Writing in Asia* describes how Spain's otherwise successful *Escuela de Escritores* taught Spanish writers for a decade but "having failed several times to approach different Spanish universities, we have also tried to make an agreement for validation and support of our master course with some British universities" (Whetter 4). The entwining of the English language and CW pedagogy is further illustrated in the smattering of continental European CW courses taught in English, as with one of the few CW master's degrees in Sweden or the CW BFA at the South Gate School of Creative Writing in Denmark (Whetter 4).

The 16 Canadian universities featured here, from our Pacific to Atlantic coasts, confront the inheritance of the founding of CW as a discipline within the Anglophone university while also welcoming the multilingual and ESL learners addressed in my recent *Teaching Creative Writing in Asia*. While *Teaching Creative Writing in Canada* is not quite the first anthology to address the national flavour of Canadian CW pedagogy, it is the most definitive. Contributors Professor Stephanie Bolster, Catherine Bush and myself were delighted to appear alongside several other university CW profs in *Writing Creative Writing*, co-edited by three other Canadian CW-prof colleagues, though that 2018 Canadian anthology did not restrict its teaching focus to university degree programs (Dunlop et al.).

While Mark McGurl's Harvard University Press *The Program Era: Postwar Fiction and the Rise of Creative Writing* is right to point out the contemporary rise in the popularity of post-secondary CW degrees (25), Canada bucks one popularity trend and leads others. Where France, with at least three doctoral programs in CW, now has more CW doctoral programs than Anglophone Canada does (just two, at the University of Calgary and the University of New Brunswick), these examples from Spain, Sweden and Denmark, combined with the fact that Ireland's first CW postgraduate degree was only offered in 1997–1998 to suggest that (Trinity), in an admittedly sweeping generalization, CW in continental Europe has not been the campus rage that it is in Anglophone countries excluding Ireland. As detailed more fully in my first chapter, the popularity of CW in Australia denies any Anglo-American-centric claims that CW is only popular in England and North America. With legal and historical ties to England, the "longest unprotected border in the world" tying us geographically to the USA (a fact cited in everything from a *New York Times* essay on the increasing murkiness between literary fiction and nonfiction (Schiff), to joint government documents ("International"), to research in surgery (Gelfand)) and a comparable postcolonial/Indigenous reckoning to that in Australia, Canadian CW pedagogy is both relevant and unique for timeless issues in what I still contend is one of the major pedagogical revolutions in, well, the history of the university. While most chapters here join the growing chorus of CW profs and veterans suspicious of the efficacy and inclusiveness of the writing workshop (Chavez, Díaz, Mura, Naga and McGill, Nguyen, Poddar, Salesses, Watkins), and David Leach and Robert McGill recount the replacement of the intimate workshop of fewer than 20 students with stadium-rock CW lecture courses of around 100, but what other university discipline foregrounds peer learning for undergrads like CW has and does? As I often regularly teach undergraduate literature courses as well, I'll never forget how illuminating it was, and how skewering, when I first read Jonathan Franzen's Denise Lambert, a university dropout who becomes a successful chef, lamenting "working hard on papers that only a professor ever saw" (379).

Where Canada is a midpoint between the UK and the USA, my four recent years directing the first CW master's degree in Singapore, in a degree then conferred by Goldsmiths, University of London (Goldsmiths), found me in a midpoint between the UK and an Australia where, as my first chapter here points out, a comparable postcolonial country has at least 8.5 times the number of CW doctoral programs compared to Canada despite having a smaller Anglophone population. The vibrant CW educations in Australia and New Zealand combine with those growing in Asia (in Singapore, the Philippines, Hong Kong, China, India; see Whetter 3–5) to welcome this examination of post-secondary CW pedagogy that is neither American nor English, while simultaneously being postcolonial, contemporary and global.

With one of if not the highest percentage of post-secondary graduates in the world, (Friesen; "Most") and now as the third-most popular destination country for international university students (Rutka; Singhal), Canada is, by design, accident or both, also a relevant laboratory for any examination of twenty-first-century tertiary education. With the first CW classes offered in Canada as long ago as 1939 (van Herk 4), Canada has long been a global voice in what was originally a pedagogical revolution—the belief that Humanities students themselves should be able to write, and not just *write about*, fiction, poetry, drama, etc. as a field of study. Terry Eagleton describes the first literary revolution in the Anglophone university, that of being able to study literature in English, not Greek or Latin: "In the early 1920s it was desperately unclear why English was worth studying at all; by the early 1930s it had become a question of why it was worth wasting your time on anything else" (27). While my own first chapter describes how the once-revolutionary field of English has not always been supportive of the next revolutionary wave—Creative Writing—McGurl is right to describe how CW courses and degrees address "insatiable student demand—that simultaneously progressive and consumerist value" (94). The novelist in me recognizes that I might sound naïve in saying that our new anthology should be both national and universal, yet my 25 years of teaching CW at five different universities, four in Canada and one in Singapore, convince me annually that hope is one requisite fuel in teaching.

Teaching and writing are the dual passions here, as partly illustrated by how almost all chapters close with some comments on student writing each prof finds herself making both regularly but subjectively, each prof's version of what Shannon Sandford et al. recognize as "writing-as-knowing" (6). As one of my own stock comments is "Get your hands dirty," it's time this introduction rolls up its sleeves and introduces the superb work of these Canadian writer-profs of geographical, pedagogical and gender diversity.

Part I, "Workshopping the (Canadian) Workshop" sets the national scene, one in which we, too, question the workshop model, before more specialized additional chapters. The first of my two chapters, revised and reprinted once again, is a bit like my version of a Modernist long poem, evolving as both its author and the world does. In my specific look at Anglophone Canada's seeming disinterest in doctoral CW programs, I provide some national history, detailing, for example, the doubling of Canada's master's CW programs in the first decade of this century but also Canada's dual (and arguably schismatic) interest in both CW MFAs and MAs in English and Creative Writing, as well as the similarities and differences in those degrees. My second chapter looks at Canadian writer-professors and postgraduate CW students in the wider context of nationally funded university research. In a scenario I find "far too Canadian," to quote the title of a song by Canadian band Spirit of the West, Canada's publicly funded Social Sciences and Humanities Research Council of Canada annually awards hundreds of millions of public-dollar research grants which could, but almost never do, fund the fiction, creative nonfiction, poetry and plays or screenplays of Canada's writer-profs. That scrutiny of national grant ledgers also addresses one sad national iteration of a global teaching phenomenon: the continued replacement of reasonably paid tenure-track and tenured teaching positions with adjunct teachers who provide superb teaching value to universities in exchange for precarious and exploitative single-course contracts.

Narratives loving change as they do, **Professor David Leach** writes of eventually chairing the Writing program at the University of Victoria, a program he himself did not finish as an undergrad. Professor Leach also propels this book into the contemporary debate about how the university writing workshop may have discouraged BIPOC writers and/or aesthetics, questioning the inherited wisdom of, for example, the workshopee staying silent during class critique. Reflecting on his role as department chair during a transformative and, read on!, heart-attack inducing time, Leach recounts his and his department's reckoning with Felicia Rose Chavez's *The Anti-Racist Writing Workshop* and Liz Lerman's *Critical Response Process*.

Continuing this trilogy of MFA program management narratives, **Professor Jeanette Lynes**, founding director of Canada's second-youngest CW MFA program, next describes the program highs and lows in the first dozen years of the CW MFA at the University of Saskatchewan. While my own first chapter can appreciate the need some of Canada's CW programs have had to not be managed by English departments and/or critical scholars, Prof. Lynes recounts a kind of institutional homelessness, including during a campus nadir of massive university cuts. Lynes rightly wonders if university CW programs might not be "so 'othered'" within the academy if they were housed in Fine Arts departments. Art on!

One good MFA program origin story follows another here as **Professor Stephen Kimber** describes the doubly unique emergence of Canada's newest CW MFA program, at the University of King's College in Halifax. In a kind of program alchemy, Prof. Kimber and his Journalism colleagues launched a new MFA specializing in creative nonfiction. Storytelling schools, Kimber and others here show us, have their own stories to tell.

I usually tell my students that the pet names we have for our writing projects might be incantations that help them get written. The pet comparison (/elevator pitch) I've always had for this anthology is "the Canadian and slightly more scholarly *MFA vs. NYC*." While Chad Harbach's illuminating *MFA vs. NYC: The Two Cultures of American Fiction* figures here most overtly in our third section, with **Professor Timothy Taylor's** valuable chapter "MFA vs. NYC vs. MBA," I invoke Harbach's crucial American anthology to describe the close of Part 1 for, sadly, somewhat crassly and unavoidably, Harbach's only inclusion of two chapters from one contributor, each with nearly the same title. Where Harbach's teammate Keith Gessen publishes "Money (2006)" and "Money (2014)," we close Part 1 with two different chapters on, in oversimplified terms, some of the economics of writing in Canada and learning to write here. The penultimate work in the landscape gallery that opens the book comes from **Dr. Olga Stein**, who distils her book-length study on the impact of Canada's ecosystem-changing Scotiabank Giller Prize for Fiction on all aspects of CanLit. Stein applies Pierre Bourdieu's concept of "cultural capital" and James English's "economy of prestige" to Canada's literary prize culture, observing increases in prize value and influence at a time when the income of Canadian writers is plummeting (Writers' 3; Degen). Switching from (some aspects of) the economics of CanLit to the new global economics of CW educations, **Professor Robert McGill's** thorough chapter charts the shift in Anglophone university teaching from the tiny writing workshop of 15 or so students to the new pressures for CW to be taught in stadium-rock-style massive lecture courses. Prof. McGill's informed fieldnotes (and how-to guide) invoke similar supersizing pressures at Canada's oldest CW degree program, at the University of British Columbia, while U. Vic's Prof. Leach addresses those same economic pressures in his field marshal's Chapter 3.

Part II, "The Canadian CW Playground: Writing-as-Knowing (in Canada and beyond)," borrows a phrase recurrent in contemporary CW scholarship (Sandford et al.) which even crosses over into Engineering pedagogy (Herman et al.) while also recalling the now-rare 1995 Canadian anthology *Poetry and Knowing*, with its chapters by, among other valuable Canadian contributors, Dr. Don McKay (my graduate CW Poetry prof) and Dr. Jan Zwicky (the graduate CW Poetry prof of **Chapter 8's Andy Weaver** (Lilburn, cf. Almon)). The Ancient Greek dual influence on education and poetics recurs even here as three seemingly different writer-profs at three very different universities—Toronto's massive York University but also its Ontario College of Craft and Design University as well as Montréal's Concordia University—each addresses the seemingly endless intersections of ekphrastic writing. **Dr. Andy Weaver**, Coordinator of the Graduate Diploma in Creative Writing and Chair of English at the enormous York University recounts, with admirably good spirits, trying to teach a large undergraduate class to write poetry after a semester studying fiction and creative nonfiction with other lecturers. Grappling with poetry's dual "image problem" and "imagery problem," Weaver reminds his students, and now us, that poetry is play.

Similarly, **Catherine Black**, across Toronto at OCAD University, channels not just ekphrasis but the pioneering role that Fine Arts had in admitting art-making into university curricula with—and what an early pedagogical revolution it was—peer critique making our fellow students also our teachers. The inventiveness of Black's urban, performative teaching and assignments nicely aligns writing students with other trained artists while also providing the crucial lesson that writing projects (if not writers) need not "think of the book as the natural end-point of text" when performance and public art spaces abound (or can be made).

Completing this second internal trilogy, one on writing and visual art (/seeing), **Professor Stephanie Bolster**, from Concordia University in Montréal, collapses the layered learning many of we writer-profs go through, replacing an artistic education and maturation we might have stumbled through with clear prompts, invitations and, in her case, art gallery visits to, for example, compress the half-accidental arrivals of many first books with the dense learning opportunities of a graduate writing syllabus. "What one tries to do in an ekphrastic poem," Bolster knows, "is what one tries to do in any poem: to capture something in a way that is faithful to all its facets and addresses both its known and unknown aspects." Yes!

While the ekphrastic trio of Weaver, Black and Bolster certainly do not ignore sonic arts, sound poetry and other appeals to the ear, naturally one of our two playwrights, the University of Calgary's **Professor Clem Martini**, invites all to listen to create. Resonant with our creative nonfiction writers here (Leach, Kimber, Meisner, Taylor, Martini himself and more), this playwright's advice for dialogue recalls writing's fundamental conversation with versions of the real: what begins as true, what might be true and maybe even what needs to be true.

Professor Gregory Betts, recent president of the Association of Canadian College and University Teachers of English, completes our sensory-lab second section with his requisitely avant-garde call for more avant-garde creation in Canada's CW courses and classrooms. To love art is, at times, to love its surprises and disruptions. No other published writer and CW prof I've ever met dares ask, as Betts compellingly does, whether teaching our students to publish might not be the big win we think, and claim, it is.

The third and final section of this anthology, **Letters Home**, begins, as most new sections of a text should, with a great title. **Professor Timothy Taylor's** "MFA vs. NYC vs. MBA" kicks off a closing section that reckons with CW educations both within and beyond the workshop and/or text. Prof. Taylor's background in commerce, including his earning an MBA en route to helping award students MFAs in Canada's oldest CW MFA program (at the Univ. of British Columbia), and also his lifetime of freelance journalism, including for *The New York Times* and Canada's *The Walrus*, gives him, he self-diagnoses, a "thinker-for-hire" mentality he recounts trying to replicate for his students.

If hope is one requisite fuel for teaching, surely surprise is another. While not all writing advice remains relevant across a writer's career, I'll always agree with Eudora Welty's line, "If you haven't surprised yourself, you haven't written" (qtd. in Burroway 214). Many if not all of us collected here, and certainly, Taylor, Kimber, myself, Natalie Meisner and Catherine Bush, did not set out to become teachers. When teaching a little as part of our own postgraduate educations then to stay alive when the scholarships ended, others may have shared my delighted surprise at how rewarding teaching can be. My esteemed colleagues probably did not, at least save **Professor Angie Abdou**, have the same soul-shocker of a surprise that only in teaching writing did I discover inside myself a coach. What for me has been a metaphor or association, admittedly one for a quarter of a century, is now a substantial focus, of research and practice, for novelist, memoirist and sports literature scholar Prof. Abdou. Coaching swimming, Dr. Abdou reveals with practical insight (e.g., "train to train" versus "train to compete"), reinvigorates her coaching of writing.

With her career attention to the impact of power on stories, lives and civilizations, Margaret Atwood is right once again when pointing out, as **Catherine Bush**'s clear-eyed chapter also does, that "It's not climate change, it's everything change" (Barnett). Long-time director of the CW MFA program at the University of Guelph, Bush dares to address not so much the elephant in the planetary room as the fact that the room, like much of Canada's wildlands have recently been, is on fire.

As anthologies are conversations, it's fitting that we close with an interview, and from another of our playwrights. LGBTAIQ2S+ **Professor Natalie Meisner** is proudly gender- and genre-fluid, writing plays devoted to the last Canadian jailed for homosexuality and African-Canadian sprinter Marjorie Turner Bailey, once the fastest woman in the world, as well as poetry collections and children's books. In her interview about the vitality of "liveness" in teaching, performance and writing, Prof. Meisner chronicles how valuable bravery and acceptance are to creation and learning.

Books often contain the seeds of others, so instead of closing with a list of what's missing, I prefer to think ahead to the Canadian CW teaching stories a second volume might include a few years from now. However vibrant CW is and has always been in Canada, no chapter here provides a post-mortem for the demise of the Canadian Creative Writers and Writing Programs, Canada's national organization comparable to America's massive Associated Writers and Writing Programs, the international Creative Writing Studies Organization or—we quote their journal and have also presented at their annual conference—the Australasian Association of Writers and Writing Programs. Most if not all of us presented at the biannual then annual conferences of the CCWWP until its seemingly abrupt suspension around 2019 (CCWWP). Some CCWWP former board members must have stories to tell. More universally, where chapters from Lynes and Meisner mention the neuro-diverse, those learners and writers will next enable and require the margin-centre transpositions that gender, BIPOC and LGTBQ+ writers and learners have already enacted in the contemporary university and especially CW courses. Canada's Indigenous CW writer-profs like Frances Koncan, Jodan Abel, Joshua Whitehead, Shannon Webb-Campbell, Armand Ruffo and Billy-Ray Belcourt could launch another valuable Canadian, international and Indigenous anthology. My other solicitations that didn't result in chapters *this time* included to the University of Guelph's fascinating International Institute for Critical Studies in Improvisation. Creative Writing pedagogy is creativity pedagogy, and I for one would love to see some of the research in improvisation, including with soundpainting, mapped onto a writing that can seem like the opposite of improvisation until, of course, it isn't! Lastly, I for one am stunned that CW pedagogy remains so removed from university Acting programs: campus writers and actors are character and voice professionals who barely interact. Our future teaching stories will hopefully be even more inclusive. Blessedly, not lamentably, these are (teaching) stories for another day.

Note

1 In the grammar of usage that capitalizes fields of study like History and Psychology, and as former writing prof David Foster Wallace recognizes, the words Creative Writing "are capitalized because they understand themselves as capitalized. Trust me on this" (73). This anthology uses "Creative Writing" to refer to the subject of academic study, where students can take courses or degrees at all post-secondary levels. Lowercase "creative writing" is used to denote the actual act of writing fiction, poetry, drama and/or creative nonfiction, the wordsmithing that can happen inside or outside a university.

Works Cited

Almon, Bert. *Review of Poetry and Knowing: Speculative Essays and Interviews*, edited by Tim Lilburn, *Canadian Book Review Annual Online*, n.d., https://cbra.library.utoronto.ca/items/show/1118.

Barnett, David. "'It's Not Climate Change, It's Everything Change': Sci-Fi Authors Take on the Global Crisis." *The Guardian*, 9 Jul. 2023, https://www.theguardian.com/books/2023/jul/09/climate-change-sci-fi-authors-global-crisis-atwood-mccarthy.

Bandukwala, Manahil. "Book Launch Season, Part One: Being an Author." 25 Aug. 2023, https://open-book.ca/Columnists/Book-Launch-Season-Part-One-Being-an-Author.

Burroway, Janet. *Writing Fiction: A Guide to Narrative Craft*. 10th ed., U. Chicago P, 2019.

Canadian Creative Writers and Writing Programs. "Home." *Canadian Creative Writers and Writing Programs*, n.d., https://ccwwp.ca/.

Chavez, Felicia Rose. *The Anti-Racist Writing Workshop: How to Decolonize the Creative Classroom*. Haymarket, 2021.

"Countries With The Longest Coastline." *World Atlas*, 2023, https://www.worldatlas.com/articles/countries-with-the-most-coastline.html.

Degen, John. "Re: Author Income Stats Post 2018?" Received by Darryl Whetter, 21 Nov. 2023.

Díaz, Junot. "MFA vs. POC." *The New Yorker*, 30 Apr. 2014, www.newyorker.com/books/page-turner/mfa-vs-poc.

Dunlop, Rishma, Daniel Scott Tysdal, and Priscilla Uppal, Eds. *Writing Creative Writing: Essays from the Field*. Dundurn, 2018.

Eagleton, Terry. *Literary Theory: An Introduction*. U of Minnesota P, 2008.

Francis, Daniel. Rev. of *Pierre Berton: A Biography* by Brian McKillop. *The Tyee*, 21 Aug. 2009, https://thetyee.ca/Books/2009/08/21/PierreBertonActivist/.

Franzen, Jonathan. *The Corrections*. Farrar, Straus and Giroux, 2001.

Friesen, Joe. "Census Shows High Rate of Undergraduate and College Education among Canadians, But Complex Trends Lie Behind It." *The Globe and Mail*, 4 Dec. 2022, https://www.theglobeandmail.com/canada/article-census-2021-university-college-graduate/.

Gelfand, Elliot. "In Celebration of our Differences." *The Journal of Thoracic and Cardiovascular Surgery*, vol. 136, no. 2, 2008, pp. 259–66. *National Institutes of Health*, https://doi.org/10.1016/j.jtcvs.2008.03.047.

Goldsmiths, University of London. "LASALLE College of the Arts." 2023, https://www.gold.ac.uk/academic-partnerships/lasalle/.

Harris, Kathleen, and Aaron Wherry. "Parliament Prorogued Until Sept. 23 as Trudeau Government Reels from WE Charity Controversy." 18 Aug. 2020, https://www.cbc.ca/news/politics/liberal-government-trudeau-prorogue-government-1.5690515.

Herman, J.L., Hall, L., Kuzawa, D., Wahlin, L., and Faure, M. "Writing as Knowing: Creative Knowing Through Multiple Messaging Modes in an Engineering Technical Communications Course." *Creative Ways of Knowing in Engineering*, edited by Diana Bairaktarova and Michele Eodice, Springer, 2017, pp. 99–120.

Hill, Mark. "Why Does Canada Produce So Many Comedians?" *Cracked*, 18 Nov. 2021, https://www.cracked.com/article_31813_why-does-canada-produce-so-many-comedians.html.

"History of the *Official Languages Act*." *Government of Canada*, 8 Sept. 2023, https://www.canada.ca/en/canadian-heritage/campaigns/canadians-official-languages-act/history-official-languages-act.html#.

"The International Joint Commission on the Great Lakes." *U.S. Department of State Archive*, n.d., https://1997-2001.state.gov/publications/statemag/statemag_jun98/bom.html.

Lilburn, Tim, editor. *Poetry and Knowing: Speculative Essays and Interviews*. Kingston, ON: Quarry, 1995.

McBride, James. "Queen Elizabeth II Is the Monarch of Fifteen Countries. What Does That Mean?" *Council on Foreign Relations*, 25 Mar. 2022, https://www.cfr.org/in-brief/queen-elizabeth-ii-monarch-fifteen-countries-what-does-mean.

McGurl, Mark. *The Program Era: Postwar Fiction and the Rise of Creative Writing*. Harvard U P, 2009.

McKillop, Brian. *Pierre Berton: A Biography*. 2008. Emblem—McClelland & Stewart, 2010.

"Most Educated Countries 2024." *World Population Review*, n.d., https://worldpopulationreview.com/country-rankings/most-educated-countries.
Mura, David. *A Stranger's Journey: Race, Identity, and Narrative Craft in Writing*. U of Georgia P, 2018.
Naga, Noor, and Robert McGill. "Negotiating Cultural Difference in Creative Writing Workshops." *Pedagogy*, vol. 18, no. 1, 2018, pp. 69–86.
Nguyen, Viet Thanh. "Viet Thanh Nguyen Reveals How Writers' Workshops Can Be Hostile." *New York Times*, 26 Apr. 2017, https://www.nytimes.com/2017/04/26/books/review/viet-thanh-nguyen-writers-workshops.html.
O'Neill, Aaron. "Population density in Canada from 2009 to 2020." *Statista*, 12 Oct. 2023, https://www.statista.com/statistics/271206/population-density-in-canada/.
Poddar, Namrata. "Is 'Show Don't Tell' a Universal Truth or a Colonial Relic?" *Literary Hub*, 20 Sept. 2016, https://lithub.com/is-show-dont-tell-a-universal-truth-or-a-colonial-relic/.
Rutka, Jacob. "The Year Ahead: Education in 2023." *MacLean's*, 6 Dec. 2022, https://macleans.ca/year-ahead/year-ahead-education-international-students-public-school-university/.
Salesses, Matthew. *Craft in the Real World: Rethinking Fiction Writing and Workshopping*. Catapult, 2021.
Sandford, Shannon, et al. "Green Encounters: Critically Creative Inter/Actions with-and-in Ecologies of Crisis." *New Writing: The International Journal for the Practice and Theory of Creative Writing*, vol. 21, no. 1, 11 Jul. 2023, https://doi.org/10.1080/14790726.2023.2223188.
Saunders, Toby. "Top 10 Largest Countries in the World 2023." *BBC: Science Focus*, 18 Jun. 2023, https://www.sciencefocus.com/planet-earth/largest-countries-in-the-world.
Schiff, Stacy. "The Interactive Truth." *New York Times*, 15 June 2005, https://www.nytimes.com/2005/06/15/opinion/the-interactive-truth.html. Op-ed.
Seinfeld. "Elaine's Movie Taste Gets Her in Trouble." Episode aired 13 Mar. 1997; *YouTube*, uploaded by *Seinfeld*, 12 Oct. 2022, https://www.youtube.com/watch?v=c5VluH1BeXo.
Shaw, George Bernard. *Arms and the Man*. Brentano's, 1913. *Project Gutenberg*, 2 Dec. 2023. https://www.gutenberg.org/cache/epub/3618/pg3618-images.html.
Singhal, Anshul. "Canada Has the Third-Largest International Student Population in the World." *Y-Axis Immigration Services*, 10 May 2023, https://www.y-axis.com/news/canada-third-largest-international-student-population/.
Trinity College Dublin. "Creative Writing (M. Phil.)." *University of Dublin*, 31 May 2024, https://www.tcd.ie/courses/postgraduate/courses/creative-writing-mphil/.
van Herk, Aritha. "'Why Should We Forgive Our Enemies?': The Passions and Persuasions of Creative Writing." *The Wascana Review*, vol. 43, no. 1, 2011. https://www.arithavanherk.com/writings/
Vanderslice, Stephanie. *Rethinking Creative Writing in Higher Education: Programs and Practices That Work*. Creative Writing Studies Ser. Kindle ed., Creative Writing Studies, 2012.
Wallace, David Foster. "The Fictional Future." *MFA vs. NYC: The Two Cultures of American Fiction*, edited by Chad Harbach, n+1, 2014, pp. 73–80.
Watkins, Claire Vaye. "On Pandering." *Tin House*, 23 Nov. 2015, https://tinhouse.com/on-pandering/.

Whetter, Darryl, Ed. "Introduction." *Teaching Creative Writing in Asia*, edited by Darryl Whetter, Routledge, 2022, pp. 1–13.

———. "Teachings from the Medicine Wheel." *qwerte*. 1997. [https://www.lib.unb.ca/Texts/QWERTY/Qweb/qwerte/mic_mal] *Internet Archive*. https://web.archive.org/web/20070205095302/https://www.lib.unb.ca/Texts/QWERTY/Qweb/qwerte/mic_mal/.

"Which Country Has the Most Lakes in the World?" *World Atlas*, 2023, https://www.worldatlas.com/articles/which-country-has-the-most-lakes-in-the-world.html.

Writers' Union of Canada. *The Diminishing Returns: Creative Culture at Risk*. The Writers' Union of Canada, 2018.

Part I

Workshopping the (Canadian) Workshop

1 Can'tLit

(Anglophone) Canada's Anomalous Disinterest in Creative Writing Doctoral Programs[1]

Darryl Whetter

Say It Ain't So

English writer Philip Hensher fulfills one core writerly duty—truth-telling—when writing novels about the idiocy of invading Afghanistan (*Mulberry*) or the challenges of monogamy (*King*), and again as a Creative Writing [CW] professor willing to blow the whistle on how vehemently some English literature departments and professors hate writers, writing and writing educations. Hensher laments,

> I learnt that there are people employed by English literature departments who hate literature and would put a stop to it if they could. They talk about literature being subversive and questioning of authority, but once they have admitted creative writing into a department they find that it can't be controlled and they don't like it.
>
> (Wroe)

Despite this palpable hatred, what recent East Anglia master's course director Andrew Cowan calls "scepticism bordering on contempt" (40), Canada's pedagogical *spécialité de la maison* is to house CW programs in university English departments—"the enemies of literature," according to Hensher (*King* 365). Examples from Canadian university programs, professorial hiring, national research funding and my own two decades of work as a Canadian Creative Writing professor who has also taught abroad (in Singapore) demonstrate a similar "hatred" between Canadian professors of English and the CW programs under their majority rule. This national preference for having those who write about literature managing the educations of those who write it has negative aesthetic, political and economic consequences in and beyond Canadian education.

Canada's art historians and musicologists don't design and manage the education of our visual artists and composers, but English profs (who have rarely published books of poetry or fiction, etc. themselves) routinely control the educations of our writers, and with obvious costs to national and personal truth-telling. As indicated in Table 1.1, the number of graduate writing

DOI: 10.4324/9781032614144-3

Table 1.1 Masters' Creative Writing Programmes in English Canada

Pre-2000	*Post-2000*
MA in English and Creative Writing	
University of Calgary	University of Toronto
Concordia University	University of Regina
University of Manitoba	
University of New Brunswick	
University of Windsor	
MFA in Creative Writing	
University of British Columbia	University of Victoria
	University of Guelph
	University of Saskatchewan
	King's University

programs in Canada *doubled* in the 2000s, yet various factors within the Canadian academy (not the internationally popular discipline of CW), find most Canadian writing programs more devoted to the head than the heart and managed, not coincidentally, by English departments. Our writing grads are much more likely to be versed in Elizabethan celibacy or Victorian diarists than what William Faulkner so rightly describes as "the human heart in conflict with itself." I've taught writing for 2.5 decades now, mostly at four Canadian universities, and am worried that—with English professors predominantly calling the shots—Canadian CW programs housed in English departments too easily downplay core writerly skills like social-emotional intelligence, revealing, engaged and accurate dialogue, dramatic tension, comedy and, most notably, plot. In his *Lectures on Literature*, Vladimir Nabokov writes:

> Let us worship the spine and its tingle.... The study of the sociological or political impact of literature [is] for those who are by temperament or education immune to the aesthetic vibrancy of authentic literature, for those who do not experience the telltale tingle between the shoulder blades.
>
> (64)

Canadian CW programs risk downplaying Nabokov's devotion to a spinal "tingle," what with many of Canada's CW programs and funding agencies generally asking writers to be scholars who simply drop the footnotes, while graduate CW education in all major Anglophone countries of comparison values the unique fusion of personal and cultural truth available to the creative writer and her reader. Even this adjacent genre of CW pedagogy can prefer the theoretical to the aesthetic. In the introduction to *The Scholarship of Creative Writing Practice*, the latest (2024) of their three recent anthologies of CW pedagogy, Marshall Moore and Sam Meekings make "an acknowledgment of the growing body of work that challenges those conventions ['of scholarly writing']: scholars such as Candace Spigelman have argued in favour of treating personal reflection as relevant in the academic realm" (7; Cf. Spiegelman).

"Only in Canada, eh? Pity"[2]

The uninformed or hostile managers of Canada's CW programs who ignore student demand, the cost-effectiveness of arts spending and the enormity of Canada's book industry do so at national cost, despite their state funding. According to Joe Friesen, the "postsecondary education reporter" at *The Globe and Mail* (a national newspaper Clement Wallace has summed up as "Canada's newspaper of record" (343)),

> Canada also had a lower share of population with a graduate degree, at just 9.3 per cent, compared with a range of 13 to 15 per cent elsewhere in the G7. A little more than 1 per cent of Canadians have a doctorate, and 8.2 per cent a master's degree.

The Organization for Economic Co-operation and Development's 2019 report *Education at a Glance* shows that Canada's per capita completion rate for PhDs is not even in the global top 29 and that we fall far below the OECD and EU23 averages (14th and 15th place respectively) (248). Canada's low per capita completion of PhDs is regrettable considering our regularly ranking in the top three (usually the top two) countries for the highest per capita undergraduate enrolment (Frisen; Grossman).

Canada's institutional disregard for CW is illustrated by the national lack of interest in capitalizing on our high interest in undergraduate education in general and our ballooning interest in CW masters' degrees in particular. Notably, the doubling of master's CW programs in Canada has not been met here—as it has in other Anglophone countries (save Ireland)—with attendant changes in the number of Canadian doctoral programs in CW. Between an archived page at the Australasian Association of Writing Programs [AAWP] site (Australasian "Category"), the comments on a query post of mine to the Australasian Postgraduate Writers Network Facebook group (a group which receives a link at the Postgraduates page of the AAWP site) (Whetter, "Darryl's"; Australasian) and a few emails with Australian CW professors I've come to know from my AAWP conference presentations, Australia appears to offer 17 PhD programs in CW;[3] English Canada offers just two.

Despite Canada's doubling of CW master's programs and, as noted below and in the next chapter, ample federal scholarship funding for CW PhD students, Canada has just two Anglophone CW doctoral programs, at the universities of Calgary (Faculty of Graduate) and New Brunswick (Department). Why does Australia, with its comparable post-colonial history but a population of 27 million (Australian Bureau), have 8.5 times the number of Anglophone CW PhD programs than Canada, with our population of 40 million (Statistics, "Canada's")? Given Canada's officially bilingual English-French population, Statistics Canada's most recent percentage of 75.5% Anglophones puts the comparator Australian and Anglo-Canadian populations at 27 million and 30 million respectively. Why do these two large countries with the same English monarchs on our currency and postage stamps demonstrate such radically different interests in writing a doctoral dissertation that is a novel instead of one about someone else's novel(s)? My answer: Canadian English (i.e., literature) departments.

The United States also shames Anglo-Canada's doctoral CW offerings. The "Guide to Writing Programs" at the Association of Writers and Writing Programs [AWP] site lists 35 American doctoral programs in CW. Coming up on a population of 336 million (United States Census), the United States has roughly 8.5 times Canada's population yet 12.5 times the number of CW PhD programs (AWP "Guide"). The former "Mission Statement" of AWP was "to advance the art of writing as essential to a good education" (qtd. in Ashton 160), and David Fenza, AWP director for 29 years (AWP, "AWP's Executive"), likes to describe CW educations as "the largest system of literary patronage the world has ever seen" (qtd in Boddy 104). Notably, this American patronage has evolved in an educational marketplace of both state-funded and privately funded universities. Unlike Canadian universities, American, Australian and United Kingdom universities do not ignore the staggering student demand for doctoral CW educations.

Even Canada makes Canadian doctoral CW offerings look bad. As a somewhat unique officially bilingual country where, for example, discussion in Parliament occurs in either English or French ("Research"), our predominantly French-speaking province of Québec, with its population approaching nine million (Statistics, "Population") has more doctoral CW programs than Canada's Anglophone universities which ostensibly serve 30 million Anglo-Canadians (Statistics, "Canada's"). The CW doctoral programs at *Université Laval ("Doctorat en études littéraires")*, *Université de Montréal* ("*Doctorat en littératures*") and *Université de Sherbrooke* ("*Programmes*") comprise one-third more CW doctoral programs for, largely, the one-fifth of Canada's population that is Francophone (Statistics, "Population"). The Anglophone Canadian doctoral story is not, compared to global and domestic comparators, adequately being told.

Unchecked discipline hostility appears to be one reason Canadian universities have not responded to the obvious market for more Canadian CW PhD programs. In *Harper's*, American author and semi-reluctant writing professor Lynn Freed refers to graduate CW programs as "the cash cow of the humanities" (69). Fenza too knows that "creative writing classes have become among the most popular classes in the humanities" ("Afterword" 167). Amazingly (and at national cost), Canadian Humanities programs are uninterested in this cash cow. If the Canadian English professors who ignore the student demand for CW PhDs (to say nothing of the intellectual and cultural opportunities they afford) were wasting their own money, I'd be slightly more forgiving.

However, their cart-before-the-horse sales strategy insists on marketing a product students no longer want to buy. Mark McGurl's *The Program Era: Postwar Fiction and the Rise of Creative Writing* contrasts the rapid growth of graduate CW with the minimal growth of graduate English degrees:

> in 2003–04 there was a total of 591 US institutions offering either an MA (428) or a PhD (143) in English literature. In 1991–92 that number had been 549. This represents an increase of 7 percent, as compared to a 39 percent increase in the number of creative writing programs over the same period.
>
> (414)

More recent American stats find "the number of English majors dropped by a third from 2011 to 2021" (Goldberg; Heller; cf. McMurtie). Countries with an abundance of CW PhD programs (such as the United States, the United Kingdom and Australia) have much higher general completion rates for PhDs per capita (OECD; *Public Education* 16). As noted below and in the next chapter, the Social Sciences and Humanities Research Council of Canada [SSHRC] is theoretically just as willing to fund a PhD thesis that *is* a Canadian novel instead of a disquisition *about* a Canadian novel. In the single most popular TED Talk ever (Fleck), on the lack of creativity in schools, Sir Ken Robinson claims that "every education system on Earth has the same hierarchy of subjects…. And in pretty much every system too, there's a hierarchy within the arts. Art and music are normally given a higher status in schools than drama and dance" (Robinson). Canada's English professors perpetually hierarchize English literature over Canadian literature *and* all literature over CW.

(Why Don't We) "Follow the Money" (?)

Canada's unique lack of interest in the growing market for a CW education hurts Canada intellectually, culturally and economically. Canada's English departments ignore what McGurl rightly describes as CW's "insatiable student demand—that simultaneously progressive and consumerist value" (94). The Victorianists and Renaissance drama scholars who run the majority of Canada's CW programs disregard not just the Canadian and global demand for a CW education in particular, but also creative education in general. Daniel Pink's *A Whole New Mind: Why Right-Brainers Will Rule the Future* observes,

> In the US, the number of graphic designers has increased tenfold in a decade; graphic designers outnumber chemical engineers by four to one. Since 1970, the US has 30% more people earning a living as writers…. Some 240 US universities have established creative writing MFA programs, up from fewer than twenty two decades ago.
>
> (55)

The well-documented efficacy of arts funding should find Canadian CW grads who are creative problem solvers and polyvocal communicators with varied employment opportunities. In the most recent report I can find from the Canada Council for the Arts [CCA], from 2023, and one using data from Statistics Canada (for 2021), Canada's culture GDP "rose 8.3% to $54.8 billion in 2021, with increases in all domains" and "[c]ulture accounted for 2.3% of total economy GDP in 2021." The Canada Council for the Arts crunches more Stats Can data to count nearly 11,000 full-time publishing jobs in Canada in the book selection alone (excluding periodicals and newspapers). In a comparison I've made with different stats over the years, Canada has had more full-time artists than autoworkers since I first published a short version of this study in 2014, with the most recent stats I can find reconfirming this fact in 2019 (Dundas). I've seen more of my CW former students (e.g., Peter Chiykowski, "Peter") become entrepreneurs than my former literature students; according to the Conference Board of Canada "the percentage of artists who are self-employed is six times the self-employment rate in the overall labour force" (*Useful* 4).

Canada's CW graduates may in fact be more employable than those Canadian English majors conscripted into professionalized Anglophilia, yet they are continually given short shrift by the John Donne experts and other scholars of non-Canadian literature who manage their educations. The University of Windsor has one of the older Canadian CW master's programs (Univ. of Windsor, "Creative"). Despite my curricular protests while a U. Windsor prof from 2001 to 2005, Windsor's CW undergrads are *still* only required to take one credit of *either* American or Canadian literature but two of "British" literature (Univ. of Windsor, "Course"). Can any reader imagine a Portuguese university allowing its literature majors to substitute a Spanish literature course for the national literature? I once did an invited campus reading in the English Department at Nipissing University in northern Ontario. Chatting with a student, I asked which of her literature courses were most stimulating for the novel she was sketching now and hoped to work on significantly following graduation ("A Conversation with"). She replied that her two remaining English courses, Restoration Drama and Prairie Realism, did not really pertain to her novel about a contemporary Canadian woman coming of age in a city.

Dick and Jane vs. the Palimpsest

Others who have taught in one of Canada's hybrid English–CW programs have surely experienced that moment when a student, usually in third year and drunk on theory, discovers the word *palimpsest* and then writes a palimpsestic poem or scene of fiction. Palimpsests are undeniably interesting, but are they the appropriate focus for a writer's education? Before proceeding to evidence on *how* Canadian CW education promotes the head [palimpsests and rhizomes; England and the past] at the expense of the heart [love, humour and plot], allow me to clarify the terms of debate. John Barth, high priest of both writing programs and, not coincidentally, postmodern fiction, utterly confuses the form and content of minimalism in his claim "a language's repertoire of other-than-basic syntactical devices permits its users to articulate other-than-basic thoughts and feelings" before going on to conclude "Dick-and-Jane prose tends to be emotionally and intellectually poorer than Henry James prose" (70–71). Given, amongst other facts, Canada's preference for making a CW education the smaller fraction in an English–CW master's, it routinely shares Barth's preference for sesquipedalian pyrotechnics over social-emotional intelligence. Robert Olen Butler, a senior professor in Florida State University's influential graduate writing program and a winner of the Pulitzer Prize for fiction, knows, "We are the yearning creatures of this planet.... Every second we yearn for something. And fiction, inescapably, is the art form of human yearning" (40). Canada's national preference for a writing degree split—almost never equally—between CW workshops and English lecture courses combines with our national refusal to serve our own market for doctoral degrees in CW with institutional biases for scholarship over creative production to provide writing educations designed to produce clever and textually deft but emotionally underdeveloped writers.

I did the hybrid MA program at the University of New Brunswick and taught for four years in the one at Windsor. At their best, these hybrid programs combine the (crucial) peer learning of graduate-level CW workshops and creative theses with a good grounding in relevant literature, the very reading that Prof. Leach's Chapter 3 laments his CW majors are not doing. At their worst, the hybrid CW-English programs are like a military education that requires a tour of duty in obligatory literature seminars, where candidates will write scholarly essays, not stories or poems. Our national preference for argumentation and citation over emotion in CW pedagogy is manifest in the oral thesis "defences" required in these half-English MAs. The title and ritual of a defence suggest that a candidate can argue the merit of her collection of poems or stories, not simply present stories or poems that are their own argument. At Columbia, one of the most influential CW MFA programs in the United States, a CW thesis passes or fails exclusively as a written document (Columbia). Columbia's posted list of degree requirements for the CW MFA states, "A thesis conference with your two faculty thesis evaluators is optional. *This is not a thesis defense*—your evaluators, in consultation with your concentration director, make the decision to pass or fail the thesis before the conference takes place" ("Graduate"; emphasis added). Canadian CW thesis defences are a clear hangover from the aped scientism of New Criticism (the zombie engine of English studies). McGurl's *The Program Era* warns,

> With its penchant for specialized vocabularies and familiarity with the less-travelled regions of the library, literary scholarship is at least partly in sync with the scientism of its wider institutional environment,

> the research university. Creative writing, by contrast, might seem to have no ties at all to the pursuit of positive knowledge. It is, rather, an experiment—but more accurately, an exercise—in subjectivity.
>
> (405)

Canada's institutional fear of the inner life wants arguments, not poems, and rarely aesthetic arguments at that. I spent two years as the Coordinator of the CW program at Dalhousie University, from 2008 to 2010 (Smulders) but on two non-renewable ten-month contracts. For years, Dal displayed the national preference for a colonial ownership of CW by an English department to such a degree that the CW program had *no* permanent faculty from 2008 until 2015. If you wanted to study Russian, German, or Sanskrit at Dal, you could study with a prof who would be there next year and was paid to answer emails in the summer and who could compete for internal research funding, vote on major committees and so forth. Not so for CW at Dal, even though, as the magazine *Canadian Art* points out, Canada's cultural industries contribute more to Canada's GDP than agricultural and forestry industries combined. During my two (limited-term) years at Dal, the English Department professors strenuously debated whether or not they should reduce their teaching load from five courses over eight months to four. Such a reduction was ultimately endorsed by a nearly unanimous departmental majority, but not before it was clarified to all stakeholders, including upper administration and most notably students, that limited-term CW professors would continue to teach a full third more than their English colleagues.

"Nobody Knows Anything"[4]

In the past half-century, CW in North America has shifted from the untutored ethos of rock and roll to the formal accreditation of a classical music education. Nonetheless, Cowan, McGurl, Pink and Fenza compellingly argue that we're long past debating whether creative writing can be taught (McGurl 24; Pink 27; Fenza "Creative"). Forty years ago, Canadian visual artists studied their craft at university, but writers largely didn't. Canadian writers educated in the 1980s like Douglas Coupland, Lisa Moore and Margaret Christakos actually majored in visual arts, not writing (Vancouver; Christakos; NSCAD). Now, graduate CW programs offer mentoring and peer critique (at a time when editors are busy marketing) as well as exposure to visiting authors, experience on literary journals and financial assistance. Fenza notes, "Academic programs [in CW!] have mustered hundreds of millions of dollars to support the study, making, and enjoyment of literature" (qtd. in Whetter, "Can'tLit" 2018, 252). In Canada, CW should be a bridge between our multi-billion-dollar industries in publishing and tertiary education.

In addition to our national preference for graduate CW degrees that must pay obeisance to codpiece poetry or radical textuality, crucial state institutions like the Social Sciences and Humanities Research Council of Canada

[SSHRC] also prefer a junior writer's scholarly potential, not her creative output. In the novel *Muriella Pent*, Russell Smith's Canadian satire of the culture of culture, an application form for a Toronto artistic residency overtly states "DO NOT ATTACH A WRITING SAMPLE" (106), and "Please note that support materials in the form of writing samples are no longer a part of the application process" (108). This same preference for explanations over art is funny in Canadian satire yet sad in public policy. The very real SSHRC will provide ample master's and PhD scholarships to CW candidates, yet the master's application similarly forbids a writing sample ("Canada Graduate"). SSHRC CW master's applicants submit a bibliography, but *not* a writing sample ("Canada Graduate"). The admittedly catch-all instructions for Canadian master's students in fields as diverse as health, engineering and CW nonetheless meet flagrantly dichotomous language in SSHRC's application instructions:

> If the output of your degree program is *an artistic creation rather than a thesis*, clearly indicate the *research component* of your proposed work. Outline the objectives of your research, the context, methodology and contribution to the advancement of knowledge.
>
> ("Canada Graduate"; emphasis added)

As detailed more fully in my next chapter, SSHRC could be a significant patron of the Canadian arts, yet very little of the billion public dollars they awarded to faculty and postgraduate students in 2022 went to storytellers and their traffic in social-emotional intelligence. In 2022, SSHRC awarded $934.1 million in grants, primarily to postsecondary faculty, in its Insight Grant program (Social, "Competition: Insight") and $106.9 million in scholarships and fellowships for master's and doctoral candidates through its Talent program (Social, "Competition: Talent"). As my next chapter shows, the average, now, of just one national CW grant a year to writer-profs finds them applying for "Research/Creation" grants in the Fine Arts program for faculty (Social, "Preparing"). Even the slash in the program title (always the hybrids!) shows our national refusal to respect art as art: English scholars and art historians may apply to this hybrid program *in addition to* other SSHRC standard research grants that exclude artist-profs. Write literature, and SSHRC has just one grant per year for the country's writer-profs; write about literature, and it has several. I served on a SSHRC Research-Creation jury for faculty grants in 2015–2016, and nearly all the projects recommended for funding were exclusively scholarly and not creative or artistic (Social, "Insight"). The same jury that was tasked with evaluating proposals for plays and novels also had proposals for exclusively scholarly articles or books on Shakespeare and Byzantine art in the same competition. The latter, not the former, received almost all the recommendations for funding. Not funding stories means not funding characters and, arguably, emotions and the inner life.

The political fallout of Canada's CW hostage-taking extends beyond where and what is studied by whom and includes, perhaps most significantly, what is written. Our national preference for arguments over art-making risks a hyper-rational ghettoization of graduate CW material. For almost half a century Susan Sontag's essay "Against Interpretation" has called for "in place of a hermeneutics ... an erotics of art," yet we keep steeping our writing students in hermeneutics, not aesthetics (7). University-trained (American) writer Sandra Cisneros states overtly that when she wrote her breakthrough novel *The House on Mango Street* she consciously used "a child's voice, a girl's voice" as an explicitly "anti-academic voice" (xv). The marginalization of emotional complexity within so-called Humanities disciplines can additionally distance the marginal voices many profs claim to serve.

"Ugly with an Explanation"[5]

Canada's disregard for emotional complexity risks providing a CW pedagogy that denies students literature's fundamental work with empathy. Scottish writer Andrew O'Hagan's novel *Be Near Me* has the best, and shortest, definition of education I've ever read: "managed revelation" (32). Aesthetic theoreticians and cognitive psychologists also recognize the ways in which literature, especially narrative literature, allow us to expand our minds by thinking like others. In a section of his *The Art Instinct* called "The Uses of Fiction," Denis Dutton argues that

> of all the arts, [fiction] is the best suited to portray the mundane imaginative structures of memory, immediate perception, planning, calculation, and decision-making, both as we experience them ourselves and as we understand others to be experiencing them. But storytelling is also capable of taking us beyond the ordinary, and therein lies its mind-expanding capacity. To understand, intellectually and emotionally, the mind of another is a distinct ability that emerges ... [an] evolved adaptation.
>
> (119)

Dutton goes on to conclude, "Fiction provides us, then, with templates, mental maps for emotional life" (122). Cognitive psychologist and Anglo-Canadian novelist Keith Oatley summarizes human conversation as "verbal grooming" and suggests, "The primary function of conversation is to maintain relationships—a large number of relationships—and *to maintain intimacy in relationships*" (86; emphasis added). The empathy-rich medium of fiction is not simply a font of emotion, but also of intelligence. Creativity scholar and educational psychologist Howard Gardner observes that "many people with IQs of 160 work for people with IQs of 100.... In the day-to-day world no intelligence is more important than the interpersonal" (qtd. in Goleman 41).

A national CW education that privileges literary analysis over literary production shuns interpersonal intelligence. George Eliot claims,

> The greatest benefit we owe to the artist, whether painter, poet or novelist, is the extension of our sympathies.... Art is the nearest thing to life; it is a mode of amplifying experience and extending our contact with our fellow-men.
>
> (qtd. in Cooke 144)

One can hear the phrase "rhizomatic poetics" in any Canadian university English department (including those that offer CW); one rarely hears the word "empathy" (or the excitement that attends to rhizomatism). We adore the fragmentary but disparage feelings. Harvard psychology PhD Daniel Goleman calls social-emotional intelligence "a meta-ability, determining how well we can use whatever other skills we have, including raw intellect" (36). In a land of methodology, thesis defences and bibliographies, the crucial "meta-ability" of social-emotional intelligence fostered by literature is not meeting its maximum audience.

"The Great Generosities"

As a university discipline, CW should be a thinking and communication tool, and it deserves a place at every institute of higher learning. Unacceptably, however, writing in Canada is managed (and sometimes even taught) by profs who have never published CW or have not published it in decades. Not even Canada would short-change its music or fine arts students in this way, yet we'll appoint unqualified English profs to direct or even teach story writing. Fenza knows:

> In addition to advancing the art of literature, creative writing workshops exercise and strengthen the resourcefulness of the human will, and it is the exercise of will not over others, but for others, as stories and poems are made as gifts for readers and listeners.
>
> ("Afterword" 167)

Henry James prefers the "great generosities" of writing: "We trust to novels to train us in the practice of great indignations and great generosities" (86). In Canada, our failure to meet the demand for CW PhDs, and to value those degrees, continues to underplay the great generosities of social-emotional intelligence central to CW pedagogy.

Notes

1 This chapter has been as revised and re-issued as a twentieth-century long poem. Most substantially, it appears, under the title "Can'tLit: What Canadian English Departments Could (but Won't) Learn from the Creative Writing Programs They

Host" in *New Writing: The International Journal for the Practice and Theory of Creative Writing*, vol. 14, no. 3, 2017, (https://doi.org/10.1080/14790726.2017.1299765), vol. 11, no. 1, 2017, 316–26. A revised version was reprinted in the only other Canadian anthology of essays about CW pedagogy, Writing Creative Writing: Essays from the Field, edited by Rishma Dunlop, Daniel Scott Tysdal and Priscila Uppal (Dundurn Press, 2018, pp. 243–59). An early version was published in Literary Review of Canada, vol. 22, no. 7, 2014, pp. 22–23 and was subsequently selected to the anthology Best Canadian Essays 2015 (Tightrope, 2016, pp. 239–48).

2 This phrase was the tagline in a Canadian series of tea commercials from the 1970s ("Red Rose").

3 In random order, here are the 17 Australian PhD programs I'm counting: (1) University of New South Wales, (2) Swinburne University of Tech, (3) Flinders University, (4) Monash University, (5) University of Wollongong, (6) Macquarie University, (7) University of Queensland, (8) University of Tech Sydney, (9) Curtin University, (10) University of Adelaide, (11) Southern Cross University, (12) University of New England (Australia), (13) Deakin University, (14) University of the Sunshine Coast, (15) RMIT, (16) University of South Australia and (17) University of Sydney.

4 Screenwriter and novelist William Goldman's famous description of the unpredictability of a movie's success (qtd. in Surowiecki).

5 *New Yorker* art critic Adam Gopnik distinguishes between art that is "Beauty Per Se" and "Ugly with an Explanation. Andy and Duchamp and so on" (83).

Works Cited

Ashton, Jennifer. *The Cambridge Companion to American Poetry Since 1945*. Cambridge, Cambridge UP, 2013.

Association of Writers and Writing Programs. "Association of Writers and Writing Programs (AWP) Receives $15,000 Grant from the McKnight Foundation to Support Writers in Minnesota." *Association of Writers and Writing Programs*, 15 Oct. 2014, https://www.google.com/search?client=firefox-b-d&q=AWP+%22mission+statement%22+%E2%80%9Cthe+art+of+writing+as+essential+to+a+good+education%E2%80%9D+. Press release.

Association of Writers and Writing Programs. "AWP's Executive Director." *Association of Writers and Writing Programs*, 16 Mar. 2018, https://www.awpwriter.org/magazine_media/writers_news_view/4431/.

Association of Writers and Writing Programs. "Guide to Writing Programs," *Association of Writers and Writing Programs*, 2023, https://awpwriter.org/AWP/AWP/Academic-Writing-Programs/Guide-to-Writing-Programs.aspx#:~:text=AWP's%20Guide%20to%20Academic%20Writing,size%2C%20and%20financial%20aid%20offered.

Australasian Association of Writing Programs. "Postgraduates," *Australasian Association of Writing Programs*, n.d., https://aawp.org.au/postgraduates/.

Australasian Association of Writing Programs. "Category Archives: Doctorate." *Australian Association of Writing Programs*, 2010, https://aawp.org.au/category/course-level/doctorate/.

Australian Bureau of Statistics. "Population Clock," *Population Clock and Pyramid*, n.d., https://www.abs.gov.au/statistics/people/population/population-clock-pyramid.

Barth, John. "A Few Words About Minimalism." *Further Fridays: Essays, Lectures, and Other Nonfiction, 1984–1994*. Little Brown, 1995.

Boddy, Kasia. *The American Short Story since 1950*. Edinburgh UP, 2010.

Butler, Robert Olen. *From Where You Dream: The Process of Writing Fiction*. Grove, 2006.

Canada Council for the Arts. "Provincial and Territorial Cultural Indicators, 2021." *Canada Council for the Arts*, 26 Jun. 2023, https://canadacouncil.ca/research/research-library/2023/06/provincial-and-territorial-indicators-2021.

"Canada Graduate Scholarships – Master's program: Steps for Completing and Submitting the Application." *Natural Sciences and Engineering Research Council of Canada*, 1 Sep. 2023, https://www.nserc-crsng.gc.ca/researchportal-portaildere-cherche/instructions-instructions/cgs_m-besc_m_eng.asp#a2.

Canadian Art. "Culture Industries Have $58.9 Billion Impact in Canada." *Canadian Art*, 25 Jun. 2019, https://canadianart.ca/news/culture-industries-have-58-9-billion-impact-in-canada/.

Christakos, Margaret. "Re: Q for mag: Vis. Art?" Received by Darryl Whetter, 7 Jun. 2011.

Cisneros, Sandra. "Introduction." *The House on Mango Street*. Vintage, 1991.

"A Conversation with Darryl Whetter." *Nipissing University*, 4 Jan. 2014, https://ccareads.nipissingu.ca/s3.htm.

Cooke, George Willis. *George Eliot: A Critical Study of Her Life, Writings and Philosophy*. Osgood, 1884.

Cowan, Andrew. "The Rise of Creative Writing." *Futures for English Studies: Teaching Language, Literature and Creative Writing in Higher Education*, edited by Ann Hewings, Lynda Prescott, and Philip Seargeant, Palgrave MacMillan, 2016, pp. 39–60.

Department of English: Faculty of Arts. "PhD in English (Creative Writing)." *University of New Brunswick*, n.d., https://www.unb.ca/fredericton/arts/departments/english/grad/phd-writing.html.

"Doctorat en littératures de langue française." *Unviersité de Montréal*, n.d., https://admission.umontreal.ca/programmes/doctorat-en-litteratures-de-langue-francaise/.

"Doctorat en études littéraires." *Université Laval*. 23 Oct. 2023, https://www.ulaval.ca/etudes/programmes/doctorat-en-etudes-litteraires.

Dundas, Deborah. "Artists Make Less Money Than Most Canadian Workers." *Toronto Star*, 29 Mar. 2019, https://www.thestar.com/entertainment/books/artists-make-less-money-than-most-canadian-workers/article_d0e34901-7c75-5b0b-8084-ead874c821d1.html.

Dutton, Denis. *The Art Instinct: Beauty, Pleasure, & Human Evolution*. Oxford UP, 2009.

Faculty of Graduate Studies. "*English: Doctor of Philosophy.*" *University of Calgary*, 2023, https://grad.ucalgary.ca/future-students/explore-programs/english-phd.

Faulkner, William. "Banquet Speech." *Nobelprize.org*, n.d., https://www.nobelprize.org/prizes/literature/1949/faulkner/speech/.

Fenza, David. "Afterword." *Creative Writing Studies: Practice, Research and Pedagogy*, edited by Graeme Harper and Jeri Kroll, Multilingual Matters, 2007, pp. 165–67.

Fenza, David. "Creative Writing and Its Discontents." *Writer's Chronicle*, Mar.-Apr. 2000, n.p., *Education Resources Information Center*, https://eric.ed.gov/?id=ED462703.

Fleck, Anna. "The Most Popular TED Talks of All Time." *Statista*, 17 Apr. 2023, https://www.statista.com/chart/29742/most-popular-ted-talks/.

Freed, Lynn. "Doing Time: My Years in the Creative Writing Gulag." *Harper's Magazine*, July 2005, pp. 65–72.

Friesen, Joe. "Census Shows High Rate of Undergraduate and College Education among Canadians, But Complex Trends Lie Behind It." *The Globe and Mail*, 5 Dec. 2022, https://www.theglobeandmail.com/canada/article-census-2021-university-college-graduate/.

Goldberg, Nicholas. "Where Have All the English Majors Gone?" *Los Angeles Times*, 24 Oct. 2023, https://www.latimes.com/opinion/story/2022-10-24/college-humanities-decline. Op-ed.

Goleman, Daniel. *Emotional Intelligence: Why It Can Matter More Than IQ*. Bantam, 1995.

Gopnik, Adam. "The Children of the Party." *New Yorker*, 12 May 1997, pp. 78–91.

Grossman, Samantha. "*And the World's Most Educated Country Is ....*" *Time*, 27 Sept. 2012, https://newsfeed.time.com/2012/09/27/and-the-worlds-most-educated-country-is/.

"Graduate Courses & Requirements." *Columbia University*, 2023, https://arts.columbia.edu/writing/graduate.

Heller, Nathan. "The End of the English Major." *The New Yorker*, 27 Feb. 2023. https://www.newyorker.com/magazine/2023/03/06/the-end-of-the-english-major.

Hensher, Philip. *King of the Badgers*. Fourth Estate, 2011.

Hensher, Philip. *The Mulberry Empire*. Knopf, 2002.

James, Henry. *Notes and Reviews with a Preface by Pierre de Chaignon La Rose: A Series of Twenty-Five Papers Hitherto Unpublished in Book Form*. 1923. Nabu, 2010.

McGurl, Mark. *The Program Era: Postwar Fiction and the Rise of Creative Writing*. Harvard UP, 2009.

McMurtie, Beth. "Can You Get Students Interested in the Humanities Again? These Colleges May Have It Figured Out." *The Chronicle of Higher Education*, 4 Nov. 2019. https://cla.purdue.edu/academic/cornerstone/documents/can-you-get-students-interested-in-the-humanities-again-these-colleges-may-have-it-figured-out---the-chronicle-of-higher-educati.pdf.

Moore, Marshall and Sam Meekings, eds. *The Scholarship of Creative Writing Practice: Beyond Craft, Pedagogy, and the Academy*. Bloomsbury, 2024.

Nabokov, Vladimir. *Lectures on Literature*. Harvest, 1982.

NSCAD University. "NSCAD Contingent Heads to MASS MoCA." *NSCAD University*, 25 May 2012, https://nscad.ca/nscad-contingent-heads-to-mass-moca/.

Oatley, Keith. *Such Stuff as Dreams: The Psychology of Fiction*. Wiley-Blackwell, 2011.

O'Hagan, Andrew. *Be Near Me*. 2006. McClelland, 2008.

Organisation for Economic Co-operation and Development. *Education at a Glance 2019*. OECD Publishing, 2019, https://doi.org/10.1787/f8d7880d-en.

"Peter Chiykowski." *LookItsPeter*, n.d., https://lookitspeter.com.

Pink, Daniel. *A Whole New Mind: Why Right-Brainers Will Rule the Future*. Riverhead, 2005.

"Research Publications: Official Languages and Parliament." *Library of Parliament*, 15 Mar. 2022, https://lop.parl.ca/sites/PublicWebsite/default/en_CA/ResearchPublications/2015131E.

"Red Rose 1977 TV Commercial." *You Tube*, n.d., https://www.youtube.com/watch?v=KAtDXOnmqiM.

"Programmes et admission: Doctorat en études littéraires et culturelles." *Université de Sherbrooke*, n.d., https://www.usherbrooke.ca/admission/programme/707/doctorat-en-etudes-litteraires-et-culturelles.

Robinson, Sir Ken. "Schools Kill Creativity." *Ideas Worth Spreading: TED Talks*, Feb. 2006, https://www.ted.com/talks/sir_ken_robinson_do_schools_kill_creativity?language=en.

Smith, Russell. *Muriella Pent*. Doubleday, 2004.

Smulders, Marilyn. "Faculty Frosh." *Dal News*, 30 Sept. 2008, https://www.dal.ca/news/2008/09/30/newprofs.html.

Social Sciences and Research Council of Canada. "Competition Results: Insight Grants." *Social Sciences and Research Council of Canada*, 1 Sept. 2023, https://app.powerbi.com/view?r=eyJrIjoiM2QxZDc1M2MtN2QyNi00MDI5LTk3ZGMtZjQzY2Y0YWFiYjE2IiwidCI6ImZiZWYwNzk4LTIwZTMtNGJlNy1iZGM4LTM3MjAzMjYxMGY2NSJ9&language=en-ca.

Social Sciences and Research Council of Canada. "Competition Results: Talent." *Social Sciences and Research Council of Canada*, 1 Sept. 2023, https://app.powerbi.com/view?r=eyJrIjoiM2QxZDc1M2MtN2QyNi00MDI5LTk3ZGMtZjQzY2Y0YWFiYjE2IiwidCI6ImZiZWYwNzk4LTIwZTMtNGJlNy1iZGM4LTM3MjAzMjYxMGY2NSJ9&language=en-ca.

Social Sciences and Research Council of Canada. "Insight Grants Selection Committees: October 2015 Competition." *Social Sciences and Humanities Research Council of Canada*, 18 May 2016, https://www.sshrc-crsh.gc.ca/funding-financement/merit_review-evaluation_du_merite/selection_committees-comites_selection/insight_grants-subventions_savoir_oct2015-eng.aspx.

Social Sciences and Research Council of Canada. "Preparing an Application Involving Research-Creation for Insight and Insight Development Grants." *Social Sciences and Research Council of Canada*, 3 May 2023, https://www.sshrc-crsh.gc.ca/funding-financement/apply-demande/background-renseignements/preparing_research_creation_application_idg-preparer_l_application_recherche-creation_sds-eng.aspx.

Sontag, Susan. "Against Interpretation." *Against Interpretation and Other Essays*. Farrar, Strauss & Giroux, 1963.

Spigelman, Candace. *Personally Speaking: Experience as Evidence in Academic Discourse*. Southern Illinois UP, 2004. Studies in Writing and Rhetoric.

Statistics Canada. "Canada's Population Reaches 40 Million." *Statistics Canada*, 19 Jun. 2023, https://www.statcan.gc.ca/en/subjects-start/population_and_demography/40-million.

Statistics Canada. "Population Estimates, Quarterly." *Statistics Canada*, 27 Sept. 2023, https://www150.statcan.gc.ca/t1/tbl1/en/tv.action?pid=1710000901.

Surowiecki, James. "The Science of Success." *New Yorker*, 2 July 2007, https://www.newyorker.com/magazine/2007/07/09/the-science-of-success.

United States Census Bureau. "U.S. and World Population Clock." *United States Census Bureau*, 2 Dec. 2023, https://www.census.gov/popclock/.

University of Windsor, Department of English and Creative Writing. "Course Planning: Honours English and Creative Writing." *University of Windsor*, 2022, https://www.uwindsor.ca/english/sites/uwindsor.ca.english/files/2022_-_honours_english_and_creative_writing.pdf.

University of Windsor, Department of English and Creative Writing. "Creative Writing." *University of Windsor*, n.d., https://www.uwindsor.ca/english/314/creative-writing.

Vancouver Art Gallery. "Douglas Coupland: Everywhere Is Anywhere Is Anything Is Everything." *Vancouver Art Gallery*. n.d., https://www.vanartgallery.bc.ca/exhibitions/douglas-coupland-everywhere-is-anywhere-is-anything-is-everything.

Wallace, Clement. *Understanding Canada: Building on the New Canadian Political Economy*. McGill-Queen's UP, 1996.

Whetter, Darryl. "Can'tLit: What Canadian English Departments Could (but Won't) Learn from the Creative Writing Programs They Host." Excerpted in *Literary Review of Canada*, vol. 22, no. 7, 2014, pp. 22–23.

Whetter, Darryl. *Best Canadian Essays 2015*. Toronto: Tightrope, 2016, pp. 239–48. Print.

Whetter, Darryl. "Can'tLit: what Canadian English departments could (but won't) learn from the creative writing programmes they host." *New Writing: The International Journal for the Practice and Theory of Creative Writing*. vol. 11, no. 1, 2017, pp. 316–26. *Taylor and Francis Online*, https://doi.org/10.1080/14790726.2017.1299765.

Whetter, Darryl. "Can'tLit: What Canadian English Departments Could (but Won't) Learn from the Creative Writing Programs They Host.In *Writing Creative Writing: Essays from the Field*. edited by Rishma Dunlop, Daniel Scott Tysdal and Priscila Uppal. Dundurn, 2018, pp. 243–59.

Whetter, Darryl. "Darryl's Post." Australasian Postgraduate Writers Network. *Facebook*, 27 Nov. 2023, 10:54, p.m., https://www.facebook.com/groups/381535468640600.

Wroe, Nicholas. "Philip Hensher: A Life in Writing." *The Guardian*, 30 Mar. 2012, https://www.theguardian.com/culture/2012/mar/30/philip-hensher-life-in-writing.

Prof. Whetter's Recurrent Comments on Student Writing.

Give this a middle. We arrived too quickly to this outburst/epiphany. What earlier action, reaction or dialogue could prepare our arrival here? Think of this as B or maybe even C. What A (or A then B) would make this feel complete, not sudden?

"Doth thou": would you use these words in conversation? Yes, writing involves and requires multiple voices and the language we use in the coffee shop need not be the same language as all writing. Still, is this phrasing, well, a little fancy?

Recall the Ghostbusters workshop warning about crossing the literal and the figurative. In a scene literally involving pregnancy, a figurative reference to a "pregnant pause" becomes a self-conscious wink-wink-nudge-nudge moment that takes us out of the illusion.

Here's the dog vs. collie issue I pointed out in workshop. We read the generic dog, while visual readers will see a collie. When you can, always let the reader see what you see.

Get your hands dirty. Notice how formal and removed the tone and diction are here. Get in there.

2 The (Funding) Stories We Tell

Faculty Creative Writing as Nationally Funded University Research[1]

Darryl Whetter

Universal Professor-Writer Questions in this Canadian Particular

What happens, as has been the case for myself and other Canadian artist-profs, when professor-writers pause their writing of fiction, poetry, creative nonfiction, stage and screenplays to write lengthy and onerous national grant applications that might, as has twice happened to me, win a professor's university (not that professor directly) roughly $50,000 CAD to support the research, publication and promotion of creative writing that earned just $1,000 in sales ("Awards Search Engine: Rowing")? Why are only a few of Canada's eligible writer-profs—who, unlike painting profs, use writing as their primary medium—either not applying or not winning these empowering and substantial federal "Research-Creation" [R-C] grants from the Social Sciences and Humanities Research Council of Canada (SSHRC), a funding organization inaccessible to Canadian writers who aren't profs? Why does SSHRC's Insight Grant program (the main funding program for developing faculty research) have an applicant success rate of 52% ("Facts"), while the "Fine Arts" sub-competition only has a success rate of 35.5% ("Insight: Area")?[2]

Switching from the writing-professor's career to the writing, for those of us who do the parallel writing of a complex federal grant application for creative writing alongside that writing, what are the aesthetic, not just professional, advantages and disadvantages of writing a novel or poetry collection (et cetera) supported by an elusive federal grant? One each of my three novels and three collections of poetry enjoyed nearly $50,000 in state support when, like many Canadian writers, I earned less than $1,000 in royalties on those books.

My first novel, *The Push & the Pull*, was, like many first novels, a fictionalized version of my youngish life. My application for SSHRC support for pre-published drafts of that first novel invoked universal issues like caregiving but not flag-snapping-in-the-wind national issues. By my second novel, the onerous SSHRC application, rejected one year but funded the next, found me in a new compositional mode of actually pre-plotting a novel (or at least the counterfeit plot summary, in a novel with counterfeiting, for the

DOI: 10.4324/9781032614144-4

grant application), what my SSHRC-funded first collection of poetry would rightly quote fossil lovers to recognize as "Parts and Counterparts" (Gould 93). Concerning both aesthetics and career advancement, has the presence of these substantial, tenure-locking, personally and professionally enabling grants prompted any evolutionary mutations in CanLit akin to the award-bait novel? Is a novel proposed for SSHRC funding more likely to receive funding if it concerns episodes of capital-H Canadian History, from the Vimy Ridge battles of the Great War to the *Front de libération du Québec* terrorist bombings of the late 1960s and 1970s, et cetera, or contemporary social issues (e.g., Canada being an early global leader in legalizing same-sex marriage, recreational marijuana and euthanasia)?

With my second novel, *Keeping Things Whole*, only in trying to find social issues to invoke in my SSHRC application did I think to turn my observations and minor reading about Windsor, Ontario's high concentration of nude dancers and escorts into a bit of plot for a law-student character: fictional law student Kate Chan founds "Safe Sisters," a legal-aid outreach network of female law students and sex-trade workers (Whetter, Darryl, *Keeping* 13–15+). Only in writing the justify-yourself grant application did I (i) finally read the research of Jacqueline Lewis (Hanger) a former campus colleague studying Canadian and Windsorian sex work then, percolation and pressure doing their work, (ii) transform that information into plot.

When the Canadian professors who teach your postgraduate writing then the deans and vice-presidents who evaluate your professorial career encourage you to apply for federal CW research grants, should you? In sum: if you're seeking tenure, hard yes! Post-tenure: only if you're feeling *very* lucky and/or need to splice a genome or travel extensively.

New Grant Footprints in the Canadian Snow

In a new research category for their career-cementing national faculty research grants and postgraduate scholarships SSHRC dubbed "Research-Creation" ("Definition"), in 2003, SSHRC began allowing postgraduate students, tenured, or tenure-track artist-professors in Music, Theatre, Fine Arts, Creative Writing and the *very* few in Dance at Canadian universities to apply for multi-year funding, often in excess of $40,000 CAD for faculty, in federal research grants that empower both research and professorial careers ("Formative").

To look at another, less hopeful column in the Canadian writer's ledger, according to The Writers' Union of Canada's report *Diminishing Returns: Creative Culture at Risk*, (i) a Canadian writer's "median net income [was] … less than $4,000" in 2018, the last year for which they reported annual income (3; Degen) and (ii) "writers are making 78% less [in 2018] than they were making in 1998" (5). To earn $17,500 from a SSHRC national scholarship in the second year of a two-year CW master's degree while working on a book of poems that may well earn just $300 as an advance on royalties in the CanLit market risks being an early lifetime income peak for Canadian writers ("Canada Graduate").

Any Canadian faculty researcher—including me twice but excluding me several times—who wins a SSHRC grant, including a Canadian writer-prof who wins a "Research-Creation" grant, enjoys several career boosts inside the profession in addition to the actual research boon of money for travel or hiring out specialized services. From 2008 to 2011, at the University of Calgary—one of the two Anglophone Canadian schools offering a CW PhD—tenure-track CW prof Dr. Christian Bök was granted $101,000 ("Awards Search Engine: Xenotext") to alter bacteria so it would write "poetry" (Vaidyanathan). Other specialized services are more affordable than genetic manipulation. For a memoir I'm writing, I have submitted three slightly revised annual applications for a SSHRC R-C grant to (a) fund brain scans and a genome mapping which could (b) be discussed with me by a co-applicant neurosurgeon regarding a neurological disease that may run in my family. As (c) I could not and (d) should not pester such a neurosurgeon within Canada's beleaguered public medical system, this collaborative federal research grant would also allow me to obtain brain MRI scans our state medical system does not need to purchase and a genome mapping it almost certainly would never purchase for a seemingly healthy citizen.

For the individual prof, the professional benefits of a Canadian writer-prof winning a SSHRC R-C grant include, beyond funds for travel or expensive technical services, the general fact of grant success tending to beget grant success; institutionally, she also helps her host university hit competitive public benchmarks. In a media iteration of what many regard as Canada's weakness for monopolies or oligarchies in various industries (Carney; Daro), *MacLean's* magazine is not wrong to bill itself as "Canada's magazine" (Macleansmag). For the past 30 years (Cision), *MacLean's* annual ranking of Canada's universities has been central to their media centrality. The *MacLean's* ranking explicitly counts SSHRC dollars towards their "20 per cent" "faculty" "score" of any one university (Dwyer, 2021). Their published "Methodology" for 2022 states:

> In addition, the magazine measures the success of faculty in securing research grants from SSHRC, NSERC and CIHR. *Maclean's* takes into account both the number and the dollar value received in the previous year, and divides the totals by each institution's full-time faculty count.
>
> (Dwyer)

With SSHRC research grants so empowering to both research and careers, why do so few Canadian writer-profs win them? I count just 44 faculty CW R-C grants awarded in nearly 20 years (although, notably, the program had some pilot phases for its first ten years, with R-C grants not always available). More significant, while two early program years, 2003 and 2006, had peaks of eight faculty CW R-C grants, from 2010 on, only one or two have been awarded each year.[3] Only three writer-profs, Ted Bishop, now emeritus at the University of Alberta, Adam Dickinson, of Brock University, and myself have won more than one SSHRC R-C grant for CW. With career-making and book-empowering grants available to Canadian writer-profs, why are so few actually awarded?

Far more Canadian postgraduate CW students have their creative research federally funded compared to CW profs. From 2004 until 2021, I count 198 master's CW R-C scholarships, 35 doctoral and just 44 faculty CW R-C grants with SSHRC's public *Awards Search Engine*.[4]

Traplines

Regardless of whether SSHRC, with its annually varied jurors, does or even can prefer big-issue Canadian novels, do professor applicants pre-assume that more personal stories are less likely to be supported than proposed novels ticking high-profile national and/or social boxes? To repeat: my first novel, with its Faulknerian "human heart in conflict with itself," was not funded, but my prescient second novel, railing against Canada's federal marijuana prohibition just five years before it would be repealed, was funded. Regardless of whether or not these examples are Canadian, does the availability of career-enhancing grant support for the writer-professor reveal programmatic biases for the programmatic, rewarding writing and/or professorial skills more bureaucratic than artistic, promoting art/writing that defends well rather than reads well? In one of David Mamet's advice essays for actors and playwrights, with the notable title "A Generation That Would Like To Stay in School," he contends, "The classroom will teach you how to obey, and obedience in the theatre will get you nowhere" (18). In Canadian universities, my CW experience and this admittedly bean-counting chapter contends, SSHRC grants will get writer-profs hired and promoted but will have little impact on whether or not the supported novel (etc.) is likely to be published or well-received. Having served on these highly subjective SSHRC juries for artist-profs three times, I have no hope they would have awarded a proposal from former Canadian CW prof Michael Ondaatje for what would become his *The English Patient*, winner not just of the Man Booker Prize but of the Golden Man Booker, "the best winner of the Booker prize of the last 50 years, in a public vote" (Flood). Like many, that good novel wouldn't look good in a summary, let alone a "theorised" proposal.

The have/have-not equity remuneration scandal in university teaching, one very much both Canadian and global in CW pedagogy, is, regrettably, also exposed by SSHRC R-C funding. In *MFA vs. NYC*, Keith Gessen is right, however nationally myopic, to say, "Practically no writer exists now who does not intersect at some point with the university system—this is unquestionably the chief sociological fact of modern American literature" (176). SSHRC faculty R-C grants are reserved for full-time, tenure, or tenure-track CW profs, thus further exacerbating the equity divide between those with permanent or at least multi-year contracts versus those impoverished adjunct instructors who are hired semester-by-semester to teach CW courses in the same department as tenure-track or tenured faculty but lack what SSHRC's "Eligibility" page loosely if not collusively defines as sufficient "affiliation" with a university ("Insight Grants: Eligibility"). In my email interviews with various Canadian CW profs, Winnipeg writer Dr Jonathan Ball replied, "I am not allowed to apply for research funding, because the U does not consider me a real prof. SSHRC does not see me as a real prof." Exemplifying the exploitation and precarity of the adjunct instructor, Ball's unpredictable and variable teaching income would consist of a meagre per-course rate times some uncertain number of courses per year at, he tells me, "two universities, in four departments, since graduating, steadily over the course of the last 13 years." In the summer of 2022, another Canadian writer and regular adjunct CW course instructor welcomed to teach but still shunned by SSHRC, Toronto poet Margaret Christakos, posted:

> 30 years ago in August 1992 I got my first Creative Writing teaching contract, at Ontario College of Art. At the time the pay was $6,089 for each course. This week there's a posting for a CW sessional position at OCAD [the same school, rebranded] this fall which is—I kid you not—paying $6,507.

The exploitation and precarity of sessional CW course instructors like Ball and Christakos does not spare them being found guilty-by-association by the fellow writers who review their books or serve on non-SSHRC arts grant juries such as those at the empowering Canada Council for the Arts. *Quill & Quire*, the Canadian equivalent of *Publisher's Weekly* (though one apparently not so keen on fact-checking), reviewed Ball's latest poetry collection, *The National Gallery*, claiming, "Ball—who belongs to a coterie of other supposedly outsider Canadian poets who are almost uniformly tenured or tenure-track university professors, white and male" (Eckerlin). In addition to the fact that Ball is not a tenured or tenure-track prof, the review's hostility towards writer-profs is central to its concluding line: "if Ball is the Poet Laureate of Hell, it is perhaps fitting that it is a Hell writ large in and sanctioned by the halls of Canadian academe" (Eckerlin). Despite teaching for 13 years and having earned a SSHRC R-C doctoral fellowship, the prolific Ball is not "sanctioned" enough by "Canadian academe" to apply for SSHRC R-C faculty grants.

SSHRC faculty R-C grants, then, have certainly not been a boon to arts funding in general in Canada or any kind of redress for academic precarity and inequity. In the email interviews I did for this chapter, several tenured or tenure-track Canadian writer-profs spoke of feeling trapped between rocks and hard places when it comes to funding their research, lamenting that the SSHRC application process is too onerous, stealing precious writing time that could otherwise produce fiction or poems, not grants to support them, but also feeling too salary-privileged to apply to the Canada Council for the Arts and its provincial equivalents. Those Canadian writer-profs who do not feel, as one correspondent who asked to remain anonymous put it, "too guilty" (a frequent interview reply) to apply to the Canada Council for the Arts worry that applications from professors for the CCA's federal two-year writing grants—capped at $25,000 for all project costs ("Research") a low figure for SSHRC R-C grants—will be rejected by the fellow writer-jurors who feel professors are too privileged to apply to the CCA and provincial equivalents, including as the rare few who can apply to SSHRC.

The opportunity costs in lost labour, if not creative concentration, incurred by CW profs applying for SSHRC R-C grants are significant. Here are the obligatory section titles and word counts of my latest 2021 (unsuccessful) SSHRC R-C grant application, from a proposal in which a neurosurgeon would consult on my seeking brain and genome scans as part of writing an illness-narrative memoir (Table 2.1).

As the references are actually a bibliography of works consulted, not just those cited, and as not all applicants will have to try to have a former formal grievance campus foe excluded as an assessor, a lighter word count here is 15,000 words to apply to win—in a meagre annual offering I did not know until I wrote this chapter—just one to two annual faculty R-C CW grants since 2013. Given how few of the Canadian CW profs I consulted endure these 15,000 slings and arrows applying for SSHRC R-C CW grants, and the (very) fewer still who receive them, most Canadian writer-profs presumably eye that labour buy-in and recognize that they could complete a few short stories or personal essays with that same amount of work. Recalling Mamet: who would rather write grant-speak than, say, fiction? My only sibling, the

Table 2.1 Required Categories and Sample Word Counts for a 2021 SSHRC Faculty R-C Grant Application

Section	*Word Count*
Request for Multi/Interdisciplinary Evaluation	456
Summary	554
Detailed Description	4,130
Knowledge Mobilization Plan	670
Expected Outcomes Summary	489
Team/Students/Output	2,199
Budget Justification	872
Exclusion of Potential Assessors	171
Relevant Research Contributions over the Last Six Years (2015–2021)	1,772
Description of R-C Support Material	201
Writing Sample R-C Support Material	3,555
References	3,695
Total	**18,764**

mediaevalist K. S. Whetter, is also a Canadian prof in an English department, a (prolific) literary scholar ("Dr. Kevin"). As my prof-brother puts it,

> With the time and work I put into a SSHRC application, which lives or dies on the reports of two judges and probably won't get funded, I could research, write, and publish two articles—articles I am confident I will be able to publish. Why would I go through the wasted hope and wasted labour of trying to get a grant to enable publication when I can just do the same amount of work and know that I will publish something at the end?
>
> (Whetter, Kevin)

SSHRC jurors are not, I must reiterate, judging only R-C applications. Each of the three SSHRC juries I served on had us (i) evaluating scholarly projects in the same ranked competition as R-C projects with (ii) a majority of non-artist scholars on the jury. At times, that lack of artistic experience leaves professor-jurors, I contend with what I contend are not sour grapes, unqualified to properly judge R-C projects. For example, I have twice now received negative comments from SSHRC jurors who regard my plan to hire a CW student researcher (strategically, a proposed expenditure which is all but obligatory) as not an effective learning strategy for that student: I have applied to have a student assistant, who would be a CW major or post-graduate CW student to, in part, copy-edit different drafts of my manuscript (while also managing research to share on social media, et cetera). If I were a student again, I could imagine few learning tasks more illuminating than watching my published writer of a supervisor revise her work, to see (and hear) how she contracts and expands a story in progress. Unimpressive, apparently, to the Victorian and Renaissance scholars likely to be serving on an SSHRC jury doling out Canadian tax dollars earmarked for Canadian faculty and post-grad research in the Humanities.

Fossilization

I received SSHRC R-C grants for two of my seven books of creative writing: one novel and one collection of poems. My SSHRC rejections for a different novel and a proposed memoir are also illuminating. What became my 2013 marijuana-smuggling novel *Keeping Things Whole* (funded from 2011 to 2014 by SSHRC at $55,000 under the [better!] working title *Rowing to Cuba*) did, as my application claimed it would, touch on fascinating national issues and history involving smuggling, sex work, the liminality of border cities like its setting of Windsor, Ontario/Detroit, Michigan, et cetera. Still, that novel does not strike me as nationally and internationally relevant as my 2020 climate-crisis novel *Our Sands*, which was rejected by SSHRC in 2015 (with, as is the norm with my SSHRC rejections, one assessor giving a *Fund-this-now!* score and the second a *Down with CW!* score). Each novel is,

I hope, prescient. My marijuana smuggling novel of 2013 questions Canada then spending hundreds of millions per year policing a drug seen, smelled, or heard about by every Canadian who has attended secondary school. By 2018, Canada surprised itself and the world by legalizing recreational, not just medicinal, cannabis (House of Commons Canada). In a notable pairing, my novel *Keeping Things Whole* includes the designer's pot leaf on the title page and the SSHRC logo and name in the non-diegetic frontispiece info. Yes, a novel set in Canada's marijuana smuggling industry captures plenty of historical and contemporary Canadian issues, including American influence both negative (with our initial cannabis prohibition following theirs) and positive (with Canada moving from importing its marijuana to growing it (well!) following the exodus of American men and women into Canada, with more of the latter both coming and staying, during America's Vietnam War) (Hagan 122–24). All fascinating, I trust, but not as relevant, surely, as my rejected SSHRC 2015 proposal to write a novel set in Canada's Alberta tar sands, which *The Guardian* rightly calls "one of the single biggest source sites of the carbon pollution that is choking the planet" (Goldenberg). Noam Chomsky and Laray Polk describe Canada's tar-sand oil as "the dirtiest oil on the planet" (160). My rejected 2015 SSHRC grant proposal for a tar-sands novel cited various sources, including whistle-blowing physician Dr. John O'Connor and Anishinaabe author Winona LaDuke, to contend that Canada's notoriously toxic tar-sands industry, the run-off of which affects predominantly Indigenous communities, was proof that Canada's Indigenous genocide was not 'just' the "cultural genocide" lamented by so many (Mako 191; Woolford & Benvenuto 374; Bolen) but actual genocide. By 2021, international media began carrying stories about the mass graves of children found on Canada's former (Indigenous) residential 'schools' (Austen).

In my analysis and experience, SSHRC's R-C CW grants, selected as they are by just two jurors, who need not even be Canadian ("Insight Grants: Merit"), give no appropriate favouritism to how pronouncedly "Canadian" or not the proposed project is. Poet/memoirist Emilia Nielsen's 2020 grant, which SSHRC's public *Awards Search Engine* and grant result tables they emailed me cross-reference to indicate was the only CW R-C awarded in 2020, seems (admirably) far more universal than Canadian ("Awards Search Engine: Life").

(Grant) "Parts and Counterparts"

For my first SSHRC CW R-C faculty grant, in 2008, I was awarded just shy of $40,000 CAD for a poetry project then called *Match Destination Formatting* which was published, in 2012, as the poetry collection *Origins* ("Awards Search Engine: Match"); my publishing contract for the book was just $300 from a publisher who, like all Canadian literary publishers, would not exist without federal and provincial grants from other, non-SSHRC government agencies.[5] The $40,000 R-C grant was substantial for its proposed period of just 12 months compared to my 2011–2014 SSHRC R-C grant of nearly $55,000 over three years ("Awards Search Engine: Rowing").

Travel costs are eligible with aSSHRC, and much of both my proposed, grant-seeking expenditures and my actual grant spending (a wiggle room which Singapore, the other country where I have been a CW prof, would never abide) for the 2008 poetry project were devoted to numerous trips which contributed both directly and indirectly to several of the published poems. The one-sentence summary I eventually developed for *Origins* was "A collection of poetry devoted to energy, evolution and extinction as they have been, can be and/or should be observed in the globally-unique fossil record found around Joggins, Nova Scotia." In a book which contrasts the chance recordings of fossils with art as purposeful fossilization, I made (undeniably fun) research trips to fossil museums and field sites in Canada: the Redpath in Montreal; the Royal Ontario Museum in Toronto; the Royal Tyrell Museum in Drumheller, and the Burgess Shale Geoscience Foundation in Yoho National Park, British Columbia. Darwin's *On the Origin of Species* is overtly indebted to Canada's Joggins fossils, where he writes of "Messrs. Lyell and Dawson found carboniferous beds 1,400 feet thick in Nova Scotia, with ancient root-bearing strata," so of course I needed to visit Down House, the Darwin museum in England (296).

With a poetry book divided into halves named after a fossil's "Part" and "Counterpart," which Harvard palaeontologist Stephen Jay Gould describes as "two for the price of one—the fossil itself (called the part) and the impression of the organism forced into layers above (called the counterpart)—thumb and thumbprint, if you will" (*Wonderful* 93), surely a flight down to Mark Rothko's counterpart (the Rothko Chapel gallery in Houston, Texas) and part (its 14 site-specific paintings) was required. Grant project and grant application, if you will.

Looking again at the 39 poems published in *Origins*, I count nine that could not have been written without those research trips but 16 that didn't need me to move beyond a bookstore or library. As the author of four books of fiction and three poetry collections, I am reasonably confident in my ability to imagine and/or extrapolate a scene from research while also simultaneously confessing that two of the book's landscape poems, "Signed Inheritance: A Drumheller Glosa," and the ekphrastic "The Rothko Chapel," that valentine to a suicidal painter, could not have been written without my travelling to those destinations. Each of those two poems has been reprinted elsewhere *after* the publication of the book, and in Canada, most anthologies and journals prefer first publication ("Rothko"; "Signed"). In a national investment SSHRC could neither have anticipated nor shunned, what would turn out to be my only solo spot in my numerous panel appearances over four years at the *very robust* Singapore Writers Festival was a full-hour reading and lecture from *Origins* (Singapore). That same Canadian federal government annually (and appropriately) spent new money, rather than capitalizing on the old it had already invested in *Origins*, flying Canadian writers to Singapore for what some regard to be one of the most vibrant literary festivals in the world (Treagus-Evans).

Having already published two books of fiction, when I wrote my SSHRC R-C application for these fossil poems, a combination of confidence, industry savvy and late-early career cynicism found me thinking of the project more like producing a film than writing a book: I would write it if the money came together (i.e., if I won a federal grant). Also, gambling that national success is easier after international success, my SSHRC application regularly mentioned that I was applying for federal funds to, in part, deepen then share knowledge I had first gained while working as the editor of the provincially and nationally funded, but internationally sanctioned, UNESCO nomination dossier for what would become one of my province's major UNESCO World Heritage sites, the Joggins Fossil Cliffs (Boon and Calder 128). I would go on to publish six more books of my own poetry and fiction but never again with such a combination of grant shrewdness and career pragmaticism. Fifteen years later, I still love a book I wouldn't have written without a SSHRC R-C grant.

Conclusion: "(Un) Inherited Design"

Between the evolutionary theory I read about while editing the Joggins Fossil Cliffs UNESCO nomination dossier then read in earnest for (i) a SSHRC R-C grant application and, even better, (ii) the poetry collection it enabled, I still think at least monthly of how evolution involves a series of gates opening and closing (for gene, species, biome, et cetera). Gould also revived attention to Dollo's law, a late nineteenth-century evolutionary breakthrough that recognizes that once evolutionary success has been achieved, reversion to less biologically viable forms becomes impossible ("Dollo"). Gould would later summarize Dollo's law as "History is irrevocable. Once you adopt the ordinary body plan of a reptile, hundreds of options are forever closed, and future possibilities must unfold within the limits of inherited design" (*Eight* 9). As a CanLit writer, scholar and professor, and having applied repeatedly to SSHRC's R-C program since their pilot-project year of 2003, and with my books funded and not by that program, but also by the Canada Council for the Arts and, provincially, Arts Nova Scotia, I cannot say that SSHRC's Research-Creation program is a substantial evolutionary success for Canadian writer-profs or even Canadian writers or for the ecosystem of CanLit. While SSHRC's R-C grants for master's and doctoral CW students are significant, with now just one or two faculty book-writing R-C grants awarded each year and many Canadian CW profs either shunning the work to apply or not being selected for funding while possibly also being rejected for writing grants from the Canada Council for the Arts, SSHRC's R-C faculty CW grants remain a chance mutation for the individual writer-prof organism in Canada, but not the species of Canadian writer-profs nor the landscape of CanLit.

Notes

1 This chapter first appeared, with a slightly different title, in the 2024 Bloomsbury anthology *The Scholarship of Creative Writing Practice*, edited by Marshall Moore and Sam Meekings.

2 The stat of only 35.5% of faculty Fine Arts grants being awarded in SSHRC's 2022–2023 is available via the URL in the citation here. However, as pick-lists focus that data, the reader's best path is to start at 2022–2023 SSHRC's "Facts and Figures" page and then (ii) launch the "Competition Results" "Interactive Dashboard." (iii) Inside that dashboard, one should select the "Insight" tab across the top, then (iv) page 5, with (vi) "Funding Opportunity" set to "Insight Grants" and (vii) "Area of Research" set to "Arts and Culture."

3 Although counting grants with SSHRC's public Awards Search Engine seems straightforward, especially with "Creative Writing" listed in a "Discipline" picklist, this iteration of their search engine does not easily find old projects with, I believe, the R-C category predating use of "Creative Writing" as a discipline searchable in that field. My 2008 poetry project Match Destination Formatting is not easy to find as an R-C grant (but it was) ("Awards Search Engine: Match").

4 Shifting names and categories within SSHRC make some data challenging to track. For example, the "code" indicating a doctoral fellowship has changed, according to a posted SSHRC document, including both 752, for "Doctoral Fellowships" and then 767 for a presumably rebranded "Canada Graduate Scholarship – Doctoral" ("List of Funding"). The slightly different "List of Sub-Disciplines and Codes" lists Creative Writing as '50818' ("List of Sub-Disciplines"). Email correspondence from SSHRC confirms that while faculty have won CW R-C "Connection" grants (to present more polished research), my count here fixates on their book-writing "Insight" and "Insight Development" grants.

5 In a generalization too simple for one direct citation, there is no such thing as a professionally published literary book in Canada that has not been supported by government grants. For extensive details, see Ultra Libris: Policy, Technology, and the Creative Economy of Book Publishing in Canada by Rowland Lorimer, the founding director of the Master of Publishing program and the Canadian Centre for Studies in Publishing at Simon Fraser University. If you read Canadian fiction, poetry, CNF or drama, the book in your hand floats on several levels of government subsidy. Note as well that while both are federal government agencies, SSHRC and the Canada Council for the Arts are no more organizationally linked than, say, Health Canada and the Ministry of National Defence.

Works Cited

Austen, Ian. "'Horrible History': Mass Grave of Indigenous Children Reported in Canada." *The New York Times*, 28 May 2021, https://www.nytimes.com/2021/05/28/world/canada/kamloops-mass-grave-residential-schools.html.

"Awards Search Engine: Life Writing and Life-Altering Disease: Engendering Counternarratives of Chronic Illness." *Social Sciences and Humanities Research Council of Canada*, n.d., http://www.outil.ost.uqam.ca/CRSH/Detail.aspx?Cle=197137&Langue=2.

"Awards Search Engine: Match Destination Formatting: A Web and Print Poetic Investigation of Evolution, Community and the Joggins Fossil Cliffs." *Social Sciences and Humanities Research Council of Canada*, n.d., http://www.outil.ost.uqam.ca/CRSH/Detail.aspx?Cle=52945&Langue=2.

"Awards Search Engine: Rowing to Cuba: A Novel." *Social Sciences and Humanities Research Council of Canada*, n.d., http://www.outil.ost.uqam.ca/CRSH/Detail.aspx?Cle=89933&Langue=2.

"Awards Search Engine: The Xenotext Experiment." *Social Sciences and Humanities Research Council of Canada*, n.d. http://www.outil.ost.uqam.ca/CRSH/Detail.aspx?Cle=73337&Langue=2.

Ball, John G. "Re: Research Qs re: Funded Cdn. Research." Received by Darryl Whetter, 16 Jul. 2022.

Boon, Jenna and John Calder. *Nomination of the Joggins Fossil Cliffs for Inscription on the World Heritage List*. Joggins Fossil Institute, 2007.

Bolen, Michael. "UN Urged to Declare Canada's Treatment of Aboriginals 'Genocide.'" *The Huffington Post Canada*, 18 Oct. 2023, https://www.huffpost.com/archive/ca/entry/un-urged-to-declare-canadas-treatment-of-aboriginals-genocide_n_4123112.

"Canada Graduate Scholarships—Master's Program." *Natural Sciences and Engineering Research Council of Canada*, 1 Sept. 2023, https://www.nserc-crsng.gc.ca/Students-Etudiants/PG-CS/CGSM-BESCM_eng.asp.

Carney, Bryan. "Monopoly-Friendly Canada 'Does Not Treat Competition Policy Seriously.'" *The Tyee*, 19 Mar. 2019, https://thetyee.ca/News/2019/03/19/Monopoly-Friendly-Canada-Competition-Policy/.

Chomsky, Noam and Laray Polk. *Nuclear War and Environmental Catastrophe*. Seven Stories, 2013.

Christakos, Margaret. OCAD Sessional CW Rates Over 30 Years. *Facebook*, 11 July 2022, https://www.facebook.com/margaret.christakos.5.

Cision. "Maclean's Unveils Its 20th Anniversary University Rankings." *Cision Canada*, 10 Nov. 2010, https://www.newswire.ca/news-releases/macleans-unveils-its-20th-anniversary-university-rankings-546250902.html.

Daro, Ishmael N. "Canada Has an Oligopoly Problem—And We Need to Fix It." *THIS Magazine*, 30 Nov. 2018, https://this.org/2018/11/30/canada-has-an-oligopoly-problem-and-we-need-to-fix-it.

Darwin, Charles. *On the Origin of Species by Means of Natural Selection, or, the Preservation of Favoured Races in the Struggle for Life*. John Murray, 1859.

"Definition of Terms: Research-Creation." *Social Sciences and Humanities Research Council of Canada*, 4 May 2021, https://www.sshrc-crsh.gc.ca/funding-financement/programs-programmes/definitions-eng.aspx?pedisable=false#a22.

Degen, John. "Re: Author Income Stats Post 2018?" Received by Darryl Whetter, 21 Nov. 2023.

"Dr. Kevin Whetter." *Acadia University*, n.d., https://english.acadiau.ca/dr-kevin-whetter.html.

Dwyer, Mary. "Maclean's University Rankings 2023: Our Methodology." *Macleans.ca*, 7 Oct. 2022, https://www.macleans.ca/education/macleans-university-rankings-2022-our-methodology.

Eckerlin, Jesse. "[Rev. of] The National Gallery by Jonathan Ball." *Quill & Quire*, Nov. 2019, https://quillandquire.com/review/the-national-gallery.

"Facts and Figures." *Social Sciences and Humanities Research Council of Canada*, 24 Oct. 2023, https://www.sshrc-crsh.gc.ca/about-au_sujet/facts-faits/index-eng.aspx.

Flood, Alison. "The English Patient Wins Public Poll of Best Man Booker in 50 Years." *The Guardian*, 8 Jul. 2018, https://www.theguardian.com/books/2018/jul/08/the-english-patient-wins-public-poll-of-best-man-booker-in-50-years.

"Formative Evaluation of SSHRC's Research/Creation in Fine Arts Program." *Social Sciences and Humanities Research Council of Canada*, 3 Apr. 2013, https://publications.gc.ca/site/eng/9.834253/publication.html.

Gessen, Keith. "Money (2006)." *MFA vs. NYC: The Two Cultures of American Fiction*, edited by Chad Harbach, n+1, pp. 175–85.

Goldenberg, Suzanne. "The Tar Sands Sell-Out." *The Guardian*, 28 May 2015, https://www.theguardian.com/environment/ng-interactive/2015/may/28/carbon-bomb-canada-tar-sands-fort-mckay-town-sold-itself.

Gould, Stephen. Jay. "Dollo on Dollo's Law: Irreversibility and the Status of Evolutionary Laws." *Journal of the History of Biology*, vol. 3, no. 2, 1970, pp. 189–212, https://doi.org/10.1007/bf00137351, https://link.springer.com/article/10.1007/BF00137351.

Gould, Stephen Jay. *Eight Little Piggies: Reflections in Natural History*. Norton, 1994.

Gould, Stephen Jay. *Wonderful Life: The Burgess Shale and the Nature Of History*. Norton, 1990.

Hagan, John. *Northern Passage: American Vietnam War Resisters in Canada*. Harvard UP, 2001.

Hanger, Art. *The Challenge of Change: A Study of Canada's Criminal Prostitution Laws*. Report of the Standing Committee on Justice and Human Rights, Dec. 2006, https://www.ourcommons.ca/Content/Committee/391/SSLR/Reports/RP2610157/391_JUST_Rpt06_PDF/391_JUST_Rpt06-e.pdf.

House of Commons Canada. Bill C-45, C-45: An Act Respecting Cannabis and to Amend the Controlled Drugs and Substances Act, the Criminal Code and other Acts States. n.d. *parl.ca*, https://www.parl.ca/legisinfo/en/bill/42-1/C-45. 1st session, 42nd Parliament.

"Insight: Area of Research: Arts and Culture." *Social Sciences and Humanities Research Council of Canada*, 1 Sept. 2023, https://app.powerbi.com/view?r=eyJrIjoiM2QxZDc1M2MtN2QyNi00MDI5LTk3ZGMtZjQzY2Y0YWFiYjE2IiwidCI6ImZiZWYwNzk4LTIwZTMtNGJlNy1iZGM4LTM3MjAzMjYxMGY2NSJ9&language=en-ca.

"Insight Development Grants." *Social Sciences and Humanities Research Council of Canada*, 20 Nov. 2023, https://www.sshrc-crsh.gc.ca/funding-financement/programs-programmes/insight_development_grants-subventions_de_developpement_savoir-eng.aspx#4.

"Insight Grants: Eligibility." *Social Sciences and Humanities Research Council of Canada*, 3 Oct. 2023, https://www.sshrc-crsh.gc.ca/funding-financement/programs-programmes/insight_grants-subventions_savoir-eng.aspx#4.

"Insight Grants: Merit Review: Evaluation Process." *Social Sciences and Humanities Research Council of Canada*, 3 Oct. 2023, https://www.sshrc-crsh.gc.ca/funding-financement/programs-programmes/insight_grants-subventions_savoir-eng.aspx#6.

"List of Funding Opportunities and Codes." *Social Sciences and Humanities Research Council of Canada*, n.d., http://www.outil.ost.uqam.ca/CRSH/Liste_Info.aspx?Info=5&Langue=2.

"List of Sub-Disciplines and Codes." *Social Sciences and Humanities Research Council of Canada*, n.d., http://www.outil.ost.uqam.ca/CRSH/Liste_Info.aspx?Info=2&Langue=2.

Lorimer, Rowland. *Ultra Libris: Policy, Technology, and the Creative Economy of Book Publishing in Canada*. ECW Press, 2012.

Macleansmag. *Maclean's Magazine*, [Instagram landing page], n.d., https://www.instagram.com/macleansmag/?hl=en.
Mako, Shamiran. "Cultural Genocide and Key International Instruments: Framing the Indigenous Experience." *International Journal on Minority and Group Rights*. vol. 19, no. 2, 2012, https://papers.ssrn.com/sol3/papers.cfm?abstract_id=2087175, *Elsevier*.
Mamet, David. *True and False: Heresy and Common Sense for the Actor*. Vintage, 1999.
Singapore, National Arts Council. *Annex B – Singapore Writers Festival 2017 Festival Tracks*, n.d., https://www.google.com/url?sa=t&rct=j&q=&esrc=s&source=web&cd=&cad=rja&uact=8&ved=2ahUKEwiP7anycH5AhVvGVkFHTiEAN8QFnoECAIQAQ&url=https%3A%2F%2Fwww.nac.gov.sg%2Fdocs%2Fdefault-source%2Fnac-news-files%2Fsingapore-writers-festival-2017-celebrates-20thedition_annexb.pdf%3Fsfvrsn%3D1099e86d_0&usg=AOvVaw3wEe2sSH6uySwfR-7asmXR.
"Research and Creation." *Canada Council for the Arts*, n.d., https://canadacouncil.ca/funding/grants/explore-and-create/research-and-creation.
Treagus-Evans, Phil. "The World's Best Literature Festivals." *The Reading Lists*, n.d., https://www.thereadinglists.com/the-worlds-best-literature-festivals/.
Vaidyanathan, Gayrathi. "Could a Bacterium Successfully Shepherd a Message through the Apocalypse?" *Proceedings of the National Academy of Sciences*, vol. 114, no. 9, 2017, pp. 2094–95, https://doi.org/10.1073/pnas.1700249114.
Whetter, Darryl. *Keeping Things Whole: A Novel*. Nimbus, 2013.
Whetter, Darryl. *Origins: Poems*. Palimpsest, 2012.
Whetter, Darryl. *Our Sands: A Novel*. Penguin Random House, 2020.
Whetter, Darryl. "The Rothko Chapel." *The Ekphrastic Review*, 2019, https://www.ekphrastic.net/ekphrastic/the-rothko-chapel-by-darryl-whetter.
Whetter, Darryl. "Signed Inheritance." *A Crystal Through Which Love Passes: Glosas for P.K. Page*, edited by Jesse Ferguson, Buschek Books, 2013, pp. 70–73.
Whetter, Kevin. "Re: Quote You re: Opportunity Cost of SSHRC Apps?" Received by Darryl Whetter, 8 Aug. 2022.
Woolford, Andrew and Jeff Benvenuto. "Canada and Colonial Genocide." *Journal of Genocide Research*, vol. 17, no. 4, Taylor & Francis, 11 Dec. 2015, pp. 373–90, https://doi.org/10.1080/14623528.2015.1096580.
Writers' Union of Canada. *The Diminishing Returns: Creative Culture at Risk*. The Writers' Union of Canada, 2018.

3 Can the Workshop Be Saved? Notes from a Writing-School Dropout—And Former Department Chair

David Leach

I've been a professor in the Department of Writing at the University of Victoria, one of Canada's oldest and largest, since 2004. Over these past two decades, and especially during my five-year term as department chair, from 2014 to 2019, I've often told prospective students and inquiring authors that, yes, creative writing can be taught and, yes, UVic is one of the finest undergraduate writing schools on the planet. At the same time, a dark and shameful secret squats within my conscience: I am, in fact, a Creative-Writing school dropout. Worse, I dropped out of the same department in which I now teach and once gamely chaired. What seemed like my own misgivings as an undergrad with the workshop system at the core of our program have soured other writing teachers as well. Even as I continue to teach and help to collegially govern a workshop-centred CW degree, I worry the workshop method might turn off aspiring authors. When, as Chair, I defended our small-class pedagogy from a thousand administrative cuts, I often wondered if the more pressing question wasn't "Can the workshop be saved?" but rather "Should it?"

***

Because our departmental history reflects a key discipline divide in CW in Canada, a little program history is important before a very contemporary discussion of the workshop controversy. In 1973, UVic expanded Creative Writing from a small "division" of courses within the Department of English into a department all its own. Robin Skelton, a Yorkshire-born poet who had been hired as an English prof in 1963, was its co-founder and original chair (Thompson and Boyd). Six years later, a committee recommended the department secede from the Arts and Sciences into the new-ish Faculty of Fine Arts. That administrative schism, sundering UVic Creative Writing from English, shaped our evolution. Nationally, Canada perpetuates that artist/humanities scholar schism in the forking CW master's path of MFAs in CW (like ours, U. Guelph's [Chapter 15] and UBC's [Chapter 13]) and MAs in English and Creative Writing (as at Concordia [Chapter 10] and the University of Toronto [Chapter 7]). Unlike all other Creative Writing programs in

DOI: 10.4324/9781032614144-5

Canada save our provincial neighbours at UBC, our department would no longer remain an annex of eccentrics serving at the whims of PhD-wielding professors and deans in a scholarly academic faculty of historians, philosophers and literature professors. Creative Writing was free to "explore and create" (as the Canada Council for the Arts currently entitles its writing grant *du jour*) like the musicians, actors and visual artists on campus ("Explore").

The contemporary challenges with the workshop manifest in our department, in large part, because the majority of our history was spent teaching undergraduates and, even now, most of our courses serve our BA/BFA programs; these students are often young writers (see below) most vulnerable to an unwelcoming workshop and least prepared to serve as peer editors. When I arrived as an undergraduate, in 1989, the Department offered a four-year bachelor's CW degree. UVic only added a small "boutique" MFA degree in 2008. New undergraduate students started their journey in a first-year class split into three cohorts of 30, rotating between sections of fiction, poetry and stage drama. Just as the influential American nonfiction journal *Fourth Genre* would later recognize creative nonfiction as the fourth genre (of four!) to be granted respect, a separate UVic course taught nonfiction ("5 Years"). Different instructors in each genre led a series of lectures, readings, exercises and drafts that concluded with a final graded assignment. Students needed at least a B- in any genre to qualify for that workshop in the following year.

"Look to the left of you and look to the right," a professor cautioned us in our first class. "Only one of you will finish this program."

In my own UVic CW undergrad, I assumed I'd be the one to cross that finish line. I was wrong.

***

From second year onwards, workshops at UVic followed the formula exported like corn from the fields of the legendary Iowa Writers' Workshop (a pedagogical crop we've only recently acknowledged might not be as nutritious as promised). Fiction prof W.D. Valgardson had completed his MFA in 1969 at the University of Iowa, which "made a tremendous impression" on him (Bukoski 27), before coming to UVic as an associate professor in 1975; Dave Godfrey, co-founder of House of Anansi Press—the Canadian publisher who released CanLit-defining 1970s books like Margaret Atwood's *Survival*, Northrop Frye's *The Bush Garden: Essays on the Canadian Imagination* ("Gnarowski et al.") and Michael Ondaatje's first novel (Kertzer)—who took over as chair of the Writing Department in 1977, had earned a BA, MFA and PhD all at Iowa in the 1960s (Adams). W.P. Kinsella, the department's most famous alumnus at the time, had graduated from UVic's BFA into an MFA at Iowa—and hated its program. (The middle-aged Kinsella had been "disappointed by the workshop's lack of deadlines and loose structure at the time … [and] felt unsatisfied with the lack of substantive feedback he received from his peers" (O'Leary).)

What I liked—what most students like—about the program was its ready-made community of fellow authors-in-the-making. I'd gone from being an angsty high-schooler filling notebooks with *Star Wars* fan fiction and confessional poetry, to sitting in seminar rooms of wannabe writers and a few future stars. The department published an undergraduate lit journal and encouraged students to get off campus to discover Victoria's small but lively literary scene. We did so with friends we'd made in workshops. My first public reading, in a cramped downtown bookstore, featured me and another fiction undergrad ... and a single audience member. The other reader, though, was Eden Robinson—future author of *Monkey Beach* and the *Trickster* trilogy of novels—who wowed us with a captivating tale of supernatural horror. We knew she was destined for greatness.

Size *did* matter. In the Science courses I'd taken before switching majors into Creative Writing, I felt invisible amid cavernous auditoriums of frantic note-takers. Even Humanities electives were mid-sized lectures of 35-plus students with professors who would occasionally look up from their notes. In Creative Writing, the undergraduate workshops had the human scale of graduate seminars. We students felt seen and heard. Few recognized, though, who *wasn't* feeling seen and/or heard: the LGBTQ+ students, writers of colour and authors with disabilities.

The workshops and required electives were not, to our delight, just groupthink. Robin Skelton had published several books on poetics and co-founded *The Malahat Review*, which informed his courses in historical and contemporary forms of poetry. Jack Hodgins, a Governor General's Literary Award winner and a former high-school teacher, designed courses in the forms and techniques of the short story and the novel ("Past"). They were the best classes in my university experience, and I still draw on his insights—especially his visualizations of complex story structures—in my own prose and teaching. I also repeat the advice that Hodgins gave us: "You can only write at a level or two below what you are reading at." And so he filled his syllabi with mandatory and recommended readings from Canadian and international authors (mostly in English, some in translation, like David Grossman's haunting Holocaust metafiction *See Under: Love*) that pushed us to expand the horizons of what was possible.

Any writing program built on a foundation of the workshop has inherent risks. One potential flaw is that too much of the reading required of students will be their peers' draft work—some of it good, some of it ... well, less good. That quality gap can feel acute in an undergraduate degree, filled with younger writers with more limited reading backgrounds than those of MFA candidates. Sure, most workshops begin by assigning and discussing a flurry of published stories, samples of favourite authors, exemplars of a sub-genre or a literary technique. Soon, however, the machinery of the workshop takes over, drafts get submitted and class time focuses fully upon students' own words.

Workshop insularity can create a hothouse: some students' work flourishes under the workshop's critical intensity; others' creativity withers from a lack of outside nourishment. As a student-writer, I could often tell who amongst my peers read—I mean, *really* read—and who didn't. It showed in their work and in their feedback. I can tell the same now as an instructor. The most promising student writers read widely and have a hunger to read more. They gravitate to our forms and techniques courses. Workshops alone can't sustain them.

Midway through my third year, I felt the sagging symptoms of what I would later diagnose, and see in my own students, as "workshop fatigue." My joy in writing declined. Deadlines became a grind. Our workshop solidarity showed cracks. We envied our more accomplished peers. We resented others who handed in dashed-off, cliché-riddled drafts. We seethed at verbose classmates who dominated discussions. (@GuyInYourMFA was once a guy in your BFA—in fact, he might have been me.) We recycled our kneejerk feedback: "What's the focus? Make this a scene! This would work better in first-person." I couldn't bring myself to sit through another workshop.

And so, in what still feels like an act of betrayal, I switched majors from Creative Writing to English literature. I read more. I wrote more. (Mostly for the campus newspaper.) I graduated on time, wrote a half-draft of a half-assed coming-of-age novel, knocked off an M.A. in English at Queen's, taught ESL overseas and then first-year composition back in Canada and stumbled into a career as a freelance writer and magazine editor.

* * *

Fast-forward to 2004. I applied for and was hired for a new position at UVic's Department of Writing. Ten years earlier, the department had dropped "Creative" from its name, and my later attempts, as chair, to reinstate the word would founder on the rocks of university bureaucracy. I was the fourth faculty member hired that year, as the department replaced retiring faculty and expanded to meet demand in a widening gyre of genres. With my hire, creative nonfiction joined fiction, poetry and drama in the introductory course. (Full disclosure: I'd never heard the term "creative nonfiction" before I applied.) A few years later, we split drama into distinct stage and screenwriting streams.

The department's ambitious growth in the early 2000s reflected both national and international interest in CW courses and soon spawned unintended downstream consequences. An undergraduate degree juggling hundreds of students across five different genres, plus a minor in professional writing and co-op work options, our program became complex and unbalanced. Faculty needed to lead more required workshops, so we were less available to offer lecture/discussion electives. For example, I taught Forms and Techniques of Short Creative Nonfiction only every other year, a schedule challenging for any student who had switched majors and hoped to graduate on time. Lacking options, students took workshops in second or third genres as senior electives. This caused registration logjams, with long waitlists for workshops in fiction and screenwriting, until students often needed five or even six years to finish four-year degrees. They complained to our chair, who begged the dean for money to offer more workshops.

Departments across Canada, however, were facing pressure from administrations to justify budgets by meeting enrolment targets, numbers known at UVic as Equivalent Enrolments Taught—or EETs ("Equivalent"). (I imagined this referred, metaphorically, to the sum of students "eaten" by the university.) Our workshops were frowned upon as "low EETs courses"; intimate enrolments might be fine for a graduate seminar or the occasional honours seminar but not for an entire undergraduate degree. Our expanding roster of required workshops, however, made it hard to meet rising EETs targets. We needed big courses to offset their small enrolments. To save our workshops, we creative writers had to think creatively.

First, we took inspiration from faculties under even more threat from enrolment drops and budget clawbacks. To compete with big-draw Social Science classes like PSYC 100, Humanities departments had launched "bums-in-seats" courses, often with few or no prerequisites and catchy cultural studies titles. At UVic, we called these "Vampire Studies" electives after a wildly popular *Nosferatu*-inspired film-and-lit elective run by the Germanic Studies Department.

Writing already offered one such large-draw course. Since the early 1990s, sessional instructor Brian Hendricks had taught a fourth-year elective in myth and film to packed lecture halls. In 2008, needing more EETs, the Department added a first-year course titled "The Writer's World in Books and Film," in which 150 students watched a movie about an author (*Capote*, say, or *The Hours*) and attended a lecture about their life and work. Later, screenwriting instructors refocused the course on storytelling methods in Pixar, Marvel and DC movies. These Hollywood iterations proved so successful that the Department bumped capacity to 250 students and ran multiple sections per year. Eventually, we couldn't find lecture halls with enough seats for the bums that wanted in.

WRIT 109—which the Department subtitles "The Pixar Story" when one lecturer is at the helm—remains a Writing course in which students do little writing; in fact, it's mostly taken by non-Writing majors, with assessment via online blogs, multiple-choice midterms and final exams. These courses require a nimble subject expertise and a special style of pedagogy that few instructors can manage: less line editor and workshop mentor and more inspirational raconteur and high-energy stage performer, with a side gig as a projectionist. It can seem a bit scammy, luring hordes of first-year students to spend tuition money to watch Hollywood flicks. But courses like The Pixar Story remain popular and keep our workshops afloat. Sort of.

Our Writing department was still asked to find other administrative "efficiencies" in our core programming to address budget issues and the backlog of students who couldn't graduate in time. We made some hard choices: we doubled the number of students in our forms and techniques electives. We dropped the requirement that Writing majors include a second fourth-year workshop as a requirement to graduate. Workshop fatigue can often plague our senior majors by their final year anyway, although no longer requiring, for example, poets to also write nonfiction at advanced (undergraduate) levels means students graduate with fewer polished drafts in their portfolios and may be slower to make the genre pivots that so many writers do.

The centrality of the workshop model to CW teaching kept recurring. Under administrative pressure in the cost-cutting new millennium, the Department also remodelled our introductory WRIT 100 course. Instead of rotating through genre-based sections taught by three or four separate instructors, we scaled up the course into a 150-student lecture that could be taught across two terms by a single faculty member, or co-taught by two instructors, with tutorials of 30 students. That "big tent" concentration freed faculty and sessionals to teach more workshops and electives. However, WRIT 100 now absorbs much of our graduate student budget, so that teaching assistants can grade assignments and run tutorials. Unlike our bums-in-seats electives *about* writing, an introduction to Creative Writing can't run without any actual writing.

Doubts also crept into our collective faith in the workshop system of peer feedback. We realized we were now sending first-year students from a large-intake class straight into small second-year workshops, hoping they could learn on the fly to be attentive and empathetic peer commenters. Dropping second-year students straight into workshop didn't always succeed, so we redesigned our second-year curriculum. Students now begin in a 30-person lecture/discussion section that focuses on critical reading and elements of craft in one genre. By the end of term, students practise the rudiments of workshop process in small groups overseen by the instructor; we now let students splash in the shallows of the workshop pool rather than drop them right into the deep end. Only in the second term do they divide into sections of 15 students for a traditional peer workshop.

***

During my first few years of teaching, I ran the workshop pedagogy I'd inherited with little critical reflection. I'd learned it as a student, from an instructor who had learned it from another instructor, who had likely learned it in Iowa. The workshop could feel like a multi-level marketing scheme; each teacher sells a new wave of students on the workshop's virtues as a product and a process. Questioning the workshop might shake the foundations on which our own careers as teachers have been built.

Most instructors, though, eventually tinker with the peer-review engine. And so, I addressed my misgivings. The workshop, I thought, was okay at addressing the "mid-level" issues of a nonfiction draft: characterization, dialogue, scene development, integration of research. However, it was less helpful at the micro- and macro-levels of a story. How could the workshop get students to reckon more precisely with the word choices and sentence structure at the core of effective writing? (I'd subbed for poetry workshops and envied how quickly poets zero in on diction and syntax.) How could the workshop step back and discuss the narrative building blocks of sections and scenes, beyond snap judgements about a story's opening or ending?

Some instructors assigned students to act as co-leaders of the workshopping of peers' drafts to decentre attention from the faculty member as the bearer of the "right" opinion. Eventually, I assigned not one but three student-leaders to each draft: the first shepherded the general discussion; the second focused on style by identifying one sentence or passage that could be revised and another passage that "sang"—and then walked us through both passages. A third student sketched a visual flowchart of the draft's structure (an idea borrowed from Jack Hodgins) that was projected on a screen so the class could step back and offer renovation tips for the story's architecture. (I shared this workshop technique of "zooming out, zeroing in" as a pedagogy paper under that title at the 2009 AWP conference in Chicago).

In theory, the workshop's focus on draft work tries to address the mysteries of the revision process. In practice, one of the biggest challenges of teaching writing remains teaching rewriting—which is roughly 95% of writing. At the end of any class, students are often left to sort through 15 often contradictory opinions on how to improve their drafts.

In most workshop courses now, I ask students to submit a revised assignment to be workshopped a second time; this middle draft, I emphasize, is the opportunity to make bold changes and take creative risks, not just tweak words or tighten scenes. Students can get feedback on which major changes work—or not. They end up writing less original work per term (by one fewer story) but go much deeper on a single assignment. They also demystify for each other what effective revision can look like—and how rewriting is a series of focused and laborious stages. Our department also added a third-year lecture/discussion elective in editing and revision, now taught by Danielle Geller, our department's graduate advisor.

* * *

Slowly, the UVic Writing Department relinquished the one-size-fits-all model of the workshop. Different genres found new ways to adapt their pedagogies to their students' needs. Hired in 2004, independent filmmaker Mo Bradley realized that, in an era of cheap video cameras and the dawn of powerful smartphones, it made little sense to ask students to draft screenplays that would rarely get produced. Bradley retooled WRIT 320, a writing and production workshop in which teams of students turn scripts into short films, and added a hands-on prerequisite (WRIT 326: Media Production for Writers) to teach the basics of digital audio, photography and film production. Then, Bradley devised an ambitious fourth-year production course, open to all students, in which the entire class co-produces one short film over several intensive weekend sessions; the results have included *Freshman's Wharf*, a ten-episode web series, and *Knot for Sale*, an innovative 360° VR short film.

Kevin Kerr, a Governor General's Literary Award-winning playwright and recent department chair, created a similar production course for stage writing based on his expertise in site-specific theatre. Students collectively devise and mount a live performance using the unique environmental features of UVic's campus, such as the labyrinthine paths of Finnerty Gardens; again, workshopping the script is only one part in the overall course experience. Fiction professor Lee Henderson leads a graphic novel workshop that invites Writing and Visual Arts students to collaborate and blends prose narratives with drawing. Gregory Scofield teaches a seminar course that combines discussions of Indigenous women's resistance writing with learning Métis beadwork. Shane Book teaches a lecture/discussion course in hip-hop culture. Sean Holman runs trauma-informed environmental journalism classes in which students co-author oral histories with survivors of climate disasters. The Department runs other electives in humour writing, writing about place and the business of writing.

In 2016, I began to teach my own production course focused on writing interactive narratives: branching-path stories, plays, poetry and other experiences in digital and analogue media. Students spend no more than half the classes demonstrating and workshopping project prototypes; before that, they learn Twine (an interactive authoring tool) and read, play and discuss a range of experimental story-games. I let students choose their own paths through branches of critical readings, how-to videos and other craft resources, genres and media of final projects and whether to work in teams or solo.

At its best, the traditional workshop pushes against the Romantic stereotype of the solitary author, toiling in a garret or waiting for their Muse and instead emphasizes the importance of communal support and peer feedback to the creative process. Our seminar-sized production courses go even further by merging traditional writing craft with collaborative creative experimentation, hands-on technical skills and intensive production experiences.

***

Over the last decade or so, Creative Writing departments could no longer ignore the critiques of the systemic racism embedded in the traditional workshop's orthodoxy. In 2014, Junot Díaz's "MFA vs. POC," a blistering account of his experiences of white supremacy and casual racism at Cornell's MFA program, opened eyes amongst white faculty to the false faith that our workshops had ever been safe spaces for all students. Essays and blog posts from other writers (such as Paola Capó-García and David Mura) affirmed Díaz's experiences as "a person of color in a workshop whose theory of reality did not include my most fundamental experiences as a person of color—that did not in other words include *me*."

UVic's Department of Writing had never been particularly diverse, in its faculty complement or student recruitment, even by the low standards of most Creative Writing programs. Founded in 1973, on the lands of the lək̓ʷəŋən and WSÁNEĆ Indigenous peoples, the Department only hired its first female faculty members in 1992 (Lorna Crozier and Margaret Hollingsworth), its first faculty member of colour in 2016 (Shane Book) and its first Indigenous faculty members in 2019 (Danielle Geller and Gregory Scofield). For much of its history, the instructors—and a substantial portion of the student body—looked a lot like ... well, *me*. While the Department celebrates the accomplishments of a diverse range of alumni (including Richard Van Camp, Esi Edugyan and Yasuko Thanh), we can't account for the many students who never felt comfortable in our workshops and dropped out ... or the potential students and even faculty members who didn't feel welcome enough to apply. Many of us needed to take a critical look at the biases embedded in our own teaching practices and reading lists—myself very much included.

In January of 2021, as we all began to emerge from our pandemic Zoom rooms, Felicia Rose Chavez published *The Anti-Racist Writing Workshop*. Her vital book underscores the damage the conventional workshop method can inflict upon black, Indigenous and students of colour, on writers from all marginalized groups. In it, she lays out a path towards an alternative and inclusive pedagogy via an adaptation of Liz Lerman's "critical response process"—a workshop open to the full range of students' experiences and creativity. This consent-based model releases student-writers from the rigid "cone of silence" I'd been taught, first as an undergraduate and then as an instructor, to impose on the workshopper, so the draft's author might listen but not debate in a misguided belief that wordless supplication was the best way, in Chavez's words, to "receive critique"—"to assume a position of passivity: step away from the page ... and don't talk back" (36). The Chavez/Lerman workshop invites students to participate in a conversation about their own work and to ensure they receive the feedback they truly need, not just the feedback their peers and instructors *think* they need.

Recently, I joined other faculty members and instructors experimenting with the Chavez/Lerman workshop. It took a few classes for students, disciplined to the default mode of the traditional workshop, to adapt and become active participants in their own workshopping rather than passive recipients of critique. It also took time to restrain my own tendency to steer the conversation. Eventually, we all learned to listen to the author and carefully offer what the Chavez/Lerman model calls "neutral questions" and "permissioned opinions" (138) rather than blurt out thoughts and advice.

The critical-response process acknowledges that every student-writer is a different person, from a different background, with different life experiences, at a different stage in their creative process—and that students often know best what kind of critical feedback will be most valuable for their own writing. This student-centred model breaks the one-size-fits-all constraints of the old workshop. Creative nonfiction workshops are often filled with confessional moments of vulnerability and trauma, so writers and readers (as well as teachers) can struggle to distinguish a critique of expression from a dismissal of the experiences expressed. The Chavez/Lerman model slows down the process to open a space for understanding, in both directions.

As an administrator and nonfiction instructor, I've also become acutely aware of the mental health crisis on our campuses. I now begin each workshop (and the occasional committee meeting) with a mindfulness exercise known as an "attunement," which I learned at Findhorn, an ecovillage in Scotland. We stand in a circle, close our eyes and extend our hands, letting fingers hover over neighbours' palms in our touch-conscious COVID era. Then, I encourage the circle to breathe deeply, "shut the open browser tabs of our minds" and focus for the next few hours on supporting each other's creative work. The attunement acts as a mental palate cleanser and segue into the workshop proper. It reminds us to treat each other like true colleagues, not like the two-dimensional avatars on a social media app.

By midterm, students run with the new, more inclusive model as though it's all they've ever known. It might just be confirmation bias, but I've found that I've received some of the strongest and bravest drafts in the two years since I've embraced the more egalitarian Chavez/Lerman process. We all feel a little less fatigued by end of term, and the open pedagogy has renewed my wavering faith in the workshop.

* * *

I'd volunteered to become chair of the Department in 2014, after several years as Director of the Professional Writing Minor and Graduate Advisor. Long-time faculty members and previous chairs Lorna Crozier and Bill Gaston had guided our Department through much of its major restructuring; I continued their legacies while drawing on nearly forgotten math skills from my Science studies to defend our budgets and course offerings from bean-counters and unrelenting EETs targets. More importantly, I oversaw the recruitment of four new colleagues, as one generation of UVic Writing faculty gave way to the next. It doesn't matter how elite your academic programming might be if you don't hire the best possible writers to teach it.

It's now 2024. I am far closer to teaching my last workshop than teaching my first one. My years of spreadsheets and other admin chores lie behind me, and I can once again lean into the undiluted joys of teaching and writing. (I only half-joke that being chair nearly killed me: I spent the final few weeks of my term, in June 2019, recovering from a "mild" heart attack.) Looking back, I liken the experience of academic administration to trying to steer the *Exxon Valdez*—while putting out electrical fires on the bridge. Even the smallest shift in our program's direction felt achingly slow to enact; it could take a year or more to navigate the hierarchy of committee approvals and then another year for effects to trickle down to students. A well-intentioned "fix" to our curriculum also risked accidentally disrupting our program's delicate ecology. After five years at the helm, I felt I didn't guide the Department as far or as fast as I'd hoped; but I hadn't run our program aground on dangerous shoals either.

Fifty years since the founding of UVic's Department of [Creative] Writing, the workshop remains core to our undergraduate degree—understandably, imperfectly but not disastrously. Our revised and renewed program feels closer to equilibrium, with a mix of retooled peer-review workshops, and production classes, and reading-rich forms-and-technique courses, and special-topics electives driven by the diverse interests and deep expertise of our new faculty members.

As other departments and faculties on campus struggle to reverse declines in enrolments, the registration numbers for our Writing major remain robust. The workshop no longer needs saving, neither from budget cutbacks nor from its own deficiencies. Despite the administrative pressures of the neoliberal university, we see our students as more than just EETs or bums in seats. They arrive to our classrooms with a yearning to learn how to write, in an expansive range of genres and media, to meet others who feel the same, to harness their tumultuous imaginations and restless emotions, to wrestle with a complex and often unjust world and to conjure visions of a new one. And then, catalyzed by a little gentle guidance, they do exactly that, with unique voices and in expressive forms that no A.I. chatbot can replicate.

That creative alchemy—whether it happens within or without a workshop—will always give me hope.

Works Cited

"5 Years of 4th Genre." *Michigan State University Press*, Home: Literary Collections, 2024, https://msupress.org/9780870137761/5-years-of-4th-genre.

Adams, James. "Late Writer Dave Godfrey Created Three Publishing Houses." *The Globe and Mail*, 3 July 2015, www.theglobeandmail.com/arts/books-and-media/late-writer-dave-godfrey-created-three-publishing-houses/article25269903.

Bradley, Mo, director. *Freshman's Wharf*, 2011.

Bradley, Mo, director. *Knot for Sale*, 2016, vimeo.com/221807753.

Bukoski, Anthony. "The Canadian Writer & the Iowa Experience." *Canadian Literature*, vol. 101, Summer 1984, pp. 15–34.

Capó-García, Paola. "Addressing the 'Too White' Problem: A Response to Junot Díaz's 'MFA vs. POC' Critique." *Remezcla*, 7 May 2014, remezcla.com/culture/junot-diaz-mfa-vs-poc-a-response.

Chavez, Felicia Rose. *The Anti-Racist Writing Workshop: How to Decolonize the Creative Classroom*. Haymarket Books, 2021.

Díaz, Junot. "MFA vs. POC." *The New Yorker*, 30 Apr. 2014, www.newyorker.com/books/page-turner/mfa-vs-poc.

"Explore and Create." *Canada Council for the Arts/Conseil des arts du Canada*, Funding: Grants. N.d. https://canadacouncil.ca/funding/grants/explore-and-create.

"Equivalent Enrolments Taught (EET)." *Definitions*. University of Victoria, Institutional Planning & Analysis. www.uvic.ca/institutionalplanning/definitions.

Gnarowski, Michael et al. "House of Anansi." *The Canadian Encyclopedia*. 15 Jan. 2015. https://www.thecanadianencyclopedia.ca/en/article/house-of-anansi.
Grossman, David. *See Under: Love*. Translated by Betsy Rosenberg, Picador Farrar, Straus and Giroux, 1989.
Hodgins, Jack. *A Passion for Narrative: A Guide for Writing Fiction*. McClelland & Stewart, 1993.
Kertzer, Jon. "Why Do I Love Most." Rev. of *Coming through Slaughter*, by Michael Ondaatje. *The Fiddlehead*, Spring, 1977, 113, pp. 126–29. https://thefiddlehead.ca/content/coming-through-slaughter-michael-ondaatje-anansi-1976.
Lerman, Liz, and John Borstel. *Liz Lerman's Critical Response Process: A Method for Getting Useful Feedback on Anything You Make, from Dance to Dessert*. Dance Exchange, 2003.
Mura, David. "On the Response to Junot Díaz's 'MFA vs. POC'." *Warscapes*, 7 May 2014, www.warscapes.com/blog/response-junot-diaz-s-mfa-vs-poc.
O'Leary, Josh. "If You Write It: The University of Iowa Author Who Inspired the Field of Dreams." *Iowa Magazine*, 12 June 2020, magazine.foriowa.org/story.php?ed=true&storyid=1968.
"Past Winners and Finalists." *Canada Council for the Arts/Conseil des arts du* Canada: GG Books, Governor General's Literary Awards, n.d., https://ggbooks.ca/past-winners-and-finalists.
Robinson, Eden. *Monkey Beach*. Vintage Canada, 2000.
Robinson, Eden. *Return of the Trickster*. Penguin Random House, 2021.
Robinson, Eden. *Son of a Trickster*. Penguin Random House, 2017.
Robinson, Eden. *Trickster Drift*. Penguin Random House, 2018.
Skelton, Robin. *Poetic Truth*. Heinemann Educational, 1978.
Skelton, Robin. *The Poet's Calling*. Heinemann Educational, 1975.
Skelton, Robin. *The Practice of Poetry*. Heinemann Educational, 1971.
Thompson, F., and Colin Boyd. "Robin Skelton." *The Canadian Encyclopedia*, 16 Dec. 2013, www.thecanadianencyclopedia.ca/en/article/robin-skelton.

Professor Leach's Recurrent Writing Comments

This *what?*

Translation: Never begin a sentence with a demonstrative pronoun (*this, that, those, these*) that has an unclear antecedent. This ambiguity might cause a reader to stop and wonder what the pronoun refers back to.

~~*utilize*~~

Translation: Use *use* instead.

Your story begins here →

Translation: Cut the first page. At least.

More CMTSU details!

Translation: Search your notes or jog your memory for the unique factoids and quirky concrete details from real life that will make a novelist envious and a reader think, "Wow, you can't make that shit up!"

Who is on your lifeboat?

Translation: There are too many names for a reader to keep track of. Which characters are most important to your story? And who can be left off the lifeboat?

4 Origin Stories, Watersheds and Gendered Politics

On Launching a New Creative Writing MFA

Jeanette Lynes

My evolution—in tenure-track or tenured appointments at three different Canadian universities—from a literature professor who published creative writing and taught Creative Writing to becoming the inaugural director of Canada's second-youngest Creative Writing MFA program has endured, and resisted, campus gender politics throughout my 35 years of teaching. Notably, peer denigration of my abilities has often been tied to my faculty role as a writer. My 14 years, since 2011, as the inaugural director of the MFA in Writing at the University of Saskatchewan, a large, research-intensive university in Canada's Prairies, revealed new yet recurrent shortcomings in institutional respect, especially as a seemingly desired MFA program was institutionally rehomed but also as our university, like many, suffered massive budgetary pressures and cuts.

My wearing two hats—administrator of a Creative Writing program and for its first six years the only professor teaching in it—made me even more aware of Creative Writing's movement from disciplinary margins closer to the centre of that species at risk, the Humanities education. Other Creative Writing (CW) professors who wear or have worn similar professional hats may understand this binary split between administration and teaching and our greater exposure to marginalization within the university. Perhaps it is Creative Writing's lot in academic life to be 'othered' within the academy, to hold an uneasy, pariah status within the Humanities and Liberal Arts (possibly less so if housed within a Fine Arts Department). Social constructions of the writer as subversive maverick within a system that, at its core, has a cultural custodianship as its project prompt Janelle Adsit to call creative writing within the academy "the *institutionalization of anti-institutionality*" (40). This margin-centre dynamic implies an ongoing dissonance, which isn't always a bad thing. Vibrant, energized initiatives can spring from the margins. However, battles happen there, too, and some of the pressure points outlined in what follows may resonate and even prove instructive to future Creative Writing professors, especially those with hybrid roles as administrator and teacher/supervisor.

Canadian universities haven't been overly friendly to Creative Writing or writers. The three universities where I've taught—and, increasingly,

DOI: 10.4324/9781032614144-6

advocated for Creative Writing—supported CW so long as it remained on the sidelines. The two previous English Departments in which I worked prior to the University of Saskatchewan each had one token poet regarded as a bit 'other,' but he (males in both cases) was tolerated; these poets had doctoral degrees and the poet-scholar has been a campus fixture for some time. That said, departmental rumours rumbled that these Creative Writing faculty members had a lighter load and weren't full participants in the English department. In other words, living Canadian writers were resented at Canadian university departments devoted to the study of literature. When I proposed more Creative Writing programming at a previous university, I was told that the job of the English Department is to teach literature. Students writing about literature was somehow more important than students writing literature. My professional life changed radically in 2011 when I was hired to direct the new MFA in Writing at the University of Saskatchewan (hereafter referred to as U of S)—but this opportunity came with a whole new set of institutional politics that in turn responded to, and/or reacted to, macro forces of respect, value and gender roles.

No CW professor needs reminding that some university disciplines are perceived as being more 'powerful' or carrying a higher social value than others or that the university itself perpetually responds to larger economic and political forces. The politics of Creative Writing at my institution has been a dance of margin and centre. More broadly, the 'outsider' status of Creative Writing within some Canadian universities is shifting given the well-documented decline of student enrolments in Humanities programs (Chiose; Johnson; Vanderwal; etc.). Creative Writing courses and degrees are moving from a marginal to more central position within some English Department curricula, nudged away from being a benign 'add on' or novelty, to a more integral part of English Studies. This journey is worth tracking as part of larger pedagogical and cultural conversations.

To narrativize the past 13 years, I will, after some initial context, identify four watershed moments in the development of Canada's second-youngest MFA program in Creative Writing (and the only MFA program in our three Prairie provinces). While what follows pertains most directly to my institution, patterns may be recognizable with respect to fundamental aspects of Creative Writing within a university culture.

I: Origin Stories

Rightly, the validity of the workshop as a pedagogical model has been questioned for some time now, especially with respect to its power dynamics and exclusionary practices (Adsit, Salesses, Chavez, et al.). The notion that 'craft' is neither value-neutral nor 'universal' is opening new pedagogical conversations in productive ways. Shortly before being recently appointed to Columbia's influential writing program (Saldarriaga), Matthew Salesses opened his 2021 book *Craft in the Real World: Rethinking Fiction Writing and Workshopping* overtly with:

> This book is a challenge to accepted models of craft and workshop, to everything from character-driven plot to the "cone of silence," or "gag rule," that in a creative writing workshop silences the manuscript's author. The challenge is this: to take craft out of some imaginary vacuum (as if meaning in fiction is separate from meaning in life) and return it to is cultural and historical context. Race, gender, sexuality, etc. affect our lives and so must affect our fiction. Real-world context, and particularly what we do with that context *is* craft. (xiii)

In recent years, my students similarly question the workshop model, pushing back, asserting their own agency and taking more ownership of the classroom—rejecting the "gag rule" (Salesses xiii) in favour of a more conversational approach, for example—and in this way more fully participate in the process of their own learning. Notably, however, one feature of this origin story of graduate-level Creative Writing study at the University of Saskatchewan was the isolation of my initially being the only full-time faculty member teaching Creative Writing, and the undeniable fact of our geographical isolation as the only CW MFA program in the Prairies. With my closest CW MFA neighbours 1500 kilometres away at the University of British Columbia (see Chapter 13) or 1650 at the University of Victoria (see Chapter 3), I, too, had my "cone of silence" and was "gagged" by Canada's famous geographic expansiveness (Salesses xiii). There were on-line resources to offset that isolation, books, journals of pedagogy, professional organizations, and to combat isolation, and I availed myself of these resources. But for much of the early phase of this story, my 'subject position' was that of a lone ranger running an odd, outlier program. The U of S MFA program was in its infanthood, its auditioning-for-credibility phase, vying for a place within the university as it vied for a place in the national CW degree landscape.

The U of S MFA in Writing faced challenges, such as its quest, like an orphan child, for a stable home, discussed in "Watershed Moment #1"; the implosion of the university itself (Watershed Moment #2); the COVID pandemic's belated confrontation of accessibility in CW (Watershed Moment #3); the margin-centre migration (Watershed Moment #4).

Watershed Moment #1: Beginnings, Improvising a Programmatic Home

In the early days of the U of S CW MFA, gendered tropes (stereotypes) and institutional biases figured strongly. After several years, campus colleagues began to pay attention to the MFA in Writing; when they wanted to say something nice about its progress and my (perceived) enabling role in that, they more than once dubbed me as a "den mother" and "cheerleader" for writers. These gender monikers rankle me to this day. I'd much rather have been called an advocate for writers or a visionary leader.

Before the MFA in Writing admitted its first students in 2011, the U of S offered a smattering of Creative Writing courses at the undergraduate level, as well as those offered on the campus of its affiliated institution, St. Peter's College in Muenster, and a small number of Creative Writing courses that ran out of St. Thomas More College on the main U of S campus. The new MFA in Writing was the province of Saskatchewan's first MFA graduate-level Creative Writing program. The University of Regina offers an MA in English with a creative concentration. As Darryl Whetter points out here in his chapter "Can'tLit," Canada's master's CW programs divide largely between MAs in Creative Writing in English, like University of Regina, and MFA programs like those at the University of British Columbia and ours. To some extent, that difference (or schism) generally finds writer-scholars in MA programs and writer-artists in the MFA programs. When I arrived at the U of S in 2011, I found it odd that while officially my institutional home was, and still remains, the Department of English, the MFA in Writing program was more practically speaking housed in the Interdisciplinary Centre for Culture and Creativity (ICCC). Back then, the ICCC was well-resourced, with its own director, an administrative staff of two and a physical office space. The Centre had some funding to which scholars could apply if their projects were deemed interdisciplinary enough. Interdisciplinarity was earmarked as a priority by the university as it is at many institutions in Canada, and at the Social Sciences and Humanities Research Council of Canada (SSHRC), the national organization that turns public funds into research grants, for everyone from historians to philosophers to poets, from master's and doctoral scholarships through to faculty grants. Notably, given my career-long campus encounters with disrespect for both my gender and my discipline, the ICCC housed, in addition to our new CW MFA, Women's and Gender Studies and a few other sundry courses. I assumed, rightly or wrongly, that enough English faculty felt disinclined to home a writing MFA, or wanted to keep a distance between themselves and what may have been seen by some as a dubious experiment. If the MFA flopped, the failure would not land in the English Department. So, the ICCC provided a parking space for the baby CW MFA program. My colleagues were kind and generous to me while I oversaw this experimental new program. This arrangement seemed to work so long as Creative Writing stayed in its own lane. I taught a few literature classes, which I enjoyed, and which helped integrate me into the English Department. It's important to note that, not always the norm for me at other Canadian universities, the U of S English Department was tolerant towards Creative Writing initiatives. The "Inspired Minds" writing program at the local correctional facility was and is run by English faculty ("Literature"). Still, I'm not the first CW prof to ask how a university in general and its (English) literature department in particular can so regularly promote the value of literature while being sceptical of including student writing in curricula? *The Fieldstone Review*, a student-run, on-line creative writing magazine has been housed in the English Department since around 2005 ("About Us"). Notable Canadian poets and fiction writers like Patrick Lane, Elizabeth Brewster, Lorna Crozier, Tim Lilburn, Guy Vanderhaeghe, Candace Savage and Barbara Langhorst have taught Creative Writing at U of S over the years. David Carpenter, poet, fiction and nonfiction writer, and Robert Calder, memoirist, biographer and scholar, were long-time members of the English Department as was poet Hilary Clark, to name a few. For more than a decade, the English Department has partnered with the Saskatchewan Writers' Guild to host an annual creative writing conference, Writing North, and still does ("Writing North"). Given this history of institutional public engagement with contemporary Canadian writing, the English Department's not hosting the University's new CW MFA struck me as puzzling. When first running a new CW MFA in a country that for a long time only had two, though, who had time to sleuth out why writing seemed to be both valued and not at U of S? I was trying to get from one day to another, teaching all the MFA classes and supervising almost all the students in addition to maintaining my own writing practice.

The irony that Women's and Gender Studies and the MFA in Writing were both housed in the ICCC wasn't lost on me. Two programs perceived as feminized were slotted into this idiosyncratic Centre. My colleague who directed Women's and Gender Studies provided illuminating critiques of institutional politics. Women's and Gender Studies had been nomadic for some time. Perhaps emblematically, after several years, the ICCC disappeared; it simply went away. It had always been a project with an identity crisis. After a few years at the ICCC, the CW MFA finally became part of the English Department. The MFA in Writing had gained enough street-cred, it seemed, to be allowed into the club, largely, I was sure, due to student demand for more Creative Writing courses. Once the MFA in Writing had proven itself, it was rewarded with a more permanent institutional home, not the nomadic, and marginal one, where we began.

It's not unheard of for the often marginalized discipline of CW to move around between different campus homes. As David Leach recounts in Chapter 3, the CW program at University of Victoria began in the Department of English, then moved to Fine Arts, a rehoming from scholars to fellow artists relevant in the contemporary role CW courses and degrees play in reviving flagging enrolment in English programs. A recent article in *Inside Higher Ed* entitled "Rewriting the English Curriculum" notes "Building a connection between the creative and analytical sides of English seems to be a priority for many institutions" (Alonso). Overall, the U of S's MFA in Writing relocation to the Department of English has been beneficial.

An additional irony in the MFA's origin story, from a gendered perspective, is that the program had been leveraged into existence by powerful male academics. It took them about five years of trailblazing to move the new graduate program through the various institutional levels for approval.

These Creative Writing trailblazers remained in people's institutional memories, and the program's aura of male authority buffered me to some extent. But when I met *alone* with senior University administrators—not the aforementioned program founders, different ones—to lobby for resources for the MFA, they took their shots. U of S identifies to a large extent as a STEM and agricultural institution. One senior administrator told me that the MFA in Writing was a "boutique" program. Think *bauble. Decoration. Small staff.* Certainly, the MFA was a smaller graduate program than those in the Sciences, Social Sciences and other programs. However, as the appetite for Creative Writing grew across the country, the MFA gained momentum.

Another early watershed moment in the program's history happened around 2013, when the program's Thesis Licence Agreement was negotiated with the College of Graduate and Postdoctoral Studies, the administrative body that oversees *all* the University's graduate programs. I explained to this senior administrator that our Thesis Licence Agreement needed to continue to allow student-writers to keep their work—hopefully, for later publication—and not have it 'harvested' by the institution's ETD (Electronic Thesis Database), essentially publishing it on-line and robbing an emerging writer of the first book-length publication which Canadian publishers, like most, seek. In this instance, the senior administrator with whom I met resented creative writers' unwillingness to give their work to the world, the "taxpayers" (his word). "Who," this administrator asked me, "did I think paid to keep the campus grounds nicely manicured, and my classrooms heated?" I told him that writers *do* share their work, through publication; it just *takes longer*. Because other universities had such an agreement in place, or policies that protected student writers' work, my institution ultimately agreed to accept protecting CW theses from becoming the database intellectual property of massive research publishing corporations, of self-sabotagingly having a young poet or novelist 'publish' online with no proper distribution or promotion instead of as a book that might be considered for career-making awards. That administrator approved our dodging this database conscription on a 'probationary' basis, for three years, if memory serves. Ultimately, a senior male colleague a couple of years after that negotiated the Licence Agreement as a permanent fixture. I often felt diminished, existing within this gendered academic culture.

Watershed Moment #2: Admin-Ageddon

In 2014, the University of Saskatchewan itself risked melting down. The previous year, a new president had been hired, a woman, to whip us all into financial shape. I'm hardly telling tales out of school, here; the story of President Ilene Busch-Vishniac's prompt dismissal after just a year was all over the media (Canadian; CBC News "University"). Her budget-cutting exercise, branded as "TransformUS" was "targeted at," as Allan Maki and Tu Thanh Ha wrote in *The Globe and Mail*, "saving $25 million by cutting staff and merging faculties" to address budget deficits. Heads rolled. Walls were literally knocked down in my college to redesign program support. The administrative staff structure was decimated. People protested in public demonstrations (CBC News "TransformUS"). It was high-drama time at U of S. Veteran of *decades* of institutional sexism, I assumed that a "boutique" program like an MFA in Writing would be axed. I'd probably still have a job unless they cut tenured positions, but the MFA in Writing I had been hired to lead would, I feared, be cancelled as part of the $25 million budget cuts. There was a great deal of anger which spearheaded the countermovement "DefendUs," which consisted of "faculty, students and alumni" (CBC News, "TransformUS Gone").

The MFA in Writing survived this Admin-ageddon. Maybe we were just too small to be noticed. Sometimes, the margins are a safe place to hide. But program support was never the same after heads rolled and walls were knocked down. The new segmentation of labour meant that support work was chopped into bits with various people performing various tasks, with constant, revolving doors. Reduced staff and support required faculty like myself devoting even more time to administrative tasks or working to determine who could or would divide tasks between so many individuals.

Watershed Moment #3: The COVID-19 Pandemic

What the pandemic did for Creative Writing pedagogy, I contend, was generate an increased appetite for online education. Because digital courses removed geographical obstacles, Creative Writing belatedly confronted accessibility, finally admitted another margin-centre transposition. How many or, rather, how few, Canadian campuses have all classrooms and faculty offices accessible to those with mobility issues, caregiving commitments, et cetera? Why did it take a lethal global virus to welcome those who cannot leave their living spaces into a CW workshop that does not, arguably, have some of the specialized on-site equipment of campus courses in Sculpture or Particle Physics? If anything, CW programming gained more traction through the pandemic. It's a bittersweet irony that during a time of massive grief, and loss, positive forces of connection through writing were also in play. There's the old adage that art can comfort and affirm and offer an antidote to widespread grief.

Watershed Moment #4: The Margin-Centre Migration

U of S's new Creative Writing MFA made it through the early days of working in the margins. We survived Admin-ageddon and then the pandemic. And my program, after 11 lonely years, was granted a second tenure-track hire in Creative Writing in 2022. Our undergraduate programming has also grown substantially. CW, when housed in an academic department like English, bolsters enrolments in Literature courses. Much has been written in recent years about declining enrolments in the Humanities and Liberal Arts. Simona Chiose, in *The Globe and Mail*, may be over-dramatizing a little in her contention that, "[o]ver the past decade, students have fled the humanities," but she's correct in asserting that "universities are having to adapt." Columnist Geoff Johnson cites a "20 percent" enrolment decline in Humanities courses in recent years, adding that this decline is "neither new nor unique to Canada." One example of programmatic adaptation is the University of Waterloo's hybrid approach to programming, a new major that combines creative and professional writing. In their institutional press, the 'selling point' of this innovation is, as lecturer Dr. Andrea Jonas states, the "strong writing skills" students acquire will "be animated by their distinct voice and creative energy, which will not only prepare them for the job market but set them apart" (qtd. in Vanderwal).

This CW origin story at one Canadian university has tracked CW from being a minor player in the margins to a growing area within the English curriculum. At U of S, at least 200 undergraduates take Introduction to Creative Writing each year. About 40–50 undergraduates take the second-year CW course. Third-year CW programming is being developed as well as a CW Certificate. While Literature faculty in English Departments may continue to regard CW with ambivalence, openly or secretly, creative writers can and do live peaceably with literature scholars. Over time, institutional priorities will change and institutional practices shift. I would welcome more hybridity, in literary-creative writing studies. I'd like to see courses in environmental writing, and Indigenous poetics, small press publishing, among other topics.

II: Workshopping the Workshop

Over the past decade, there have, of course, been other watershed moments in Canadian universities' CW programs and the broader cultural landscape. In many ways, the origin story of graduate Creative Writing programming at U of S has tracked with a general ascent of CW within the academy; CW research is nationally recognized by SSHRC. Now that CW at U of S has a firmer footing and is, for the time being at least, on a relatively even keel, I can, as program director, focus less on institutional politics and more on pedagogy. I want to continue to interrogate the workshop and explore alternatives. In addition to a more diverse range of course materials I've implemented, I need to think more deeply about what a decolonized Creative Writing class looks like; Janelle Adsit's book is an exciting resource, and starting point, as is Felicia Rose Chavez's *The Anti-Racist Writing Workshop: How To Decolonize the Creative Classroom*. I'd like to think more deeply about questions of genre, what story is and what cultural values it reflects. I need to address how better to help my students who are neurodivergent or who have suffered trauma, in sensitive and respectful ways. In my graduate teaching, I'd like to introduce a broader range of narrative forms, including graphic forms, in my fiction writing course. The MFA has always emphasized community engagement; that should be fostered even more. I'd love to collaborate with colleagues in Drama, Fine Arts, Indigenous Studies and other areas. These are productive times for CW programming in Canada. Mentoring more than 60 graduate writing students at U of S since 2011, plus all the undergraduates I've taught, has been a great gift. It's heartening to see CW students gain more agency over their own learning. My days as 'den mother' and 'cheerleader' begin to recede, rightfully, into the mists of the past. Many more things feel possible now with respect to CW programs. The conversation has blown wide open. The story will have many more chapters.

Works Cited

"About Us." *The Fieldstone Review*, The Fieldstone Review, 2023, https://thefieldstonereview.ca/about%2Fcontact.

Adsit, Janelle. *Toward an Inclusive Creative Writing: Threshold Concepts to Guide the Literary Writing Curriculum*. Bloomsbury, 2017.

Alonso, Johanna. "Rewriting the English Curriculum." *Inside Higher* Ed, 4 Apr. 2023, https://www.insidehighered.com/news/2023/04/04/colleges-deploy-new-strategies-revive-english-programs#.

Canadian Press. "University of Saskatchewan Fires President Ilene Busch-Vishniac amid Controversy over Professor's Dismissal." *National Post*, Postmedia, 22 May 2014, https://nationalpost.com/news/canada/university-of-saskatchewan-fires-president-ilene-busch-vishniac-amid-controversy-over-professors-dismissal.

CBC News. "TransformUS Gone, U of S in 'Recovery Mode' Says Prof." *Canadian Broadcasting Corporation*, 10 Sept. 2014, https://www.cbc.ca/news/canada/saskatoon/transformus-gone-u-of-s-in-recovery-mode-says-prof-1.2761399.

CBC News. "TransformUS Target of Protest Rally Today at U of S." *Canadian Broadcasting Corporation*, 1 May 2014, https://www.cbc.ca/news/canada/saskatoon/transformus-target-of-protest-rally-today-at-u-of-s-1.2628829.

CBC News. "University of Saskatchewan Board Fires President Ilene Busch-Vishniac." *Canadian Broadcasting Corporation*, 22 May 2014, https://www.cbc.ca/news/canada/saskatoon/university-of-saskatchewan-board-fires-president-ilene-busch-vishniac-1.2650301.

Chavez, Felicia Rose. *The Anti-Racist Writing Workshop: How to Decolonize the Creative Classroom*. Haymarket Books, 2021.

Chiose, Simona. "As Students Move away from the Humanities, Universities Adapt." *The Globe and Mail*, 3 Mar. 2017, https://www.theglobeandmail.com/news/national/as-students-move-away-from-humanities-programs-universities-adapt/article34207300/.

English Department. University of Saskatchewan, n.d., https://catalogue.usask.ca/ENG-120#top.

Haldoupis, Nicole. *Tiny Ruins*. Radiant Press, 2020.

Johnson, Geoff. "Why Are Humanities Programs in Decline?" 19 Mar. 2023. https://www.timescolonist.com/opinion/geoff-johnson-why-are-humanities-programs-in-decline-6723587.

"Literature Matters: Arts-Based Programming in Prisons." College of Arts and Science, *University of Saskatchewan*, 30 Nov. 2022. https://artsandscience.usask.ca/news/articles/8009/Literature_Matters_Arts_Based_Programming_in_Prisons.

Maki, Allan and Tu Thanh Ha. "University of Saskatchewan Re-Evaluates Restructuring Plan." 22 May 2014, https://www.theglobeandmail.com/news/national/university-of-saskatchewan-president-fired/article18790498/.

Saldarriaga, Nicole. "Matthew Salesses Joins Writing Faculty." *Columbia University School of the Arts*, 31 May 2022, https://arts.columbia.edu/news/matthew-salesses-joins-writing-faculty.

Salesses, Matthew. *Craft in the Real World: Rethinking Fiction Writing and Workshopping*. Catapult, 2021.

Vanderwal, Olivia. "Students Combine Creative and Professional Writing in New Program." 23 Feb. 2023. https://uwaterloo.ca/news/arts/students-combine-creative-and-professional-writing-new.

"Writing North." College of Arts and Science, *University of Saskatchewan*, n.d., https://artsandscience.usask.ca/english/outreach/writing-north.php.

Recurrent Comments on Student Writing from Professor Lynes

When you return to this piece, focus on spots where the writing leaches energy—for example, adverbs. "She shouted loudly." Excessive use of 'to be' verbs. These are common culprits.

Where are we? What is happening? Can you provide a few details of setting?

Make your title work harder.

I think you've written past the story's ending. Consider lopping off the last four sentences.

The first three lines of your poem function as an 'on ramp.' The poem would be stronger if you made Line Four your new opening line.

The story bogs down in flashback, in places and loses momentum. Strive for a triangulated balance between forward-movement, interiority and backward-movement.

5 Postcards from the Edge

On Launching Canada's Most Recent MFA Creative Writing Program from a School of Journalism

Stephen Kimber

Beginnings

Every program has its creation story. The University of King's College's Master of Fine Arts in Creative Nonfiction program began as an afterthought. In the spring of 2009, the university was cobbling together yet another iteration of yet another strategic academic plan. As part of that exercise, each program was tasked with coming up with its own answer to the question of what it wanted to be in five years. We faculty in the School of Journalism decided to tackle that topic, among others, during a three-day post-academic-year retreat. Before we plunge into what happened there, there are some facts you need to know about King's, plus a few trivialities that might be helpful.

The University of King's College was founded in Windsor, Nova Scotia, in 1789; King's is, as we like to boast, "the first university to be established in English Canada … the first in Canada to receive a charter and … the oldest English-speaking Commonwealth university outside the United Kingdom" (University of King's, "History"). When we really like to brag, we add that our university is (sort-of) descended from the original King's College, the one founded by King George II in New York in 1754 and then reorganized after the American Revolution as today's Columbia University.

Nearly 100 years before the launch of our CNF MFA, the university itself had an even larger phoenix-rising moment. In 1920, the university's main building in Windsor, Nova Scotia, burned to the ground (University of King's, "100"). To survive, the university accepted a strings-attached financial lifeline from the Carnegie Corporation of New York, which Andrew Carnegie had established in 1911 "to promote the advancement and diffusion of knowledge and understanding" (Carnegie). The best way to do that, its board of directors decided, was for King's to relocate to Halifax, the provincial capital and a larger city, and enter into "an association" there with the already sizeable Dalhousie University. Under the Articles of Association agreed to in September 1920:

> King's agreed to pay the salaries of a number of Dalhousie professors, who in turn would help in the management and academic life of King's

DOI: 10.4324/9781032614144-7

> College. Students at King's would also study at Dalhousie and have access to all of the amenities of the larger school, and the academic programs at King's (except for Divinity) would fold into the College of Arts and Sciences at Dalhousie. (University of King's, "History")

Here in the twenty-first century, an army of MBAs and CPAs would be required to unravel the complexities of all that has evolved from those original articles, but for the fresh history of CW at King's, let us look at one tiny sub-clause in a much broader university agreement. Under its terms, King's is not permitted to offer any degree programs Dalhousie offers. Since Dalhousie was—and is—a major urban university with a complete table-setting of undergraduate and graduate programs, one of the three largest universities in the four Maritime provinces, King's was not left with much academic wiggle room.

In the early 1970s, the academic custody battle went from worse to worst. After the opening of the Atlantic School of Theology, which subsumed King's Divinity School, the already small King's finally had no degree programs at all. Enter the Foundation Year Programme (FYP), a standalone first-year "Great Books" program launched in 1972 that deftly navigated the Carnegie restrictions—it was not, on its own, a degree program—while adding undergraduate academic cachet and heft to Dalhousie's Arts offerings.

Six years later, in 1978, King's launched the School of Journalism, instantly becoming the university's only degree-granting program. There were two programs, in fact: a four-year honours program that combined Journalism with FYP and Arts electives, and a one-year post-baccalaureate Journalism-specific degree for students who already had an undergraduate degree in another discipline. The choice to start a Journalism School had little to do with how comfortably Journalism's practical, learn-to-do-by-doing, here-and-now ethos would sit beside FYP's original-text, classical and philosophical focus. In the end, the program-launch decision came down to President Godfrey's personal fascination with politics and media (he later served as Editor in Chief of *The Financial Post* before being appointed to the Senate), coupled with the never-far-from-consideration reality that Dalhousie did not offer a degree in Journalism.

This shared custody between Dalhousie and King's worked out well enough for long enough. For the next 30 years, Journalism and FYP, along with FYP's eventual upper-year offspring—honours programs in Early Modern Studies, Contemporary Studies and the History of Science and Technology, all jointly offered with Dalhousie—provided King's with a small-school, Humanities-rich *raison d'être*. By the end of the first decade of the twenty-first century, however, technology and the Internet, to say nothing of the global economy, had produced a tectonic shift in the relative popularity of university programs. Science, technology, engineering and mathematics (STEM) were in; Journalism and the liberal arts were suddenly out.

Worse, King's FYP, once seen as the model for Canadian Great Books programs, now faced competition as other Canadian universities copied its model—from the Humanities Colloquium at St. Francis Xavier University in Antigonish, Nova Scotia (St. Francis), to Arts One at the University of British Columbia in Vancouver (University of British Columbia). Our School of Journalism's crisis was exacerbated by the twenty-first-century decimation of the traditional news media business model on which its program was based and by the creeping "academization" of Journalism education. There was a time when an undergraduate journalism degree was all you needed to land a media job. But as more and more Canadian Journalism schools began to offer their own master's degrees in journalism, an MJ increasingly became the *sine qua non* credential, for journalists, employers and job-seeking journalists. Consequently, King's longstanding one-year post-baccalaureate bachelor's degree—still, for my money, excellent preparation for journalism—seemed less attractive.

Over the next decade, enrolment in both Journalism and FYP declined precipitously. In 2010, FYP topped out at 308 students. By 2020, the number had shrunk to 175. The one-year Journalism program attracted 50 students in 2009, but only 24 a decade later. While large multidisciplinary institutions like Dalhousie could easily weather such shifts, they produced yet another existential crisis for liberal arts and Journalism-focused King's.

The crisis was real. King's was a *small* small college—about 1,000 students, not much bigger than some Canadian secondary schools, and that's counting those enrolled in our programs and those registered at King's for its small college experience but taking their courses at Dal. We desperately needed to attract new students.

That compulsion provided the backdrop to the Journalism Faculty's 2009 retreat. Should we offer our own master's degree? How would we distinguish it from the degrees at other Canadian Journalism schools? Should we emphasize a niche focus on investigative journalism or/and entrepreneurial journalism, areas in which our faculty already had expertise?

Hanging over all of that, of course, was a more fundamental question. King's was an exclusively undergraduate university. Given our Genesis-story Carnegie limitations, would we even be permitted to offer a master's degree in journalism?

I have taught in the School of Journalism since 1982 and served several terms as Director. But I was even more intrigued by another, very different possibility. Over the years, my own Journalism practice—and teaching—had increasingly gravitated to what could loosely be termed longform journalism for magazines and books. In 1999, while casting about for sabbatical study opportunities, back when Google was novel, I Googled "creative nonfiction." The first link was for an MFA in Creative Nonfiction offered at an institution I had never heard of. Goucher College, a small private liberal arts college in Maryland which offered some specialized graduate programs, including a two-year MFA in Creative Nonfiction. The program appealed to me for many reasons. It was limited-residency, so I wouldn't have to relocate to study there. Second, it focused on a single genre. Although I was intrigued by and had published fiction, I considered myself primarily a journalist/nonfiction writer. I wasn't interested in studying poetry or playwriting. Perhaps most appealing, the overriding goal of the Goucher program was to help students write their nonfiction books.

At the time, I was completing two nonfiction books, *Not Guilty: The Trial of Gerald Regan* and *Flight 111: The Tragedy of the Swissair Crash*. I had already written two previous nonfiction books. But I was writing those books on the foundation of a shaky self-education, operating primarily on instinct. I wanted to know more about how to write the kind of creative nonfiction books I liked to read, understand the history and ethics of the genre and work with experienced writer-teacher mentors to improve my craft. I also wanted to find my "writing people" because I did not know many in Halifax's journalism community who shared my passion for writing longform nonfiction.

Goucher's MFA was everything I hoped for as a writer and teacher, helping me hone my craft and making me—I hoped—a more thoughtful, constructive writing teacher for my own students. I also picked up a few other ideas at Goucher I wanted to bring home to King's. Because Goucher's limited residency program allowed students to focus on writing a nonfiction book while living and working wherever they wanted, it attracted a different (and generally older) group of students than traditional graduate programs. Most of my fellow MFA students were well past their undergraduate years and often accomplished in other fields. There were journalists looking to expand the horizons of their work, traditional academics hoping to broaden the audience for their research, professionals with wisdom to impart, individuals with fascinating personal stories to share in memoirs, retired folks with time on their hands and a project they wanted to research and write about. A dozen years later, we at King's would see much of the same intake in our cohorts.

After graduating from Goucher in 2001, I created elective courses like Intro to Narrative Nonfiction ("Creative" was not a label that would have found favour with my Journalism colleagues) to my Journalism teaching load at King's. The courses became popular among Journalism majors and attracted Dalhousie students from other disciplines and even community learners simply interested in learning more so they could pursue their nonfiction projects.

What If ...?

I became intrigued by the idea of developing a Goucher-like program at King's. By the time I broached the idea in 2009, my colleagues were intrigued and generally supportive. Understandably, however, creating a new not-Journalism master's degree was not at the top of the priority list for my colleagues in a Journalism program that had previously specialized in undergraduate degrees. While the School of Journalism's process of pitching a conventional Master in Journalism program was ongoing, I was encouraged to develop a separate proposal for a Master in Creative Nonfiction, which would be ready when/if the time came. That fork in the road turned out to be fortuitous.

King's vice-president, Kim Kierans, a former director of the School of Journalism, and Kelly Toughill, its current director, had to push the rock of a Master of Journalism program proposal up an academic Everest. Remember Andrew Carnegie *et al.*? We were promptly informed that King's could only offer master's programs as joint ventures with Dalhousie, meaning the King's Master in Journalism proposal had to navigate through sundry administrative and faculty committee hurdles at *both* universities, then be approved by King's Faculty *and* the Dalhousie Senate, the Boards of Governors at both institutions and finally, of course, receive the imprimatur of the Maritime Provinces Higher Education Commission, the agency that must bless new academic programs here in Canada's four Atlantic provinces. Thanks mainly to the tireless efforts of Kierans and Toughill, the MJ was approved in record academic time—less than two years from faculty retreat to governmental MPHEC approval—and welcomed its first students in June 2011.

Because of that seemingly swift approval, we hoped to launch our CNF MFA one year later. However, an MFA in Creative Nonfiction, the first genre-specific CW master's degree in Canada and an unfamiliar beast in our academic world, would prove even more challenging. Although we had done what we thought was the seeding work with both institutions before submitting our proposal, there were still many questions. Should we be a Master of Arts program? No. Dal already offered MAs aplenty, including in English, and that department might someday decide to launch its own Creative Writing MA. And, oh yes, Carnegie. No need to poke that bear.

What about a Master of Fine Arts degree? Some administrators (not to mention some Journalism faculty) fretted that that sounded too much like the fine *art* degree offered at NSCAD University, our local and celebrated art school. We should be clear to people about what we were all about. In the end, however, we settled on calling it an MFA, mainly because—as we noted in our proposal—that was what similar non-English-department writing programs at universities and colleges across North America were most often called, from America's famous Iowa to Canada's University of British Columbia.

With that question answered, we smacked against the next conundrum: an MFA in…? Most Journalism faculty were not keen on calling it Creative Nonfiction because that made it sound like we made things up—not a good look for a Journalism school. For my part, I was not keen on calling it an MFA in Literary Journalism because that seemed too limiting, given that we hoped to attract memoirists, historians and others who would not see themselves in a journalism mirror. Although we finally landed on calling it an MFA in Creative Nonfiction, those two questions continued to dog us. They were the two most asked questions as we navigated through the process. But there was another frequently asked—and far more encouraging—question many of our academic colleagues asked after we had explained the program we had in mind.

How Do I Apply?

Our fledgling program quickly attracted the interest of Donald Sedgwick, a 35-year veteran of the Canadian publishing industry. He had been the publisher of Doubleday Canada, editorial director of Scholastic Canada and national marketing director at McClelland & Stewart. Don used his publishing connections to put together an advisory board of key players in Canadian publishing—writers, editors, agents and publishers—who could not only advise us on curriculum but also serve, by their presence, as a signal to potential students that we were serious about helping them become published writers.

By late 2012, we had official approval from both universities. Don was appointed the program's half-time Executive Director; I would be its half-time Cohort Director while continuing to teach half-time in the School of Journalism. We lined up a roster of four stellar writer-teacher mentors and opened for application business.

On the morning of August 3, 2013, in the King's Theatrical Society classroom on the second floor of the university's New Academic Building, Don and I and our four mentors—accomplished professional writer-mentors David Hayes, Lori A. May, Ken McGoogan and Lorri Neilsen Glenn[1]—welcomed the 19 members of the Class of 2015.

We had been hoping for 15.

Now, we had to deliver on our cheeky marketing promise: "We've got your book."

The Low-Residency King's CW MFA Program

Initially, students attended four intense residencies during their two-year low-residency program: two, two-week summer residencies in Halifax and two, one-week winter residencies, alternating between the North American publishing capitals of Toronto and New York.[2]

During the rest of the academic year, students could, even before COVID, complete their program—submit course assignments and work one-to-one on their manuscripts with their mentors—at a distance, meaning they could remain in their own communities while earning their degrees and writing their books. From the beginning, our primary focus has been on helping students master the art and craft of creative nonfiction while—and by—producing a submission-ready professional book proposal, plus as much of a complete nonfiction manuscript as possible. Every assignment—craft essays, sources essays, read-like-a-writer book reports, book-related op-eds and journal articles, marketing assignments, etc.—was structured to advance the student's book project while expanding their understanding of the genre they wanted to write. All would-be students had to submit a brief description of their book idea as part of the application process. Sometimes, during the admissions process, we worked with otherwise promising applicants to refine, revise or even rethink their less promising original ideas. That is how central the book idea was to the program.

Occasionally, students still changed their minds about the book they wanted to write after they arrived. That creative evolution is often part of the process too. One notable change of subject happened during the first week of the program's first-year summer residency, when each student had to elevator-pitch their project to fellow students, mentors and faculty, then answer questions and receive feedback. Pauline Dakin, a well-known CBC journalist, was a member of that first class. A national health reporter, she had applied to the program with a well-considered plan to write a book about how the internet affected children's health. She had already done much of the research. She was excited about the idea. So were we. But after listening to other students pitch memoir projects, Dakin stood up in front of the group. "I've never told anyone else this before," she began. That was how she decided to write *Run, Hide, Repeat: A Memoir of a Fugitive Childhood*, her award-winning, bestselling nonfiction book about growing up "on the run from the 'Mafia.'" Everyone who heard her pitch said this is the book she needed to write.

While students' previous academic records were a factor in our admissions decisions, their book ideas, their writing track records and the portfolios they submitted with their applications were usually more significant to us. In part, that's because many of our applicants were "mature." The majority ranged in age from late 30s to early 60s; we have even graduated a few students in their 80s. They may not have had the opportunity to earn degrees when they were of university age, or they ended up with old-school three-year degrees (when we officially require four) or lower GPAs (than our standard B+) from the days before grade inflation. To complicate matters, our parent university, Dalhousie, only counted undergraduate marks when calculating an applicant's GPA. Many of our under-achieving undergrads had gone on to star in other graduate and professional schools. One applicant, who had earned a graduate law degree and been teaching medical-legal ethics at a major Canadian university for decades, did not qualify for admission to our program because his undergraduate marks at Dalhousie law school 50 years before did not meet current academic standards. Another student, who had advanced degrees from prestigious American universities, including Harvard, and a Dalhousie master's degree(!), did not qualify, again because his decades-old undergraduate marks were not deemed acceptable.

Thankfully, we established a Prior Learning Assessment Review (PLAR) process with Dal's Faculty of Graduate Studies. This more real-world appraisal has become a crucial instrument in our admissions toolbox, allowing us to admit promising students—like those above—who didn't meet Dalhousie's self-defined academic criteria but had earned a place in our program on other, equally legitimate life grounds. Some of our most successful students have been PLAR admits.

Some students, including a few recent university grads and others who had retired from the workforce, chose to make the MFA their full-time job;

others, usually with excellent time management skills, juggled their MFA with ongoing work and family responsibilities.

The primary focus of the summer residencies was writing, with the goal of deepening students' understanding of the art and craft of creative nonfiction. During the winter residencies, business-related writing issues took centre stage. That said, we incorporated discussions about the writing business into our summer residencies and included author talks and craft-related presentations in the winter sessions.

During the summer residencies, the mentors—all accomplished professional writers, editors and writing teachers—conducted morning craft workshops for up to seven students. (During their first year in the program, students worked one-to-one with the same mentor; in the second year, they had the opportunity to choose two new mentors, one each semester.) In the afternoons, students attended lectures and panels featuring faculty, mentors and guests. The evenings included mentor, student and guest readings and organized and unorganized getting-to-know-each-other social time.

In the early years of the program, thanks mainly to Don's personal connections, we had the financial support of two of Canada's most prominent publishers—HarperCollins Canada and Penguin Random House Canada—to host a writer-in-residence and an editor-in-residence in each summer residency.[3] They taught master classes, met formally and informally with students and, in the case of the writers-in-residence, offered public readings of their work.

During our Toronto and New York residencies, our guests included key editors and publishers from large and small houses, literary agents, publicists, book designers, booksellers, critics and writers. During the rest of the winter semester, students completed assignments at a distance in their publishing course as well as continued to work on their manuscripts in consultation with their mentors.

Measuring Success

So far, more than 65 graduates have published their book projects or signed book deals (University of King's, "MFA"). That number, nearly one quarter of graduates, is even more impressive because the program has only graduated 241 students to date, and more of them, especially recent graduates, are likely to end up with book contracts too. Books by our alumni have been published in Canada, the United States and the United Kingdom, by international publishing houses and independent national, regional and local publishers. Some grads have chosen to self-publish, another of the publishing avenues we discuss in the program.

The range of alumni book subjects is breathtaking—from big-issue books such as Gregor Craigie's geo-apocalyptic *On Borrowed Time: North America's Next Big Quake* and *On Class* by Deborah Dundas, Book Reviews Editor at *The Toronto Star*, to investigative journalism (McDiarmid;

Heffernen), to travel (Cabral), to big ideas (McKeon; Benembarek), to historical nonfiction (Faubert; Fogarty), to self-help (Fraser), and, of course, memoir (Lampert; Pratt; Stiller). There have also been a few one-offs like Christian Smith's *The Scientist and the Psychic*, a neuroscientist son writing about his relationship with his famous psychic mother, and even a graphic memoir (MacLeod).

As icing on that cake, many of our graduates' books have won or been shortlisted for national and regional literary awards. There are, of course, other important markers of success, including the sense of community a writing program like ours can create. Consider that all but one of the 19 members of the first graduating low-residency class returned to Halifax from all over North America to graduate together in May 2015. The only student who couldn't be present for graduation was in Lebanon researching his book project; he sent a long email to his fellow grads to share in their celebration.

Given that graduation happens more than four months after their last online winter residency class together and that most of our students do not live in east-coast Nova Scotia, the significant numbers of students who continue to return to graduate in person post-COVID indicate both a level of satisfaction with their experience and a determination to build on the sense of community the program fosters. Several grads, for example, have organized their own in-person or online writing groups. One group has been meeting weekly since 2017; all five of its members have published books.

In 2015, Richard Levangie, a member of the first graduating class, organized a private King's CNF MFA Facebook group so students, alumni, mentors and faculty could share news of their successes and offer each other support and advice. Today, the group has 250 members, most of whom, of course, would not have been students in the program at the same time (Levangie). Still, it's common for alumni to offer online encouragement to grads they've never met, show up at their book launch events or go out of the way to make sure a fellow MFA's new book gets prominent display in their local bookstore.

Many of our grads have become Creative Writing teachers themselves. Some are even mentors in our MFA program. Gillian Turnbull, in fact, graduated in 2017, became a mentor in 2019 and was appointed the first full-time director of our newly named Writing & Publishing program in 2023 (University of King's, "Dr.").

In 2018, after five years, the MFA in Creative Nonfiction underwent its first—gratifyingly successful—program review. External reviewers from Ryerson and the University of Victoria (the latter another CW MFA school, see Chapter 3) described the King's MFA in Creative Nonfiction as "a unique and highly successful program," while internal Dal/King's reviewers praised it as "both distinctive and successful: unique in Canada, it has a growing reputation based on the quality and profile of its instructors ... and on the calibre of students and their projects."

That, of course, raised the inevitable question—what next?

Onward

In 2018, the university's board of governors once again asked all departments and programs to "assess their current offerings and consider possible future directions," a version of the same question that had inspired my CNF MFA program suggestion back in 2009. Born of a Journalism school and unique in Canada for focusing exclusively on Creative Nonfiction, we had reached our own crossroads. When we initially proposed the program, we projected we would achieve our enrolment sweet spot—which we believed was a maximum of 25 qualified students per cohort—by 2018. In reality, we have been admitting 30–35 students per cohort for several years now.

We were able to make that expanded enrolment work because the program's structure is elastic. Our faculty—director and cohort directors—are on contract. Mentors are hired on annual per-student contracts to work with up to seven students per semester. Despite that flexibility, we had already concluded that for pedagogical and market reasons, as well as to maintain the vital sense of community, we had really reached maximum enrolment. Consequently, we considered several options before deciding our most logical future direction was to create a parallel limited-residency MFA in Fiction program. Thanks to our successful track record with nonfiction, the approvals process for King's second CW MFA was *somewhat* smoother. But it came with its own complications. Dalhousie's English department was initially concerned that our master's program in Fiction might get in the way of its own hope to someday launch its own more traditional Master of Arts in Creative Writing degree. However, in discussions with them, it became clear our target audiences were different. And we both saw collaboration possibilities down the road.

The School of Journalism was concerned too. It understandably—particularly in the aftermath of Trump—did not want to be tarred, even indirectly, with a fictional brush. The solution, still a work in progress, has been to rebrand ourselves as the School of Journalism, Writing & Publishing, with separate directors and faculty for what are now two relatively independent and autonomous Journalism and Writing & Publishing programs. On June 17, 2023, King's welcomed the first 22 students into the first cohort of our new MFA in Fiction. There are more stories to be told.

Notes

1 Today, the program boasts 18 writer-mentors, including four who joined the first cohort of our new MFA in Fiction program in June 2023.

2 During the pandemic, we—like everyone else—ended up on online. Although we have since returned to in-person summer residencies, we discovered there were distinct advantages to continuing the winter residencies online, from costs for both students and the university to convenience for guests. It didn't take more than a winter blizzard in one part of North America, for example, to create attendance pandemonium when students and faculty had travelled from all over. That said, we have continued to focus on the online winter residencies on those publishing with our online guests based in those cities.

3 Our publisher-sponsored guests have included writers Andrew Westoll, Taras Grescoe, Charlotte Gray and Cea Sunrise Person, and senior book editors such as Pamela Murray, Craig Pyette, Diane Turbide and Bhavna Chauhan.

Works Cited

Benembarek, Sheima. *Halal Sex: The Intimate Lives of Muslim Women in North America*. Viking, 2023.

Cabral, Esmeralda. *How to Clean a Fish: And Other Adventures in Portugal*. U Alberta P, 2023.

Carnegie Corporation of New York. "Our History." *Carnegie Corporation of New York*, 2023. https://www.carnegie.org/about/our-history.

Craigie, Gregor. *On Borrowed Time: Shaking Complacency in North America's Seismic Zones*. Goose Lane, 2021.

Dakin, Pauline. *Run, Hide, Repeat: A Memoir of a Fugitive Childhood*. Viking Canada, 2017.

Dundas, Deborah. *On Class*. Biblioasis, 2023.

Faubert, Marsha. *Wanda's War: An Untold Story of Nazi Europe, Forced Labour, and a Canadian Immigration Scandal*. Goose Lane, 2023.

Fogarty, Catherine. *Murder on the Inside: The True Story of the Deadly Riot at Kingston Penitentiary*. Biblioasis, 2021.

Fraser, Kimberly. *The Accidental Caregiver: Wisdom and Guidance for the Unexpected Challenges of Family Caregiving*. Sutherland House, 2022.

Heffernan, Virginia. *Ring of Fire: High-Stakes Mining in a Lowlands Wilderness*. ECW, 2023.

Lampert, Nellwyn. *Every Boy I Ever*. Dundurn, 2019.

Levangie, Richard, ed. King's MFA in Creative Nonfiction. *Facebook*, n.d. https://www.facebook.com/kingsmfa.

Kimber, Stephen. *Flight 111: The Tragedy of the Swissair Crash*. Doubleday, 1999.

———. *Not Guilty: The Trial of Gerald Regan*. Stoddart, 1999.

MacLeod, Susan. *Dying for Attention: A Graphic Memoir of Nursing Home Care*. Conundrum, 2021.

McDiarmid, Jessica. *Highway of Tears*. Penguin Random House Canada, 2020.

McKeon, Lauren. *F-Bomb: Dispatches from the War on Feminism*. Goose Lane Editions, 2017.

Pratt, Laura. *Heartbroken: Field Notes on a Constant Condition*. Random House Canada, 2023.

St. Francis Xavier University. "Humanities Colloquium." *St. Francis Xavier University*, 2023, https://www.stfx.ca/department/humanities-colloquium.

Smith, Christian. *The Scientist and the Psychic: A Son's Exploration of His Mother's Gift*. Random House Canada, 2020.

Stiller, Karen. *The Minister's Wife: A Memoir of Faith, Doubt, Friendship, Loneliness, Forgiveness, and More*. Tyndale Momentum, 2020.

University of British Columbia. "Arts One." *Program*, University of British Columbia, n.d., https://artsone.arts.ubc.ca.

University of King's College. "100 Years after the Fire, King's Community Gathers to Remember." *University of King's College*, n.d., https://ukings.ca/news/100-years-after-the-fire-kings-community-gathers-to-remember.

University of King's College. "Dr. Gillian Turnbull Named Inaugural Director of Writing & Publishing." *University of King's College*, n.d., https://ukings.ca/news/dr-gillian-turnbull-named-inaugural-director-of-writing-publishing.
University of King's College. "History." *University of King's College*, 2023, https://ukings.ca/campus-community/about-kings/history.
University of King's College. "MFA Book Deals." *University of King's College*, 2023, https://ukings.ca/mfa-book-deals.

Professor Kimber's Recurrent Comments on Student Writing

You can be a plodder or a seat-of-the-pantser; just write the damn thing.

As a writer, I spent a lot of time coming to a full stop in my story but then thinking, well, I should also say this, and then this and then that. My endings dribbled off into nothingness. A wise editor once told me to go back three or four paragraphs from the bottom, cut the rest and then re-read to decide if I really needed all those endings or just one good one. Try it.

One of the best ways to think about scenic construction is to watch a movie with the pause button in your hand. Stop after every scene. Why did the director end the scene where they did? Why does the next scene begin where it does? Do this with your favourite movies, but also the ones you liked least. What have you learned about scenic construction from the exercise?

That ... Most of the time, "that" is one of those meaningless space-waster words. Go through your manuscript and see if each "that" is necessary. If not, cut it.

6 Why, and How, Literary Prizes Matter

Olga Stein

Canada is not exempt from the various discourses that have always surrounded prestigious literary awards. Still, commentary on prizes has grown more frequent and voluble since social media became ubiquitous, and since prizes themselves became the literary equivalent of the Oscars. Gala evenings, press conferences and a slew of other activities—like embossings on the front covers of shortlisted or winning books—enhance the visibility of prizes, including Canada's Giller. These spectacles and displays of cultural authority project glamour and gravitas. Indeed, they are meant to build followers, increase audience engagement, and, in some cases, prompt participation in the selection of nominees and winners (as with Canada Reads, from the Canadian Broadcasting Corporation's Anglophone side). Accordingly, increased online presence, televised presentations and offshoots, such as the elegantly staged readings of nominated books Canadians and CanLit watchers have come to associate with the annual Scotiabank Giller Prize, augment and amplify the resulting scrutiny. Following prize-related announcements, journalists, literary critics and academics routinely opine about shortlists and winners, as well as the implications for the nation's publishers and literary culture in general. Thus, publicity and voluminous commentary are essential features of today's prizing institutions. Currently, then, the two spheres—one made up of reviewers, critics and audiences/readers in Canada and abroad, the other, of institutions and their elect proxy—are linked by design in more ways and with harder to parse consequences for literary culture than could have been envisioned before the era of the Internet and social media.

Unlike their predecessors, which emerged from the elite academies of Europe, such as the *Académie Royale* in Paris and its offshoot, the *Académie de France* in Rome, cultural prizes of the present operate independently of academic institutions. Regardless of academic, private or corporate pedigree, literary awards elicit more interest among literary critics and readers/followers when they are perceived as wielding comparable cultural clout. This is particularly true of older prizes, like the Nobel Prize in Literature (awarded annually since 1901) and the Booker Prize (first awarded in 1969) ("All"), or when, as with these two awards, they are international and evoke interest worldwide ("Booker").

DOI: 10.4324/9781032614144-8

The Pulitzer Prize in the US, established in 1917 to commemorate the achievements of the American newspaper publisher Joseph Pulitzer, is as influential as the 55-year-old Booker in terms of the excitement it generates and the esteem it garners for its laureates.[1] The National Book Awards is another highly feted American literary prize, founded in 1950. The same can be said of prizes in the UK, like the Costa Book Awards (before 2005 Whitbread Book of the Year), the David Cohen British Literature Prize in the English Language, the Orange Prize and the Commonwealth. However, the Booker and Pulitzer remain the most influential in their respected national-cultural spheres and are eclipsed only by the Nobel Prize, awarded for literature since 1901 (worth $1.1 million USD as of 2018).[2]

Literary prizes are an ineluctable feature of our world due to the imprimatur they confer on particular works (or an entire oeuvre) and their authors. Richard Todd, James F. English, Barbara Herrnstein Smith and Timothy Brennan and Graham Huggan, among others, made groundlaying contributions to the critical study of prizes, their influence and impact, which includes the kind of affirmation or "credentialing" that might motivate an aspiring writer to pursue a Creative Writing master's degree in Canada.[3] Yet, the regard shown for such 'venerable' prizing institutions as the Nobel and Booker cannot be explained without reference to French sociologist and philosopher Pierre Bourdieu's seminal works on the sociology of culture and literature, *Distinction: A Social Critique of the Judgement of Taste* (1984) and *The Rules of Art: Genesis and Structure of the Literary Field* (1996). Bourdieu laid the ground for theorizing the "field of literature" (*le champ littéraire*) and the "literary institution" (*l'institution littéraire*), as social and cultural hierarchies that formed over time, and whose elites determined cultural/aesthetic values (and corresponding "distinctions"). More precisely, for Bourdieu and certainly with regard to CanLit's award culture, what must be grasped is:

> the emergence of a set of specific institutions which are required for the functioning of the economy of cultural goods—places of exhibition (galleries, museums, etc.), institutions of consecration (academies, salons, etc.), and specialized agents (dealers, critics, art historians, collectors, etc.), endowed with the *dispositions* objectively required by the field and with *specific categories of perception and appreciation* which are irreducible to those in common use and which are capable of imposing a specific measure on the value of artists and their products. (*The Rules of Art* 292)

Literary awards, as Bourdieu, Todd, Feldman and other observers of "cultural capital" illustrate, are part of contemporary canon-making and, therefore, never irrelevant to a writer's education. Prizing agencies have a claim to authority because they are integrated into the socially sanctioned hierarchies of literary experts and professionals, which exist in every nation.[4]

Significantly, Bourdieu also argues that the cultural domain on the whole is always competitive, tiered and fluctuating. In this arena, individual creators, movements and institutions vie with one another to establish criteria, confer value and consecrate, not unlike the vaunted "credentialing" of competing Creative Writing master's programs across Canada.

The Meanings and Uses of Cultural Capital (in and beyond Canada)

A key aspect of Bourdieu's argument is that all who participate in the cultural field rely on a host of factors to maintain and bolster their status. For Bourdieu, these factors draw on, contribute or augment what he conceived of as "cultural capital." Although a thorough account of the theoretical framework Bourdieu developed over the course of several books is not possible in just one chapter, what is most relevant to this examination of the impact of Canadian literary awards on Canadian writing programs can be condensed as follows: Cultural capital consists of an amalgam of the skills, resources and objectives that make cultural projects practicable and endows them with the meanings most likely to win societal approval. This latter enabling factor is the symbolic value attached to endeavours seen as vital to society, including the work of conferring distinction on particular books and authors, not entirely unlike the value of conferring a master's degree in Creative Writing. For example, prizes are known for distinguishing writers from communities that were under-represented in the literary field, from Salman Rushdie's canon-expanding Booker win for *Midnight's Children* or,[5] here in Canada, black writers like Austin Clarke [2002], Esi Edugyan [2011 and 2018] ("Esi Edugyan Is"), Suzette Mayr [2022] ("Suzette Mayr Wins"), or when they honour fiction that identifies or highlights the distinctive perceived features of a nation's culture, they increase their own stock of cultural and symbolic capital. The Carol Shields Prize for Fiction draws symbolic capital from its support for writers from a community that has historically been disadvantaged by androcentric priorities in the publishing industry. The Carol Shields Prize sums up its symbolic value as follows: "By putting the work of women writers in the spotlight—and by creating charitable grants and mentorships for marginalized and underrepresented writers—this new annual literary award will acknowledge, celebrate and promote fiction by a wider, more diverse and inclusive group of women and non-binary writers" ("What").

In *Prizing Literature: The Celebration and Circulation of National Culture* (2011), Gillian Roberts examines literary awards' strategic accrual of cultural capital in the Canadian context. Roberts pays particular attention to the national(ist) dimensions of literary awards: "The notion of national capital suggests that nationality becomes a kind of currency in the cultural marketplace" (21). The Giller Prize is a case in point: after its founding by real-estate developer Jack Rabinovitch in 1994, the nascent, privately owned (and funded) award managed to situate itself advantageously within the shifting and uncertain hierarchy of Canada's literary field by raising the cultural and symbolic import of its mission; it promised to celebrate the 'best' of literary achievement across all of Canada, while obtaining political cogency or "national capital" by promoting the "consumption of Canadianness," to use Roberts's phrase (and all as the Web took off in the late 1990s). To be clear, what is being consumed in connection with the Giller is a grand image—one relentlessly projected by the government, and by Canada's public and privately owned institutions—of an open, democratic, multicultural nation-state.

To recap, cultural capital, as per Bourdieu, can be conceived of as a mix of assets, which enable or equip an actor or organization to pursue their cultural goals, as when master's writing programs hope that having their graduates nominated for prizes will attract new students who might be future prize nominees, winners or judges. Literary prizes, the Giller included, amass diverse types of "cultural capital" with a view to preserving and raising their quotient of prestige in the cultural hierarchy. James F. English, whose book, *The Economy of Prestige: Prizes, Awards, and the Circulation of Cultural Value* (2005), is an indispensable reference for any student of contemporary canon-making and cultural validation, surmises that the primary objective of a literary prize may well be to wrest for itself as much cultural authority and legitimacy for conferring value on works of literature—or, to put it another way, as much cultural or symbolic capital as possible. For English, an ambitious prize will strive to make itself "culture's bureaucratic epicenter" (41). In many ways, too, the big winner of the Giller, or any prize, is the prize itself, not any one year's prize-winning fiction writer. University of Victoria Creative Writing BFA 1999 alumnus Esi Edugyan (M. Huston) went on to be a very rare two-time winner of the Giller, in 2011 and 2018 ("Esi Edugyan Is"), then (and no doubt partially because) the chair of the 2023 Man Booker Prize jury ("Esi Edugyan"). Prizes beget prizes, because, well, prizes beget prizes.

Scholars and observers of disruption, not just those devoted to Creative Writing pedagogy and/or CanLit, might make more of the Giller's nearly instantaneous leap from Canada's new literary prize to its most influential. As detailed further below, the (private) (public) Giller's dominance in Canadian fiction's prize culture, one previously fixated largely on the Governor General's Literary Awards, is a successionary example of Bourdieu's "cultural capital." Initially, as the citations below attest, the Giller scored points with the literary community by vowing to compensate for the inadequacies of the state-funded Governor General's Literary Awards for fiction ("Canada Council"). As a privately funded prize, and/or simply as a new one, the Giller could generate glamour and hype on a scale that was unprecedented for a Canadian prize. Yet more importantly still, it was able to avoid the kind of institutional rigidity and accountability that tends to discredit the work of government-run organizations. Gillian Roberts's *Prizing Literature* has a brief but helpful section comparing the Giller and the Governor General's Literary Awards (31–34). Roberts includes criticisms levelled at the GGs. She quotes Noah Richler from a 2002 *National Post* article: "The Governor General Awards' English-language fiction juries concern themselves too deeply with mapping the parameters of Canadian-ness" (Richler qtd. in Roberts 23–24). Roberts also refers to Dionne Brand's "own experience of sitting on the jury for the Governor General's Award for poetry, [which] demonstrates the ways in which the guidelines for representativeness do not adequately address the assumptions behind dominant aesthetics" (26). In an interview, Brand challenged the "self-congratulatory" quota systems of Canadian writing organizations: "the writers' Union and PEN...seem to feel that you can quantify culture into six per cent of this and two per cent of that.... This approach assumes that the contradictions of Canadian culture can be handled by putting them into discrete and isolated packages" (Brand qtd. in Roberts 27). In contrast to these laments about the longstanding Governor General's awards ("Canada Council"), consider the feting of Rabinovitch and the Giller Prize during the 2000 "Celebrate Canada" festival in New York. Journalist Leo Carey viewed the occasion as a chance to level "tacit criticism of the Governor General's Awards, which have become unpopular within the industry for what are seen as deliberately perverse decisions." According to Carey, one editor was especially forthright: "The Governor General's prize is just a disaster. The choices are hopeless—always really political" (Carey B23). Justified or not, such judgements are illustrative of the relative rankings of cultural institutions. Literary awards, as English asserts in *The Economy of Prestige*, are "part of a system or relational field" (257). In this context, prizes, not unlike competing master's Creative Writing programs, elevate their cultural standing by exploiting others' limitations.

Like any other prize, the Giller must continue to demonstrate that it is fulfilling its mandate in its cultural space better than the competition. To that end, it must consistently reward high levels of literary accomplishment while outperforming other major Canadian prizes on several fronts, including the literary criteria used to select nominees and winners. Since 2007, the Giller has been the only Canadian fiction prize to employ foreign judges (Dundas). Spokespeople for the Giller claim that international judges ensure that lists and winners are seen to be chosen with minimum bias, while adhering to the highest criteria for literary excellence. Additionally, it is apparent that since its founding, the Giller has been adapting to changing expectations and calls from numerous constituencies of readers and writers for greater representativeness. Writers from visible minorities regularly serve on judging panels or count among the nominees and winners. As well, the Giller's long- and shortlists tend to include books from small or independent Canadian presses, despite the dominance in Canada of large, multinational publishers.

Related to the international and inclusive efforts described above is the decision in 2015 to grow the judging panel from three to five judges. Journalist Victoria Ahearn quoted Elana Rabinovitch, the Giller's executive director (and daughter of its creator), in "Scotiabank Giller Prize Jury Expands to 5 Members": "I think that it will make for a much more diverse list ... it's important to include voices outside of that really insular community of CanLit" (Ahearn, n.p.). The following year, Lawrence Hill described his inclusive priorities as chair of the Giller's 2016 jury panel: "I worked very hard to devise a system ... where each juror would be heard and be able to express their preferences.... The main preoccupation was fairness to the writers whose books are being submitted" ("Q&A: Lawrence Hill," Carter n.p.). In the context of a hierarchical literary field, we must recognize that a literary award's reputation for astute and even-handed adjudication, essentially the jury's autonomy from any type of interference, safeguards respect for its selections and the prize as a whole.

Finally, although the monetary value of a prize does not always match the esteem an award is accorded, the Giller remains the most important literary prize in Canada partly because it has the largest purse. The Pulitzer may remain negligible in monetary terms, as do the sought-after Goncourt and Strega awards, but, increasingly, the size of the purse is perceived in symbolic terms, thereby translating it into a measure of both institutional legitimacy and a recipient's artistic accomplishment.[6] Accordingly, Adam McDowell's article on the founding of a new prize worth $25,000 announced that the Giller is "intended to overshadow other Canadian literary awards, including the Governor-General's" (McDowell D9). In 2005, Martin Knelman wrote in the *Toronto Star*, "The stakes have been raised," before revealing the Giller's newly minted partnership with a corporate sponsor, Scotiabank, and informing readers that the cash value of the award had climbed to $50,000. In 2008, the Scotiabank Giller Prize grew to $70,000. Its current value (since September 2014) is $100,000 for the winner, a staggering increase from the amount it started with in 1994 when privately funded. The increase illustrates that the Giller's founders and administrators believed their prize would achieve higher cultural standing on the bases of the economic capital allocated to the annual cash prize and the solidity of its corporate sponsor, which also covers the Giller's annual operating expenses.

However compelling it may seem to generally regard the richest prize or award as the most influential, Creative Writing pedagogy in Canada provides an apt example of how the seemingly empirical issue of monetary value can still create apples-and-oranges comparisons of cultural influence. The University of Calgary is one of just two Canadian English universities to offer a PhD for a creative writing dissertation. U. Cal.'s CW prof Dr. Suzette Mayr won nearly equivalent amounts for what would ultimately become her Giller-winning novel, *The Sleeping Car Porter* ("Suzette Mayr Wins"), in first a national university research grant ("Suzette Mayr"), then, *much* more publicly, in the Scotiabank Giller Prize ("Suzette Mayr Wins"). Notably, Mayr's novel was first empowered, and affirmed, by an extremely rare Research-Creation grant, awarded by the Social Sciences and Humanities Research Council of Canada [SSHRC] [described here in detail in Chapter 2 by Darryl Whetter] ("Suzette Mayr"). While that national SSHRC grant would have received internal university respect and influence, this four-year grant of $94,300 ("Suzette Mayr") would not confer nearly as much of Bourdieu's "cultural capital" as her 2022 win of the $100,000 Scotiabank Giller Prize ("Suzette Mayr Wins"). Among post-graduate students choosing whether to pursue a CW Ph.D. at the University of Calgary or the University of New Brunswick, few are likely to be as impressed by a federal grant compared to the book-sale-boosting Giller Prize.

Two recent developments attest to the growing importance of prize moneys. First, Canada's Griffin Poetry Prize, now two decades old, consolidated its two awards into a single prize: originally, one prize was given to a Canadian poet, a second to a non-Canadian ("About"). By way of explanation, the Griffin offers the following on its website: "The Griffin Poetry Prize is one of the world's most generous poetry awards.…As of 2023, the prize is [now] worth CAD$130,000, making it the world's largest international prize for a single book of poetry written in, or translated into English" ("About"). The correlation of purse size and perceived cultural cachet can also be inferred from the amount offered by the newly established Carol Shields Prize for Fiction. After attending its inaugural celebrations, Margaret Atwood shared with her Substack followers the prize founders' rationale for turning the award into a veritable jackpot. At USD$150,000, it is undoubtedly "one of the world's richest," wrote Atwood. Less money, she was told, would mean that "no one will pay attention to it, and it won't sell books, and our aim—[of] levelling the financial playing field a bit—will not be achieved" (Atwood). Atwood's comment suggests that the symbolic capital being signalled relies on both the amount of money on offer, and the fact that it is directed at writers who identify as women.

Press releases, institutional messaging, as well as statements of the sort made by Canadian writers like Atwood reveal several crucial facets of contemporary prizes' "cultural capital" and general influence. Most obviously, prizes maneuver to capture public attention and maximize impact for themselves and the books they crown. In *The Economy of Prestige*, English equates these strategies with "hard-nosed financial calculation, [and] national or municipal self-promotion" (31). The higher the monetary value of the award, the more conviction (and authority) the endorsement of a book and its author appears to carry. Of note too is that a lucrative prize demonstrates how one form of capital (money, in this instance) is leveraged or "converted" into cultural and symbolic capital (the concept of "interconvertibility" is central to Bourdieu's theory). The largesse of an award is often perceived to be commensurate with the winning book's literary achievement. This perceived value is one of the reasons for English's contention that prizes serve as agents of legitimization, instruments of the "middle-zone of cultural space" that have "in our time … become by far the most widespread and powerful of all such instruments" (12–13). The more money and resources at their disposal, the more forcefully prizes can play up their standing in the cultural field.

It should also be evident, however, that outsized monetary awards are just one of the instruments used by prizes to obtain higher cultural status. Ambitious prizing agencies have diversified their tactics, forcing us to grapple with the impact of their strategies on the literary marketplace: we have to ask, do today's big literary prizes affect the writing, publishing and consumption of books and even the education of young writers? As a corollary, we need to determine the extent to which the observed institutional jockeying for prominence, such as the more recent emphasis on popular appeal and audience/reader participation, has redefined "cultural capital"; relatedly, we need to look at which of the accompanying changes—seen in the ways prizes promote their activities more broadly and across more varied communities of readers—both validate and complicate the Bourdieusian schema of a national cultural field. These questions and others raised below are indicative of the larger problematic and corresponding set of scholarly inquiries that address the cultural phenomenon of contemporary prizes and their impact on national literatures, including their shaping in university CW programs.

In practical terms, it is hard to separate the impact of any single one of the Giller's institutional practices from the numerous commercial spin-offs the prize generates as a matter of course.[7] For instance, for purposes of measuring the effect on book sales, it is impossible to distinguish an operational aspect of the institution, such as a book's nomination or the broadcasting of the annual gala, from the publishers' marketing efforts, which piggyback on the publicity generated by announcements of shortlists and winners. Nevertheless, and significantly, certain metrics can be applied to gauge the influence wielded by a major Canadian book prize—the quantity and quality of journalistic coverage in Canada and abroad being one reliable marker. Implicitly, these and other measures of public and journalistic interest suggest that there is consensus, among analysts and readers of literary fiction, concerning the Giller's legitimacy as an arbiter of literary works (and authors) and as an advocate for their nation-wide recognition, including in CW programs.

Nominated and winning books are presented to the public, reviewers and academic critics through the certifying mechanism of a prestigious cultural institution and have a marked impact on prize-related discourse and on circulation. Consequently, we must acknowledge that literary awards create material (extra-literary) conditions which govern the success of books that are nominated and win. For this same reason, prizes also determine the kinds of fiction that gets written, published and discussed in CW programs. Soon after the Giller's founding, CanLit writers and critics began referring to the "Giller Bait" novel. One GG-nominee and eventual 2013 Giller winner, Lynn Coady, described this aspect of a book:

> To refer to a novel as 'Giller Bait' denotes a strain of thought in Canadian publishing which insists that serious, relevant, and therefore successful literature must be about something besides 1) here and 2) now. If it involves some kind of horrible war or, even better, a genocide, this

> makes it doubly prize-worthy because it shows our authors to be such a grave tribe of thinkers, unafraid to tackle The Big Issues. (Coady)

Once more, the Giller offers an example of an ongoing process that is effectively curatorial, a curation not unrelated to those lamented by current critics of the CW workshop [see chapters here by Leach, Lynes, McGill, etc.]. Shortlisted and winning books, along with the entire body of prized texts that it fashions and enlarges year after year, become representative of the Giller's literary standards or the criteria for excellence it stands by. Given its concerted insistence on the importance to the nation of the books it selects annually for celebration (and in view of the large volume of laudatory rhetoric surrounding Giller events), one must recognize that its lists and winners contribute substantially to what Benedict Anderson termed the "imagined community" (39), or what Roberts describes as the "the (imagined) life of the nation" (22). Consequently, it is evident that any inquiry into prestigious prizes like the Giller must assess the types of decisions they can compel authors to make, and how they shape or reshape national literature, including in CW programs.[8]

Furthermore, these prize-related interventions must be juxtaposed with other increasingly common prestige-building practices—such as the Griffin's aforementioned decision to consolidate its two poetry prizes into one and thereby internationalize itself as an award-giving institution, or, as is the case with the founders of the Carol Shields Prize for Fiction, to forge a binational award. For its move, the Griffin, not surprisingly, drew criticism from Canada's literary community. Reflecting on recent literary awards-related events on his *Grain of Salt* blog, poet George Murray made pointed comments about this year's Griffin:

> The Griffin Prize released its first shortlist since dropping the Canadian half of its prize and it looks like the jury was at least conscious of the optics of this terrible decision and they've included both a longlist and a shortlist with two (sort of) Canadians on it.... [N]ot only are Canadian poets being shuffled aside, Canadian independent publishers are also benched.

For Murray, "this change smacks of a couple things, [one of which is] a sort of delusion of grandeur as it tries to position itself as a mini-Nobel Prize" (Murray). Yet, the Giller, too, though less overtly (or perhaps more adroitly), behaves like an international prize by consciously working to build its reputation nationally and internationally. If the Griffin can be said to have deterritorialized its mandate by eliminating its Canadian prize, then the Giller's ambitions and other prestige-securing practices paradoxically also deterritorialize its cultural purview and mission to celebrate Canadian culture through its employment of foreign judges, its commitments to diverse settings (narratives that are not set in Canada) and international aesthetics and concerns.

Prestige as Recognition at Home and Abroad

The Giller aims to secure its position at the top of a domestic and international hierarchy of literary prizes as a value-conferring institution that selects books worthy of a global readership. Such motives, and the literary and aesthetic criteria generated as a result, are in no small way driven by the observable competition between major international prizes like the Booker and the IMPAC. This brings us back to Benedict Anderson, and the unsettling of the more traditional notion of the "national." The national has come to be what is constructed (imagined) for the sake of both popular—which is to say, biggest national audiences—as well as international appeal. The Giller, like the Griffin, was never immune from the pressures to increase its audiences and prestige both domestically and worldwide. Paradoxically, enhancement of national prestige—the effort to grow into a "super prize"—entails the exchange of local scales of value for international ones; this is also a prerequisite for achieving global reach and impact (English 262).

The "World Context" is also a reference to the political and economic climate of transnational capital and national discourse of globalization wherein prizes operate. In the case of the Giller, the aim to be representative of a national culture is to some extent made problematic by its "paratextual" function: the prize is both privately funded by Rabinovitch's estate/foundation and sponsored by the Scotiabank, a major national banking institution that operates globally; the Giller is closely associated with multinational book publishers (through the books it nominates and its judges, whose literary careers are often bound up with these same publishers); relevant also is the perennial over-representation on shortlists of the Bertelsmann group of publishers, all part of Random House, which assumed the controlling part of Penguin Group in 2013, after the 2012 takeover of "Canada's publisher" (Mason 108; cf. "How Canada's"; cf. Dewar) McClelland & Stewart by a Random House Canada that purchased a backlist including Leonard Cohen, Margaret Atwood, Michael Ondaatje, Alice Munro et cetera (Dewar). Consequently, the Giller's mandate to assist Canadian literary culture is one that competes with the realities of book publishing in Canada, as well as other exigencies.

Yet, the Giller's transnational tendencies are tempered by its concomitant aim to publicize and popularize its prize-winning books. It is deeply invested in engaging with the Canadian public, aiming to influence a wide range of readers by highlighting the combined virtues of a work's "Canadianness" and its literary merits. It employs television and social media platforms to connect with Canadians, publicize its long- and shortlisted books and promote its judging panels. Since making its long-list public, the Giller has only intensified its efforts to construct itself as a "coast-to-coast" or "national" prize. An example of such efforts, "Between the Pages," consists of a series of readings held in cities across Canada, by "a cast of local celebrit[ies] … who read selections of the [shortlisted] works."

Giller Fiction

Like the Booker, the Giller strives to make itself the most consequential prizing institution in Canada; the Booker makes this point explicitly in its "Facts and Figures" page discussion of "the Booker bounce" [in sales] (Booker, "Prize Facts"). As well, like the Booker, and as a way of meeting the expectations of diverse readers, its selections are based on a number of well-defined criteria. Several of these are on view in the judges' comments about the Giller's 2018 long-list:

> Our sole criteria going into this process was literary excellence. We were looking for books that were written in elevated, idiosyncratic, original prose that exhibited an exquisite command of the art of language, and unparalleled mastery of structure and storytelling.... This list reflects the landscape of the current Canadian imagination: diverse, bold, edgy, exciting, reflective, aware, angry and joyous. Leave it to our literature to speak out beautifully from the far-flung edge of this huge mysterious land, and sing about the erased, the immigrants, the oppressed, the survivors, the entitled. It also reflects the myriad genres that Canadian writers are working in: auto-fiction, science-fiction, epic family sagas, historical novels, coming of age dramas, short-stories, satire. These are stories about and beyond Canada, a list so exciting, exhibiting such pure excellence, it stands up to any list in the world, and it is great, great fun to read. ("2018 Scotiabank")

The passage underscores the Giller's *worldly* dimensions. Its corpus is meant to "stand up" to any other major prize list on the basis of its listed books' prose, and their varied perspectives, positions and moods, subject matter, historical and geographic purview. The ecumenicalism of the Giller's lists is seen when comparing the comment above with the description offered by Booker judges in 2018:

> All of our six finalists are miracles of stylistic invention. In each of them the language takes centre stage. And yet in every other respect they are remarkably diverse, exploring a multitude of subjects ranging across space and time. From Ireland to California, in Barbados and the Arctic, they inhabit worlds that not everyone will have been to, but which we can all be enriched by getting to know. Each one explores the anatomy of pain—among the incarcerated and on a slave plantation, in a society fractured by sectarian violence, and even in the natural world. But there are also in each of them moments of hope. These books speak very much to our moment, but we believe that they will endure. ("Man Booker")

Juxtaposing these statements exposes a number of similarities (including the presence of Esi Edugyan's novel on both lists). In addition to the liberal-democratic values the lists represent, both offer a panoramic view of the world.

Their narratives "range across space and time" in the same way that movies or television series carry viewers across continents and swaths of time for purposes of edification and entertainment. This is a form of literary cosmopolitanism—one that the globalization of media increasingly shapes. The Giller is a modern-day literary prize in more than one sense. As well as relying on various broadcasts and online strategies to promote itself and its books to readers in Canada and abroad (by highlighting features readers are most likely to identify with entertainment), its lists contain books with narratives that cross multiple borders. Or else they recreate history, events that were momentous, thrilling and function as springboards to adventure or mystery.

Conclusion

The judges' statements reveal that the Giller, like the Booker, celebrates books with an imagined readership that is international. This is one side of the Giller's corpus: its targeting of readers who have only a partial affiliation with Canada (or who have hyphenated identities) or none at all. The other side, the one more explicitly linked with Canadianness, is meant to guide readers, if not writers, to portrayals of the nation. Note, the judges praise writers' versatility, as well as the heterogeneity of perspectives, although their assumption is that any book lover with an interest in the world, history, but also in fiction that is "bold, edgy, exciting" ("2018 Scotiabank") would enjoy these works. Canadian readers are thereby constructed as an audience that values literature as art and as a window on many things—though not necessarily on that which is uniquely Canadian. Hegemonic or assimilationist constructions of Canadian literature certainly predate broadcasted programming, but the latter play a role in exacerbating omissions, particularly where all Giller nominees are labeled in the simplest terms as Canadian writers, and where descriptions of nominated books omit or underplay references to distinct or, as would sometimes be more accurate, separate cultural communities. In other words, such constructions exclude a large number of constituencies in Canada: readers and the literature of particular regions and societies with distinct linguistic and cultural traditions and histories, including those of French Canadians, Indigenous peoples (First Nations, Inuit and Métis), Acadians, the smaller communities of Mennonites and the Maritime provinces' descendants of European Scots or Celts.

To be clear, portrayals of Canada or Canadianness the Giller proffers reflect complex sets of preferences or, as per Bourdieu, tastes. The resulting corpus represents certain perspectives on Canada, but not all. Moreover, even this selective *framing* of the nation reflects an effort to represent Canadianness through the screen of liberal-humanist nationalism and cultural pluralism and is intended to appeal to readers across Canada and abroad. The Giller, then, like the Booker, reconciles the requirement to showcase national or local culture and values by aligning the national—even those instances where it appears most distinct—with that of the global through selections that "stand up to any list in the world" ("2018 Scotiabank").

There are cultural and ideological aspects to the Giller's corpus, the contemporary canon to which it contributes, and the readers it targets. The corpus serves as an affirmation of cultural pluralism, inclusion (of writers and readerships) and support for democratic processes, which include free speech. However, such overarching criteria invariably exclude books that are valuable windows on life in Canada. In other words, there is less visibility for books that authentically depict national culture but do not meet the Giller's criteria—for example, books that focus on regional life and concerns, or fiction by Indigenous authors which adhere to different narrative forms and aesthetics. This is the "concealment" Frank Davey discusses in *Post-National Arguments: The Politics of the Anglophone-Canadian Novel since 1967*. Davey's assertion that Canada's brand of humanism is conflated with Western or universal humanism and tends to go uncontested as an ethical-creative template for Canadian writers has even more relevance today, when prestige is equated with popularity, including in the writing workshop, and a growing following at home and abroad.

Notes

1 For authoritative histories of the Nobel and Pulitzer Prizes, see Burton Feldman. *The Nobel Prize: A History of Genius, Controversy, and Prestige*. 1st ed., Arcade Pub., 2000, and Douglas J. Bates. *The Pulitzer Prize: The Inside History of America's Most Prestigious Award*. Birch Lane, 1991. For a book-length study of the Booker Prize and superb analysis of its fiction, see Richard Todd. *Consuming Fictions: The Booker Prize and Fiction in Britain Today*. Bloomsbury, 1996. Essays on the Booker and other British prizes appear in "The (Booker) Prize for Fiction and the Tenor of the Times." *Fiction and Literary Prizes in Great Britain*. Eds. Wolfgang Görtschacher and Holder Klein. Vienna: Praesens Verlag, 2006.

2 Since the 1970s, numerous international prizes, modeled on the Nobel, were founded. These include the Neustadt International Prize for Literature (founded in 1970) and Pegasus Prize (founded in 1977). The International Dublin Literary Award was established in 1996 as the International IMPAC Dublin Literary Award. In US, the most notable is the National Book Critics Circle (founded in 1974). For a 25-year overview of the National Book Awards, see Joseph F. Trimmer. *The National Book Awards for Fiction: An Index to the First Twenty-Five Years*. G. K. Hall, 1978.

3 Economist Danny Quah discusses the transition to a "weightless economy" of "dematerialized" products, suggesting a "greatly expanded economic market for symbolic goods such as, among other things, artistic prestige" (Quah qtd. in English 77). See also the discussion regarding investment in creative capital in Veselinović Branislav and Drobnjakovic Maja. "The Importance of the 'Weightless Economy' and Investment in Intangible Assets." *Semantic Scholar*, 2015, https://www.semanticscholar.org/paper/THE-IMPORTANCE-OF-THE-%22WEIGHTLESS-ECONOMY%22-AND-IN-Branislav-Maja/ee293b5c8bc086c4fcfb31c07544e5cd1d1552d4.

4 This is certainly not unproblematic. See Luke Strongman: "Conclusion: The Booker Prize and the Culture of Post-Imperialism." In *The Booker Prize and the Legacy of Empire*. Rodopi, 2002.

5 Todd states that Rushdie was able to successfully introduce an-Other subjectivity to Western readers. He adds, however: "The postcolonial dimension probably

only became fully apparent to Rushdie's reader after the subsequent publication of Shame (1983) and the polemical Granta essay 'Outside the Whale' (1984)" (82).

6 Though note, founder of the Dublin Literary Award, formerly the IMPAC ("the prize that would succeed as the world's largest for a single work of fiction"), James B. Irwin, cautioned: "I don't think prestige can be bought.... Prestige is built by the decision of the judges over a period of years" (qtd. in English 124).

7 For example, Todd observes with regard to Booker announcements: "A shrewd publisher can in effect bring about a 'double publication', by releasing a potential (but not all too well-known) winner early in the year, and capitalizing on press coverage in the event of its being shortlisted later the same year" (72).

8 See important discussions regarding the writing life and self-conscious authorship in Sarah Brouillette. *Literature and the Creative Economy*. Stanford UP, 2014, and her earlier *Postcolonial Writers in the Global Literary Marketplace*. Palgrave Macmillan, 2007. Brouillettte argues convincingly that contrary to neoliberalism's focus on economic outcomes and creative entrepreneurship, which relies on notions of "the solo author's self-validation and self-sufficiency," authors are just as likely to be motivated by the ambition to win over a discriminating literary readership and secure regard within a community of author/artist peers.

Works Cited

"2018 Scotiabank Giller Prize Winner." *Scotiabank Giller Prize*, 2018, https://scotiabankgillerprize.ca/2018-finalists.

"About the Prize." *Griffin Poetry Prize*, 2022, The Griffin Trust for Excellence in Poetry, https://griffinpoetryprize.com/about.

"All Nobel Prizes in Literature." *The Nobel Prize*, 2023, https://www.nobelprize.org/prizes/lists/all-nobel-prizes-in-literature.

Ahearn, Victoria. "Scotiabank Giller Prize Jury Expands to 5 Members." *Canadian Press*, 14 Jan. 2015, https://www.ctvnews.ca/entertainment/scotiabank-giller-prize-jury-expands-to-5-members-1.2188040

Anderson, Benedict. *Imagined Communities: Reflections on the Origin and Spread of Nationalism*. Verso, 1983.

Atwood, Margaret. "The Shields Prize, Amazingly." *In the Writing Burrow*, Substack, 7 May 2023, https://margaretatwood.substack.com/p/the-shields-prize-amazingly.

Bates, J. Douglas. *The Pulitzer Prize: The Inside History of America's Most Prestigious Award*. Birch Lane, 1991.

"Booker Prize Facts and Figures." *The Booker Prizes*, Booker Prize Foundation, 1 Aug. 2023, https://thebookerprizes.com/the-booker-library/features/booker-prize-facts-and-figures.

Bourdieu, Pierre. *Distinction: A Social Critique of the Judgment of Taste*. Trans. Richard Nice. Harvard UP, 1984.

Bourdieu, Pierre. "Structures, *Habitus*, Practices" and "Belief and the Body." *The Logic of Practice*. Trans. Richard Nice. Stanford UP, 1990, pp. 52–79.

Bourdieu, Pierre. *The Rules of Art: Genesis and Structure of the Literary Field*. Trans. Susan Emanuel. Stanford UP, 1996.

Branislav, Veselinović and Drobnjakovic Maja. "The Importance of the 'Weightless Economy' and Investment in Intangible Assets." *Semantic Scholar*, 2015, https://www.semanticscholar.org/paper/THE-IMPORTANCE-OF-THE-%22WEIGHTLESS-ECONOMY%22-AND-IN-Branislav-Maja/ee293b5c8bc086c4fcfb31c07544e5cd1d1552d4.

Brennan, Timothy. *At Home in the World: Cosmopolitanism Now*. Harvard UP, 1997.

Brouillette, Sarah. *Literature and the Creative Economy*. Stanford UP, 2014.
Brouillette, Sarah. *Postcolonial Writers in the Global Literary Marketplace*. Palgrave Macmillan, 2007.
Brouillette, Sarah. "The Canada Council for the Arts Reveals the Governor General's Literary Awards Winners." *Canada Council for the Arts*, 16 Nov. 2022. https://canadacouncil.ca/press/2022/11/the-canada-council-for-the-arts-reveals-the-governor-generals-literary-awards-winners.
Carey, Leo. "The Giller Crowd Goes to New York: 'Celebrate Canada' Festival Brings out Prize's Founded and a Busload of Authors." *National Post*. 2000: B23. ProQuest. Web. 14 Jan. 2015.
Coady, Lynn. "The Book Killers: Why the Publishing World Hates the Giller and Governor General's Awards." *The Tyee*. 1 Nov. 2004, https://thetyee.ca/Entertainment/2004/11/01/BookKillers.
Davey, Frank. *Post-National Arguments: The Politics of the Anglophone-Canadian Novel Since 1967*. U of Toronto P, 1993.
Dewar, Elaine. *The Handover: How Bigwigs and Bureaucrats Transferred Canada's Best Publisher and the Best Part of Our Literary Heritage to a Foreign Multinational*. Biblioasis, 2017.
Dundas, Deborah. "25 years of the Giller Prize, the Gala that Changed Canadian Literature." *The Toronto Star*, 16 Nov. 2018, https://www.thestar.com/entertainment/books/25-years-of-the-giller-prize-the-gala-that-changed-canadian-literature/article_df16054f-653c-5de9-a972-4e82f5764cc8.html.
English, F. James. *The Economy of Prestige: Prizes, Awards, and the Circulation of Cultural Value*. Harvard UP, 2005.
English, F. James. "Everywhere and Nowhere: The Sociology of Literature After 'The Sociology of Literature.'" *New Literary History*, vol. 41, no. 2, Spring 2010, pp. v–xxiii.
"Esi Edugyan." *The Booker Prizes*, 2023, https://thebookerprizes.com/the-booker-library/authors/esi-edugyan.
"Esi Edugyan Is the Winner of the 2018 Scotiabank Giller Prize." *Scotiabank Giller Prize*, 19 Nov. 2018. https://scotiabankgillerprize.ca/esi-dugyan-winner-2018-scotiabank-giller-prize.
Feldman, Burton. *The Nobel Prize: A History of Genius, Controversy, and Prestige*. 1st ed., Arcade Pub., 2000.
Franková, Milada. "The (Booker) Prize for Fiction and the Tenor of the Times." *Fiction and Literary Prizes in Great Britain*. Eds. Wolfgang Görtschacher and Holder Klein. Vienna: Praesens Verlag, 2006.
"How Canada's Book Publisher McClelland & Stewart Became German-Owned." *CBC Radio: The Current*, 14 Jul. 2017, https://www.cbc.ca/radio/thecurrent/the-current-for-july-14-2017-1.4203051/how-canada-s-book-publisher-mcclelland-stewart-became-german-owned-author-1.4203067.
Huggan, Graham. *The Post-Colonial Exotic: Marketing the Margins*. Routledge, 2001.
Jewell, Richard. "The Nobel Prize: History and Canonicity." *The Journal of the Midwest Modern Language Association*, vol. 33, no. 1, 2000, pp. 97–113, https://doi.org/10.2307/1315120.
"Man Booker Prize Announces 2018 Shortlist." *Man Group*, 20 Sept. 2018, https://www.man.com/man-booker-prize-2018-shortlist.

Mason, Jody. "Janet B. Friskney. New Canadian Library: The Ross-McClelland Years, 1952-1978." *Papers of the Bibliographical Society of Canada*, vol. 46, no. 1, Spring 2008, pp. 108+. Gale Academic OneFile, link.gale.com/apps/doc/A183983002/AONE?u=anon~eb62a447&sid=googleScholar&xid=84c0fa1e.

McDowell, Adam. "New Giller Is among Richest for English Writers." *Gazette:* D9, 20 Jan. 1994.

M. Huston. "The Show Can Go On." *University of Victoria: Fine Arts*, 25 Mar. 2020. https://finearts.uvic.ca/research/blog/category/writing/page/15.

Murray, George. "Spring Update, or, 'Oh, yeah... This Thing...'." *Grain of Salt*, Substack, 9 May 2023. https://georgemurray.substack.com/p/spring-update-or-oh-yeah-this-thing.

Quah, Danny. "The Weightless Economy in Growth." *Business Economist*, vol. 30, 1999, 40–53.

Roberts, Gillian. *Prizing Literature: The Celebration and Circulation of National Culture*. U of Toronto P, 2011.

Stein, Olga. *The Scotiabank Giller Prize: How Canadian*. 2020. York U, PhD dissertation.

Strongman, Luke. "Conclusion: The Booker Prize and the Culture of Post-Imperialism." In *The Booker Prize and the Legacy of Empire*. Rodopi, 2002.

"Suzette Mayr." *Department of English: University of Calgary*, n.d. https://profiles.ucalgary.ca/suzette-mayr.

"Suzette Mayr Wins 100K Scotiabank Giller Prize for Novel *The Sleeping Car Porter*." *CBC Books*, 7 Nov. 2022, https://www.cbc.ca/books/suzette-mayr-wins-100k-scotiabank-giller-prize-for-novel-the-sleeping-car-porter-1.6643257.

Todd, Richard. *Consuming Fictions: The Booker Prize and Fiction in Britain Today*. Bloomsbury, 1996.

Trimmer, Joseph F. *The National Book Awards for Fiction: An Index to the First Twenty-Five Years*. G. K. Hall, 1978.

"What We Do." *The Carol Shields Prize for Fiction*, 2023, https://carolshieldsprizeforfiction.com/what-we-do.

7 Supporting First-Time Workshop Leaders in Large Introductory Courses

Robert McGill

If your only experience of Creative Writing in postsecondary education has involved workshops with a dozen or so people, you might struggle to imagine how a Creative Writing course can succeed with a class size of a hundred or more students. As the demand for Creative Writing courses has grown, however, large lecture-based courses have become increasingly common, especially at universities where courses have long been a feature in other disciplines. At the University of Toronto, it fell to me in 2018 to design and teach an Introduction to Creative Writing course with just such characteristics.[1] Previously, my only teaching of Creative Writing had taken place in small, workshop-based courses that, for all their joys, frequently frustrated students with their substantial enrolment waitlists. In contrast, a lecture-based course would allow me and its subsequent instructors to work with many more students. Still, I knew that the workshop has its advantages: in-depth attention to each student's writing; the development of students' ability to speak and listen as editors and authors; the building of close-knit creative communities. It also seemed to me that in a large introductory course, the kind of personalized support and social bonds that a workshop facilitates would be all the more important as a complement to the lecture hours. So, for my course, in addition to the two lecture hours each week, we included weekly hour-long small-group workshops led by graduate teaching assistants.

Making such workshops work depends in no small part on the TAs. In the first edition of my course, they were five Creative Writing MA program students, along with a program graduate who'd returned to the department for doctoral studies. Each TA led a workshop group of 16 students and graded their assignments. None of the TAs had previously graded creative writing, and none had led an undergraduate workshop, but they'd participated in such workshops as students. More specifically, they'd all been in the MA workshop with me, so I could draw on our shared experience when preparing them for the course.

In such a course, readying the TAs to grade fairly, attentively and with confidence from the start is crucial. So is training them to lead, with assurance and joy, workshops that are inclusive, supportive, culturally and aesthetically

DOI: 10.4324/9781032614144-9

pluralistic and rigorous in their attention to craft. For all the benefits and pleasures of workshops, even the best ones are susceptible to problems such as hurtful criticism and the assertion of particular tastes as if they're norms.[2] What's more, the student-led nature of the conversation and the fact that everyone's discussing writing by people in the class can entail intense vulnerability among the participants. The TAs need to be ready to intervene in difficult moments, and they need to foster an environment in which such moments happen rarely, if at all.

The course instructor has perhaps an even greater role to play in cultivating this environment, both through the lectures and through other elements ranging from the syllabus to the assignments. It's fundamental that an introductory course supports students in learning not only about matters of craft but also about delight in the process, sustainable creative practices and modes of mutual support. It's just as fundamental that the TAs' workshop-leading and grading be well supported by the instructor and helpful in the TAs' development as teachers.

Indeed, the instructor's essentially teaching two subjects in parallel, each with a different set of learners: Creative Writing with the undergraduates and Creative Writing pedagogy with the TAs. For the undergraduates, one might plan units on topics such as narratorial perspective, verse forms, sound and rhythm, plotting, characterization, dialogue, setting, relations to realism, intertextuality and ethics. With the TAs, one needs to address how good workshop leaders both cultivate in students and practise themselves such virtues as:

- an encouraging disposition towards students' writing and in-class comments;
- close, comprehensive engagement with workshop submissions;
- carefully articulated, substantive praise and constructive criticism;
- precision in discussing elements of craft;
- the embrace of a range of subjects, genres, styles and forms;
- curiosity about what a text's seeking to accomplish, along with open-mindedness about what counts as success;
- sensitivity to cultural diversity and the limitations of one's cultural repertoire when considering texts;
- promoting class participation from everyone without putting anyone on the spot;
- alertness for signs of student unwellness in the writing and in class.

While hardly exhaustive, this list stands as a reminder of just how many balls are up in the air at any moment in a workshop and of how many skills a good workshop leader possesses. If granted unlimited time for TA training, an instructor could offer a term-long course devoted to discussing and developing these skills. It would be a pedagogical epic journey together, undertaken in tandem with the collective teaching of the undergraduate course.

The reality of many courses, though, is that the TAs' contracts allow them only a few training hours with the instructor, often only before or even as the term begins. In such cases, the training must be less an epic than a sonnet. Within that tighter form, however, preparing the TAs can still be relatively comprehensive. In my case, it has involved elements as varied as a handbook, practice grading and workshop visits. I've also undertaken lecture-hour activities such as workshop-style discussion that are ostensibly only for the undergraduates but that are geared towards helping the workshops and grading to succeed. The results have been heartening. I've taught the course three times with workshops included, and the students' term-end evaluations have frequently identified the workshops as a favourite part of the course. I've also never had to regrade student work due to a complaint. Much of the credit goes to the TAs, who are talented, conscientious and committed to their students' success. Likewise, the undergraduates have made me literally, publicly weep in gratitude for the insight, creativity, collegiality and sensitivity that they've brought to the lectures and workshops. (Usually, I can hold it together until the last lecture. Then the tears flow.) With the hope that the parts of the course geared towards TA training and support have played a role in the course's flourishing, too, I provide details about those elements in what follows.

Model Questions, Model Feedback

Because most students in an introductory Creative Writing course are new to commenting on peers' creative work and having their own creative work graded, and because most of the TAs haven't previously graded such writing or led workshops, it's essential that both groups share an understanding of what valuable feedback and fair assessment involve.[3] To that end, a strategy for me has been to include in the syllabus a document titled "Questions to Ask of Creative Writing" (appended to this chapter). Divided into sections corresponding to the lecture units, it's both a course map and a guide to issues that the students might consider as they're writing and revising, not to mention as they're considering each other's work. The document also indicates the sorts of questions that the TAs will ask as they assess the students' writing.[4]

Another key document to share with the students and TAs at the start of the term is a sample workshop submission—whether preserved from a previous edition of the course with the author's permission or mocked up for pedagogical purposes—with model feedback attached. That feedback should include annotations and end-comments that demonstrate editorial best practices: for instance, a careful balance of appreciative remarks, questions and constructive criticism; a close attention to particular words and phrases; the use of appropriate critical terminology; the discussion of formal elements; and an expression of enthusiasm for specific elements of the text, along with stated reasons for that enthusiasm.[5] This document, together with an in-class discussion of it, puts the students and TAs in a better position to offer good feedback themselves. Not trivially, it also stands as an example of how much written feedback to offer.

Practice Grading and a TA Handbook

Having sample workshop submissions in hand at the start of the course also allows the instructor to offer the TAs practice in grading before the workshops have begun.[6] After the TAs have individually written up feedback on the samples and determined grades for them, a group meeting with the instructor can be convened in which everyone discusses their assessments. In such meetings with my own TAs, it typically becomes evident that some TAs' grades are much lower or higher than others'. While I reassure the TAs that their grading will grow more in line with one another's as they read more student writing, the exercise in itself does important work in helping them to calibrate their standards. In the meeting, we also discuss how the TAs' written feedback can best establish that the grades are clearly divorced from personal taste.[7]

The same meeting provides an opportunity for the instructor to offer affirmations to the TAs, who are, often enough, nervous about leading workshops for the first time. It can be helpful to remind them of their substantial experience relative to their students'; to note that their principal role is to facilitate conversation, not to lecture; and to assure them that their students will be not only excited to be there but also grateful for the TAs' encouragement.

The group meeting serves one more important purpose, too: as a forum for the TAs' questions and concerns about aspects of their work. In my course, because the time available for training is limited, I further prepare the TAs for the course and for our group meeting by sharing with them a handbook that contains a guide to workshopping, grading tips and a troubleshooting section featuring hypothetical scenarios, from offensive student comments to complaints about grades. (Excerpts are appended to this chapter.) The group meeting then affords the TAs a chance to ask questions relating to the handbook and for me to underscore key points in it.

Syllabus Guidelines

In a course with multiple workshop groups, it's critical that there be consistency across the groups with regard to workshop conventions, not least because the instructor needs to be able, during lecture hours, to introduce everyone to the best practices that attend those conventions. In this regard, the syllabus is a key document, articulating guidelines in sufficient detail that the students know what to expect. For instance, it's important to apprise everyone that, while the TAs will do their best to apportion the workshop time equally, students won't be at a disadvantage if their submission doesn't receive exactly the same amount of workshop discussion as others', because they'll still be receiving ample written feedback from their TA and peers. In my syllabus, I also mention that the workshopping of each text will begin with appreciative comments before the group moves on to constructive criticism. While this format can feel contrived at first, it reduces students' anxiety about whether their work will be praised or criticized, and the TAs can point to the syllabus if a student starts to offer criticism right off the bat.

Additionally, the syllabus should address the importance of students' wellbeing and the need for a safe workshop environment. For instance, anticipating the potential submission of writing that could be understood as signalling its author's psychological unwellness, I use the syllabus to make this request: "[B]ecause your TAs and I have your wellbeing in mind when we read your work, I'd ask that if you plan to submit a text with content that you think a reader could take to indicate unwellness on your part, please email your TA about your intentions before you submit the text." Even with this language in place, some students who produce such writing don't always pre-inform their TA. In those cases, the request's presence on the syllabus opens the door for the TA to reach out, remind the student of the policy and inquire as to how they are. (I also ask the TAs to let me know about such situations so that if further concerns arise, the TAs aren't left to deal with student-welfare issues that are better addressed by others.)[8]

The syllabus further takes up the matter of content warnings (often called "trigger warnings"). While many people value these warnings and expect them to be included with creative work when appropriate,[9] it would be unfair to expect that students always recognize when their writing merits one. Consequently, in my course, I don't require content warnings. Instead, if a student finds engagement with certain subject-matter harmful, I suggest that they and I devise a personalized accommodation in conjunction with the university's Accessibility Services office. Still, some students want to attach content warnings to their work regardless of whether it's demanded of them. In view of that desire, the syllabus for my course advises the class as follows:

> You're welcome, but not required, to identify the presence in your work of topics that you think might upset certain readers: write "Content Warning" at the top of the first page and list the topic/s in question.
>
> Warnings won't appear on all course texts that contain challenging material. If it makes you unwell to read about a topic, please contact me so that we can address your needs.

This policy seeks to support vulnerable students, avoid placing an undue burden of responsibility on the students when sharing their work and provide clear guidelines for the TAs as they lead the workshops.

Mock Workshopping

A 12-week course with groups of 16 students meeting weekly for a single hour doesn't leave much time in those meetings for anything but workshopping, even with the students each receiving just one opportunity to have their work discussed. Nevertheless, it's fundamental to the workshops' success that the students have a chance to participate in a workshop-style discussion before any of them is also in the position of having their creative work being considered by the group. Likewise, the TAs benefit from getting their feet wet as facilitators without the further challenge of having to negotiate the sensitivities of a submission's author. Accordingly, there are excellent reasons to make time at the start of the course for each group to conduct a mock workshop session discussing sample texts assigned by the instructor.

For this session, I've chosen texts that clearly have room for improvement. One is a version of a not particularly good poem that I wrote as an undergraduate, modified to include further problems that a workshop might address: arbitrary line breaks, ungainly rhythms, uneconomical phrasings, unduly obscure allusions and on-the-nose metaphors. Most of the students enter the course more experienced with prose than with poetry, so a poem with obvious flaws is useful as an introduction regarding what to watch out for and how to discuss it. In becoming acquainted at the course's outset with a poem that's a long way from successful, the students are also liable subsequently to feel more confident about their own writing.

Lecturing to Support the Workshops

It's not just in establishing workshop guidelines that the course instructor can use the lecture hours to help the workshops go well. Introducing craft terms to be deployed in oral and written feedback is also an important lecture activity, while the instructor's leading of class discussion about published literary texts can model an approach to appreciation and critique for the students to take up: an approach that emphasizes substantive, perceptive, well-articulated responses emerging from careful attempts to apprehend and respect the author's goals, as well as from a recognition of the limitations of one's own perspective. Equally important are in-class conversations about literary value's contingencies and the fact that there are good reasons not to be reductive about what counts as "successful" writing.[10]

In the lectures for my course, I also reflect on the workshops' importance, noting the frequent solitude of writing, along with the value of participating in a community that understands such solitude's difficulties and necessity while providing a counterpoint to it. I discuss how my own workshop participation as a student led to friendships that continue in the present day, involving people with whom I still exchange work. Such self-reflexivity helps the students to keep in the foreground the importance of supporting each other, and it helps them to recognize the support that they're receiving in turn.

Workshop Visits and Grading Reviews

The instructor can further support the workshops' success by sitting in on them to provide the TAs with feedback on their teaching. Ideally, the visits will occur far enough into the term that the workshop has had a chance to find its feet, but with enough weeks remaining for any suggestions to be meaningfully implemented.

After each visit in my course, I write a report that I share with the TA and keep on file in case they ever need a reference or a letter for their teaching dossier. There's also a post-class meeting with each TA in which they can ask questions and share their perspective on how the class went.[11] In my feedback, I'm keen to point out evidence that the TA has fostered an environment in which the students appear happy to be there, glad of each other's company and comfortable speaking.[12] I'm eager to compliment the TA for discussing the students' writing supportively and with sophistication. I laud the TAs for using their students' names and speaking assuredly without a script. I celebrate the moments of impromptu insight and collective laughter. I also offer points of critique: for instance, I once noted that a TA needed to address the fact that almost all of the students were sitting on one side of the room and, as a result, straining to see each other as they talked. Another time, I pointed out that one student hadn't spoken at all, and I suggested that, in future weeks, the TA ask a couple of survey-type questions—for example, "How old would you guess the narrator is?"—to get everyone talking in a low-stakes way. But most importantly in these meetings, I want the TAs to know that I admire how many balls they're juggling with such finesse.

Beyond aiding the TAs' development as teachers, the visits have other benefits. For one, the instructor's presence in the workshop allows the students to see the instructor as someone comprehensively committed to the course and not just the face at the front of the lecture hall. As well, for the instructor to witness how the students approach each other's writing in the workshop and how the lectures influence the discussion there can vitally shape future lectures and further iterations of the course.

Meanwhile, to ensure that the TAs' evaluations of student work are fair and their written feedback effective, it's important for the instructor to undertake checks of each graded assignment. In my course, I ask the TAs to send me graded samples for me to review. I also keep an eye on the average grades for each workshop group. I don't require that the TAs' grades fall within certain ranges, but if one TA's average is an outlier, I consider their grading more extensively, and if it turns out that the TA has been more or less generous than their peers, I invite that person to consider whether adjustments might be in order.

Accounting for Labour and Accepting Changes

Because the TAs' commitment to giving good feedback and preparing conscientiously for the workshops can tempt them toward putting more time into those activities than the TAs' contracts permit, one of the course instructor's key responsibilities is to ensure that the TAs' duties remain accomplishable within those hours. At the same time, training the TAs, reviewing their grading, visiting their workshops and giving them feedback on their work entails substantial labour on the instructor's part, to say nothing of a large course's demands in terms of dealing with individual student issues. The opportunity to work closely with talented graduate students and witness them developing and thriving as teachers is a privilege, but one that shouldn't come at the price of an untenable workload. There's a crucial need for the labour involved in teaching such large courses to be recognized and accounted for by the institutions involved.

Meanwhile, I should report that when I most recently taught my large-enrolment course, there was an enormous change: the workshop element was dropped. The reason was logistical: a second, equally large section of the course led by another instructor had been added, and we couldn't ensure that there'd be enough TAs available to lead all the workshops. To maintain a student-centred pedagogy in the new lecture-only version of the course, I "flipped" the classroom:[13] each week, there was an hourlong recorded lecture for the students to watch asynchronously, along with two hours of in-class time with me, during which we reviewed the lecture material, discussed the week's readings and undertook prompt-based writing exercises. The exercises, in particular, turned out to be a hit: when I asked the students to complete an anonymous midterm questionnaire, all of them agreed that the exercises were a valuable part of our work together.

For this new version of the course, four TAs were hired as graders. Once again, they were graduate students without experience grading creative work, so the related training elements from the course's previous version remained in place. They became all the more important, in fact, given that the TAs didn't get to know their students through workshops, which meant that there was an added impetus for the TAs to earn the students' trust via excellent written feedback. I also encouraged the students to meet with their TAs individually, both before and after they submitted work. Face to face, the TAs could make clear through their words, tone and body language their enthusiasm for the students' writing and their investment in the students' success. One-on-one meetings also made it easier for the TAs to apprehend the difference that their work was making in their students' academic and creative lives.

For me, after teaching only small, workshop-based Creative Writing courses, teaching the large introductory course, with or without the workshops, has meant a reduction in how well I'm able to get to know the undergraduates in my courses, as their primary relationships with the course's teaching personnel are with their TAs. I love reading the students' work as I review the grades, but I miss becoming acquainted with the works' authors in the same way that I do when leading a workshop. Still, the large course offers some serious consolations: for one thing, it's wonderful that so many students are getting to pursue creative writing; also, it's heartening that they're developing meaningful professional relationships with their TAs; and, not least, the course has granted me the manifold pleasures of working with exceptional graduate student-writers as they gain their first experience teaching in the field they most love.

Notes

1 My inspiration was the School of Creative Writing at the University of British Columbia, which had established such a course for its undergraduate program. I'm particularly grateful to Tariq Hussain, Sarah Leavitt, Nancy Lee, Emily Pohl-Weary and John Vigna, who gave a wonderful presentation about the course at the 2018 Canadian Creative Writers and Writing Programs conference.

2 Commentators have noted other pitfalls, too. For instance, Blumenkranz considers the potential for instructors to abuse the presence of transference and the "extreme imbalance of power" that a workshop can involve. Blythe and Sweet note several concerns, including that "[s]tudents' works are not given equal shrift (sometimes because the workshops are too large), alpha apprentices often dominate the conversation, shy students disappear into the woodwork, and negative comments rip apart works and souls" (314).

3 In the first version of my course, the assessed creative work included two workshop submissions, along with two other prompt-driven exercises that were read only by the TAs and me. All these assignments were each worth 5% of the course grade. Other graded components included workshop participation, written peer feedback, a final portfolio with a preface, and an in-person exam. In a later version of the course, I removed the grading of the workshop pieces to reduce students' anxiety around submitting their work and to better encourage them to take risks. As part of the change, the students were simply required to submit workshop texts during the term to receive feedback and to "qualify" the texts for inclusion in the students' final portfolios. I also replaced the exam, which hadn't allowed for students to produce creative work, with a take-home assignment in which the students write both creatively (in response to a lecture reading) and critically (about one of their own creative pieces in relation to another reading).

4 I've considered providing rubrics to help make the TAs' grading more time-efficient and ensure clarity in terms of their grades' rationales, but rubrics risk reductiveness, and they can make feedback seem impersonal, even rote, so I ask the TAs to approach assessment holistically while always being specific about which elements of a text are successful and which could bear rethinking.

5 The importance of displaying enthusiasm for others' work is something that Lad Tobin articulates well in describing his teaching of writing: "I try to reveal myself as someone who is deeply invested in and demonstrably fascinated by each of my students' ideas or drafts" (201).

6 There's a healthy debate about whether undergraduate creative writing should be graded in terms of its "quality." For an argument against the idea, see Wurzbacher, who makes the case for assessing students "on their ability to analyze and articulate their implementation of strategies, techniques, and concepts discussed throughout the course" (24). In my course, as I observe above, a take-home assignment requires that students demonstrate this ability.

7 For a discussion of best practices in grading, see Weldon.

8 For further discussion regarding student writing that might signal unwellness, see McGill.

9 For an overview of the debate around content warnings' efficacy, see Russon.

10 For discussions of these contingencies, especially with critical attention to the role of common workshop norms and axioms in histories of oppression, see Chavez, Mura, Nguyen, Poddar, Rubinstein, Salesses, Smith and Watkins.

11 In each edition of the course, a graduate of the Creative Writing MA program has served as the course's administrative TA. Their role has included joining me in the workshop visits and convening one-on-one follow-up meeting with the TAs. This arrangement allows for the TAs to receive two perspectives on their teaching via my report and the administrative TA's oral feedback. Witnessing others' teaching is also a valuable pedagogical experience for the administrative TA.

12 I'm eternally grateful to my colleague Nick Mount for offering similar feedback to me when, decades ago, I was a TA leading a tutorial group for one of his courses and he sat in on a session. His observations boosted my confidence as a new teacher and continue to inform my own feedback to TAs.

13 The Flipped Learning Network defines flipped learning as "a pedagogical approach in which direct instruction moves from the group learning space to the individual learning space, and the resulting group space is transformed into a dynamic, interactive learning environment where the educator guides students as they apply concepts and engage creatively in the subject matter" ("What Is Flipped Learning?").

Works Cited

Blythe, Hal, and Charlie Sweet. "The Writing Community: A New Model for the Creative Writing Classroom." *Pedagogy: Critical Approaches to Teaching Literature, Language, Composition, and Culture*, vol. 8, no. 2, 2008, pp. 305–25.

Blumenkranz, Carla. "Seduce the Whole World." *MFA vs NYC: The Two Cultures of American Fiction*, edited by Chad Harbach. n+1/Faber, 2014, pp. 209–21.

Chavez, Felicia Rose. *The Anti-Racist Writing Workshop: How to Decolonize the Creative Classroom*. Haymarket, 2021.

McGill, Robert. "The Place of Biographical Interpretation in Fiction Workshops." *New Writing: The International Journal for the Practice and Theory of Creative Writing*, vol. 12, no. 2, 2015, pp. 155–68.

Mura, David. *A Stranger's Journey: Race, Identity, and Narrative Craft in Writing*. U of Georgia P, 2018.

Naga, Noor, and Robert McGill. "Negotiating Cultural Difference in Creative Writing Workshops." *Pedagogy*, vol. 18, no. 1, 2018, pp. 69–86.

Nguyen, Viet Thanh. "Viet Thanh Nguyen Reveals How Writers' Workshops Can Be Hostile." *New York Times*, 26 Apr. 2017, https://www.nytimes.com/2017/04/26/books/review/viet-thanh-nguyen-writers-workshops.html.

Poddar, Namrata. "Is 'Show Don't Tell' a Universal Truth or a Colonial Relic?" *Literary Hub*, 20 Sept. 2016, https://lithub.com/is-show-dont-tell-a-universal-truth-or-a-colonial-relic.

Rubinstein, Helen Betya. "Toward Changing the Language of Creative Writing Classrooms." *Literary Hub*, 7 Jan. 2019, https://lithub.com/toward-changing-the-language-of-creative-writing-classrooms.

Russon, Penni. "Beyond Trigger Warnings: Working towards a Strengths-Based, Trauma-Informed Model of Resilience in the University Creative Writing Workshop." *TEXT*, vol. 21, no. 42, 2017, https://www.textjournal.com.au/speciss/issue42/content.htm.

Salesses, Matthew. *Craft in the Real World: Rethinking Fiction Writing and Workshopping*. Catapult, 2021.

Smith, Barbara Herrnstein. "Contingencies of Value." *Critical Inquiry*, vol. 10, no. 1, 1983, pp. 1–35.

Tobin, Lad. "Self-Disclosure as a Strategic Teaching Tool: What I Do—and Don't—Tell My Students." *College English*, vol. 73, no. 2, 2010, pp. 196–206.

Watkins, Claire Vaye. "On Pandering." *Tin House*, 23 Nov. 2015, https://tinhouse.com/on-pandering. Accessed 14 Aug. 2023.

Weldon, Fay. "On Assessing Creative Writing." *International Journal for the Practice and Theory of Creative Writing*, vol. 6, no. 3, 2009, pp. 168–74.

"What Is Flipped Learning?" *Flip Learning*, 12 Mar. 2014, https://flippedlearning.org/definition-of-flipped-learning. Accessed 14 Aug. 2023.

Wurzbacher, Ashley. "Confronting the Unavoidable: Grading Creative Writing." *Dispatches from the Classroom: Graduate Students on Creative Writing Pedagogy*, edited by Chris Drew, Joseph Rein, and David Yost, Continuum, 2012, pp. 23–41.

Appendix 1

Introduction to Creative Writing Teaching Assistant Handbook: Edited Excerpts

The Workshop

There are many ways to lead a workshop, but for the sake of course coherence, I'd ask that as you lead your workshop for our course, you follow the guidelines below. A weekly 50-minute, introductory, multi-genre workshop with 16 students and only 12 weeks of class raises challenges that these guidelines are here to address. If something isn't working for you, let me know, and we can discuss the situation.

I A primary purpose of tutorials is for students to learn how to give each other good feedback and how to discuss writing productively. The keys: respect for the texts and each other; the proper use of critical terminology; a collective open-mindedness about what constitutes good writing; an atmosphere of mutual encouragement and support that includes both precise, insightful praise (not just "I liked X" but "I liked X *because* Y") and constructive criticism.

II *Time management*: You need to start each class promptly to ensure that there's sufficient time for workshopping; you need to finish on time so that the students can get to their next classes. It's better to stop a few minutes early than a few minutes late. Also, it's critical that you give equal time to each week's two authors.

III *Starting the conversation*: Start the discussion of each submission by asking the appropriate student to read from it aloud. After the reading, ask the reader to say why they chose the excerpt/poem in question. Doing so will create an entry-point to class discussion.

IV *Balancing praise and criticism*: It's important to balance the time for praise and for criticism. The authors need to hear about the specific ways in which their work has succeeded for people, and it's important for the class to develop a shared understanding and vocabulary regarding the different ways of thinking about what counts as success.

V *Your comments*: In class, personally offer one or two points of praise and one or two constructively critical points about each text workshopped. Ideally, you'll often use these points as opportunities to make broader observations about writing. (If you're able to incorporate terms and ideas from the lectures, that's great.) Otherwise, your focus should be on encouraging student contributions.

a A good number of your comments should involve you pointing to particular elements of the text in question, not just talking about the text as a whole. Don't shy from discussing specific passages, lines, or even single words.
b Generally, it's best for you to offer your comments only after a number of students have spoken. If you go first, students might not feel as free to voice their own opinions for fear of seeming to disagree with you.
c It's especially important that you personally offer at least one point of praise about every text. If you don't do this, the author's liable to feel discouraged.

VI *Your questions*: The questions that you ask the students to consider with respect to each text should include not just "What do you think this text does well?" and "What do you think could be improved?" but also questions like "What's this text about?" and questions asking students to consider particular textual elements: e.g., the diction; the characters; the beginning; the ending; particular scenes or lines. Ask open-ended questions that are easy to grasp and invite a range of viewpoints; e.g., "What emotions did [some part of the text] make you feel?"
VII *Creating conversational flow*: Encourage students to engage with each other's ideas. For example, you might follow up on a student's question or comment regarding an aspect of a text by asking everyone else what they think.
VIII *Responding to student comments*: It's important that you respond positively to comments so that the students know that they've been heard and that their contributions have been valued. As the weeks go on and the conversations proceed more organically, you might respond less often as students respond directly to each other more frequently.
IX Other Elements of Good Workshop Leadership:

a Make eye contact around the room as you speak.
b Speak slowly and with sufficient volume for everyone to hear you clearly.
c Bring energy and good humour. You should give the students a sense that workshopping is both fun and important, riveting stuff.
d Conduct yourself with the same degree of professionalism that you expect of professors.
e Always keep in mind the cultural diversity of your students. Don't make assumptions about their background, expertise, or beliefs. Don't ask any student to speak authoritatively about or on behalf of a particular cultural group.

X Some Things to Keep in Mind about Your Students:

- a Some have never written creatively before. They'll need special encouragement, as well as careful explanations regarding how to improve.
- b Some are reluctant to share work. They'll be especially appreciative of a workshop that begins with substantial praise.
- c Some will be sharing very personal material. They'll be grateful if you're sensitive to this possibility without making assumptions that their fiction and poetry are autobiographical or asking them in class about the work's connections to their lives.
- d Some students won't trust your assessments right away. You'll earn their respect by showing them that you've thought carefully about their work, appreciating its strengths while offering insightful, encouraging, well-justified suggestions for revision.
- e Some will carry your feedback around in their minds for decades. Be careful in choosing your words!

Troubleshooting the Workshop

I *The class doesn't reach consensus about an aspect of a text.* That's fine! Remind everyone that different readers value different things and that it's up to the author to decide whether and how to accommodate various readers' preferences.

II *One element of a text ends up generating a lot of discussion.* Allow it to get due treatment, but make sure that other elements are addressed, too. You don't want the author to feel that their work wasn't considered comprehensively.

III A text strikes you as offensive (e.g., racist, homophobic, ableist, misogynist) in some respect and/or it features a problematic stereotype. Be sure to address this issue in class, as well as in your written feedback. If you don't, you risk seeming complicit through your silence. But you also want to avoid seeming to dress down the author. Rather than issuing a direct opinion, it can be more effective for you to identify how readers are liable to respond to the problematic element. Then, explain why they're liable to do so, even as you also identify what the author might have been trying to do. Assume the best intentions, and focus on solutions rather than on belabouring the criticism. In an article that Noor Naga and I wrote, we make this case

> It needs to be a common practice for instructors to ask their classes whether there are stereotypes in a text and to consider what the text is doing with them. Such a practice models a process of questioning for students to incorporate into their own reading and writing. Moreover, while teachers need to make it clear that stereotypes, as forms of cliché, can be aesthetic flaws, they also need to identify stereotyping as an

act of negligence with regard to human beings' particularity and as a rehearsal of oppressive histories of misrepresentation. For teachers to avoid shaming students, though, discussions of stereotyping in student work should not seem prosecutorial. Rather, instructors should turn such discussions into opportunities for collective reflection on how stereotyping functions in literature. In this respect, teachers will be more effective asking questions than issuing dictates or drawing conclusions about the ethics of a particular representation. In many cases, students whose work features cultural stereotypes are unaware that the stereotypes are even there until they are pointed out, and the mere identification of them as such is sufficient to transform the writers' subsequent practice. Teachers can also avoid shaming students by modeling humility, making it clear that virtually every writer falls into stereotyping at some point. (80–81)

IV *A student uses offensive language.* Identify the problematic language as such immediately. In a friendly, non-confrontational manner, ask the student whether there's a more precise way of putting things. Or, if the student invokes a problematic stereotype, identify it as such and ask the class to consider how the text itself might rehearse or challenge the stereotype. It's important to intervene at such moments but also not to leave the student feeling humiliated.

Grading Submissions

I Don't annotate extensively: it can eat up time, and students are more liable to read your end-comments. Don't stint on offering brief points of appreciation, though; authors are grateful to know when something has worked for a reader.

II Don't copyedit. Over-annotating can be counterproductive, discouraging the author. However, draw attention to recurring issues with things such as grammar, punctuation and spelling.

III Open your end-comments with at least a few points of praise before identifying things that need attention. Then, close your comments with words of encouragement. Identify where the student has been successful, noting what kinds of talents and potential are on display, and let them know that you're looking forward to reading more from them.

IV Your written feedback should be professional, precise, and carefully edited. Students are liable to distrust your judgement if your own writing isn't polished.

V If a student submits a piece that might be cause for concern about their wellbeing (due to, say, dramatizations of self-harm, interpersonal violence, abuse, assault, or mental illness, or due to expressions of anger/hatred directed toward the self or others), please contact me and send me the submission.

Appendix 2
Questions to Ask of Creative Writing

Below are questions to ask when assessing or revising prose and poetry. Keep in mind that the list isn't exhaustive and that not all the questions will be appropriate to all texts.

Narratorial Perspective

- Is the choice of perspective/s the best one for the text?
- Does the text exploit the potential in its choices regarding narratorial situation, mediation, reliability, and/or distance?
- Is the narrator's/speaker's voice compelling and consistent?

Verse Forms

- If there's rhyme, is there a canny use of perfect and/or imperfect rhyme?
- If there's a meter, is there an appropriate adherence to and variation on it?
- Does the choice of verse form make sense given the subject matter? Does the poem exploit its form to complicate and/or heighten the poem's effects and engagement with its subject matter?

Sound, Rhythm, Voice

- How distinctive, economical and exact is the language?
- Do the sentences have interesting rhythms?
- In the case of poetry, is there an adept use of line breaks, enjambment, end-stopping, stresses, and/or caesurae?
- Is punctuation used in a consistent way?
- If there's repetition, is it used to good effect?

Plot and Action

- How distinctive is the dramatic premise/situation?
- Is there an intriguing opening?

- Are there smooth (and/or appropriately jarring) transitions between parts?
- How well do the parts cohere?
- Is every part of the text necessary?
- Is there a sufficient sense of tension (e.g., dramatic, intellectual, emotional) and surprise?
- Is the pacing appropriate?
- How interesting is the ending? How satisfyingly does it follow on from what precedes it?
- Is exposition kept to a minimum and/or presented artfully? Do readers receive all the information they need for the text to succeed?

Characters and Dialogue

- How vivid and non-stereotypical are the characters physically, behaviourally, and/or psychologically?
- How distinct from (and/or resonantly similar to) one another are they?
- How interesting are their relationships to one another?
- Are new aspects of the characters revealed as the narrative progresses?
- Are all of the characters necessary? Do all of them get their due?
- How compelling and efficient is the dialogue (if there is any)?
- Do the characters' voices sound duly authentic in terms of their time, place, and culture?

Time and Place

- Is there a vivid, persuasive representation of time and/or place?
- How specific and memorable are the details?
- Is any research involved sufficiently integrated so as not to feel overly conspicuous?

Relations to Realism

- Are the dramatic situation and events as believable as they need to be?
- How well does the text use (i.e., deploy, exploit and/or upend) generic conventions?
- How compelling and well-integrated/dramatized are the text's themes, ideas, debates, allusions, symbols, and/or questions?

Intertextuality

- Does the text work well both for people familiar with its intertexts (i.e., texts that the writing evokes) and for people unfamiliar with them?
- Does the text avoid seeming merely derivative of its intertexts?
- Does the text help readers to see its intertexts in a new light?

Ethics and Appropriation

- As the author, are you aware of the stereotypes that circulate about the cultures you're representing, and have you avoided rehearsing them? Are your characters individuals and not types?
- Have concerns been voiced regarding stories told by outsiders about the cultures you're representing? If so, how are you addressing those concerns?
- How would you best answer readers who might accuse your text of being an inauthentic representation of a particular culture?
- Have you substantially changed the distinguishing features of any characters based on real people who might otherwise reasonably accuse you of defaming them or violating their privacy?

Part II

The Canadian CW Playground

Writing-as-Knowing (in Canada and Beyond)

8 Poetry as Play

Teaching Poetry to Not-Yet-Poets

Andy Weaver

Poetry has an image problem. Lamenting the lack of influence or respect for poetry is hardly an insightful or a novel thing to say—if one assumes that "image" means "public opinion." As someone who has spent the majority of his career reading, writing and thinking about poetry, I can attest from personal experience that the fastest way for me to end a polite conversation with a new acquaintance is to actually answer their question "What do you do for a living?" honestly. The general population's opinion of poetry is so bad that only the most craven of civilians punches so low as to make it a target; benign indifference is the best that most poets (and poems) can usually hope for from non-poets.

What I really mean by "image problem" is an *imagery* problem: for over a century, one of the most central, untouchable truths of "good" poetry is that it emphasizes imagery. Ezra Pound's "A Few Don'ts by an Imagiste," in which he explains that "An 'Image' is that which presents an intellectual and emotional complex in an instant of time," and then argues that "It is better to present one Image in a lifetime than to produce voluminous works" (200, 201), was first published in the March 1913 issue of *Poetry*; Pound's own "In a Station of the Metro," in my opinion, the purest example of an Imagist poem, appeared in the next month's issue. Pound bolsters his argument for imagism by tying the centrality of imagery with notions such as condensation ("Use no superfluous word…" [201]), a focus on concrete objects ("Go in fear of abstractions"), a distrust of personal perspective ("Don't be descriptive" [203]) and an implicit privileging of the visual over the aural: "That part of your poetry which strikes upon the imaginative *eye* of the reader will lose nothing by translation into a foreign tongue; that which appeals to the ear can reach only those who take it in the original" (205). Time and politics have displaced Pound from the centre of poetry, but the centrality of the image he championed still underpins so much of what poetry—and Creative Writing poetry courses—takes for granted. Indeed, Pound's pronouncements underpin the slogan taught in almost any contemporary Creative Writing course: *show, don't tell.* Rather than say something directly, Pound et al. advise, use an image to imply an idea or emotion whenever possible.

DOI: 10.4324/9781032614144-11

For the past several years, I have joined a second-year undergraduate Introduction to Creative Writing course already in progress, teaching the winter term of a full-year course. The fall term instructors have focused on fiction and creative nonfiction, leaving me to focus only on poetry in my term. When I ask the students in my first class who is in the course because they have been waiting for the poetry section, one or two of the roughly 25 students usually enthusiastically put up their hands, while the lion's share of the class squirms and tries to suss out whether they should be honest or tell me what they think I want to hear. Honesty usually wins out—and often slips into its brutal form once we start discussing why they are not interested in poetry: enthusiasm tends to take hold, and they offer judgements such as "irrelevant," "boring," "out of touch/date/step," and, most interesting to me, "obscure" and "rules based"—by which they mean that poetry is riddled with hidden meanings and arcane rules (such as the mysteries of rhyme scheme and fixed meter). In many ways, though, what they hate about poetry is that it refuses to say what it means: it insists on using imagery to imply its ideas, showing rather than telling. Pound's intricate "intellectual and emotional complex in an instant of time" is just so much obfuscating gobbledygook to them. Similarly, in a 2024 study, Berkeley's Andrew King notes

> invok[ing] poetry is in many ways to invoke the problem of teaching creative writing *par excellence*, dealing as it does with the literary form arguably encountered least often in our shared cultural life. I suspect that what makes poetry more intrinsically anticanonical, more resistant to taming and taxonimisation, that explains the difficulties in teaching it as a craft, is precisely its focus on the materiality of language itself: what Kenneth Koch describes as a raising of sound to the importance of sense. (30)

At first, my response to a vast majority of CW students not wanting to read or write poetry was basically "These young philistines need to be taught so much." Gradually, though, I started to wonder if the well-wrought image really was so central, so important to contemporary poetry in an era of economic disenfranchisement and environmental precarity. I found my default appreciation for imagism to be a very uncomfortable, confusing line of inquiry; the image was absolutely central when I was a young undergrad in the early 1990s, and the examples of good poetry we were given as models all highlighted it. Academically, I have certainly studied (and loved) poetry that tends to decentre the image, including Fluxus, language poetry, conceptual poetry, etc., but I also consider those poets to be examples of the maxim "one must first learn the rules before one can break them." But what if the rules had actually changed without Creative Writing courses noticing?

One of the poems I like to use as an icebreaker, after the students' onslaught of reasons why they do not like, read, or pay attention to poetry, is Evie Shockley's "truth in advertising," a poem (readily found online) that mimics the visual form and content of a North American nutritional label. Eschewing narrative, Shockley instead provides a list of "nutrition facts" that borrow a nutritional label's gram and percentage breakdowns for the "sugar," "spice" and "everything nice" for the "little girls" of Robert Southey's Victorian poem "What All the World Is Made of." Continuing the structure of a nutritional label, and mimicking their sans-serif, boxed typography, Shockley adds an ingredients list: "wood (*hard-headed*), sponge (*absorbing juice and juicy words*)" (89). Students find this text baffling and often initially rebel against it: their most common response is usually "That is not a poem!" After explaining why it is (the importance of authorial intention and context: "We read it as a poem because Shockley wants us to read it that way, with that attention"), I make my fundamental statement for the term: poetry is a place of play, where the author can play with ideas, sounds and images (the latter are downplayed, not forbidden!) but also where language can play with us, working beyond our desire to control it. I show them concrete poems (Steve McCaffery's *Carnival* panels, Mary Ellen Solt's *Flowers in Concrete*, Indigenous Canadian author Jordan Abel's *The Place of Scraps*), play them sound poems (The Four Horsemen's "Emotional Poetry," various recordings of Kurt Schwitter's "Ursonate") and recordings of poets who tend to work outside image-based poetry (Amiri Baraka, Fred Wah, Mei-mei Berssenbrugge, Wanda Coleman, Lyn Hejinian). Imagery is not so much absent from these examples, but simply not the central technique or aesthetic concern. At the end of our first class together, I tell the students that the only rule for our course is not "show, don't tell" but rather "play, play, play," and that play should be the North Star in everything they write for the course. I qualify that "play" means at least three things:

1 enjoy the action (in our case, take pleasure in creating in and with language);
2 ignore/forget/break the rules (of poetry, but also of standard language use);
3 relish in the amount of "wiggle" or "freedom" in any system.

I like to end the class by playing a bit of John Cage's "Lecture on Nothing" as an example of a poem that plays with language, plays in language and plays with our expectations.

"Play, play, play" operates as the course's rule against rules. It downplays maxims like "show, don't tell," but it also encourages students to try whatever they can think of, and I assure them that one question that I will never ask them is "How is this a poem?" Instead, I want them to ask themselves "How did I play in this poem?"

Having said that, undergraduate students balancing, at minimum, GPAs and student loans, can often be a most serious, cautious and risk-averse group, and it is important to acknowledge that asking them to play often goes directly against what (and how) they are learning in their other courses.

Play does not come naturally for them—especially playing with language, because years of rules both explicit (grammar, spelling, etc.) and implicit (the discursive norms of language games) have taught them that there are distinctly right and wrong ways to write and speak. So, the assignments in the course are designed to help the students learn to move beyond the rules. I will focus on those unsettling assignments, and how and why students encounter them, for the remainder of my discussion.

To promote actual writing over a pre-writing that can be paralyzing or distracting, my assignment schedule is brisk: the first is due in our second class, and all subsequent assignments are due one week after we discuss the assignment. This rapid pace is intended to force students to just write rather than to excessively plan their writing, and this lack of planning promotes writing as play. I also emphasize that they are submitting only a draft—the assignments are exercises/first drafts—and I return their drafts the following week with careful comments on what is working well and what could be improved. Most importantly, I emphasize that these assignments are not graded. The students need to see these assignments as places where they can safely play around freely; play does not take place when the student feels they are being evaluated. Students do eventually pass in revised versions of each of the assignments for grades (the revised versions of the first three exercises come in as a set in class six, and the last three exercises come in as a set in class ten), but only after they have received my feedback and have had a chance to absorb my suggestions and to ask me follow-up questions.

Each assignment is also discussed as a group at the beginning of class when the exercises are submitted. We take approximately 20–30 minutes to follow up on how—not what—the students created their drafts. I ask a series of questions that emphasize the process of creation: what surprised you about writing your assignment; what was easier/harder about it than you expected, and why; what did you try that did not work, and why; how did you begin; how did you know when the poem was finished; how did you choose your topic/form? This discussion is meant to help demystify the creative process, shifting it from the shadows of "inspiration" and towards the actions of playing around, trying different things, seeing multiple avenues for addressing each exercise. This discussion also helps students become more excited and free to write playfully, because by hearing their peers model different creative processes they develop an appreciation for the action of writing poetry rather than focusing only on the created poem. By the end of the course, students are often more excited to discuss how they created their draft than they are to talk about the draft itself.

Assignment One: Ekphrastic Poem Exercise (Playing with Description; the Play between Artistic Discourses)

The textbook for the course, containing most of the readings and insightful discussions of the issues surrounding the poems, is Susan Holbrook's excellent, brief and inexpensive *How to Read (and Write About) Poetry*.

Models read and discussed in class

- William Carlos Williams, "The Dance"
- W.H. Auden, "Musée des Beaux Arts"
- Amy Lowell, "Venus Transiens"
- Gertrude Stein, "Preciosilla"
- Frank O'Hara, "Why I Am Not a Painter"
- Anne Sexton, "The Starry Night"
- Fred Wah, "from Pictograms from the Interior of B.C."
- Valerie Martinez, "Granite Weaving"

Write a poem (of any length and in any free verse or fixed form you choose) about a piece of visual art (painting, photograph, sculpture). As part of the process of creating your poem, think about how directly you want to describe the artwork, how much your reader needs to be told about it for the poem to be successful, how directly tied to the artwork you want your poem to be, etc. These thoughts do not have to be included in the poem—but maybe some of them should be?

Ekphrasis ties together issues of influence, creative response, communal creativity and the role of the poet's emotions, all of which relate to different aspects of play. Writing in response to a piece of visual art, I explain, emphasizes that influence shapes our creativity and is important to acknowledge, and that point usually lowers the students' concerns about their own creativity. Looking at the model poems, I show them that "real poets" often openly respond to existing artistic creations, and we discuss how creativity does not occur in a vacuum—that everyone from Shakespeare to Quentin Tarantino has created new work by responding to and reimagining existing work. I explain that we are beginning with ekphrasis to help them get started by openly responding, but also that ekphrasis necessarily plays in the gap between visual and linguistic discourses, that the translation from one medium to another encourages them to play with language in response to what they see in the visual piece. We also discuss the necessity of responding in an ethical fashion, by openly showing the influence behind their poem; I direct them to how different poems do this, from Williams's and Auden's direct discussion of Brueghel's work in their poems, to Stein's oblique reference. We also talk about how each poem plays with its subject matter, sometimes relying on direct description (O'Hara and Sexton) and sometimes leaving the inspiring piece as a playful extra-textual reference (Moroles). We also discuss how different poems create different responsive places for the reader, and that playful techniques such as Wah's can force the reader to become playful in their response to the poem. Wah's "from Pictograms from the Interior of B.C.," for example, reproduces the stick figure, crescents and simple quadruped illustrations of an Indigenous pictogram next to his lipogrammatic, enjambed phrase "nv s ble / tr ck" [presumably "invisible trick"] (42). The removal of the "I" creates spaces where the reader needs to play to solve the poem's riddle—and we extend these absences to work through how the poem suggests that the reader must insert their own "I" into the poem while simultaneously suggesting that the reader must keep their "I" respectfully distanced from the poem. What such reciprocity of play means, I explain, is that one way of thinking about writing a poem is that the poet builds the playground for the reader, a site where the poet encourages the reader to read actively and playfully, something that both Wah and Stein encourage. A poem, I hope students see and feel, can be a meeting place, a place where community can gather—usually figuratively but, occasionally, literally, through audience participation. I encourage students to think of their poems as communal spaces, places where they can decide to playfully invite the reader in or playfully block the reader from entering aspects of their poem.

This focus on response also implicitly downplays the students' own emotions in their poems. While high school teachers and public perception tend to instil in young writers a belief that poetry is mostly about gazing at the poet's emotional navel, I do not think it is productive to simply tell students not to be emotional in their poetry, especially since emotion is obviously a part of poetry. In the discussion at the beginning of the second class, I ask students to discuss what role their personal feelings played in their ekphrastic poems. Sometimes it is a major part of a poem—but often it is not, and so we can organically move into a discussion that highlights that poetry is not just about writing one's own emotions—it is much larger than that. Poetry is a place to think, to communicate, to respond; that certainly can involve emotions, but it can also downplay emotions in order to encourage the reader to engage more strongly. This brings in the "show, don't tell" rule without actually stating it, and so students focus on what they can create by being playful rather than what they should avoid.

Assignment Two: Meditative Ode (with Apostrophe) Exercise (Playing in/as Thought)

Models read and discussed in class:

- John Keats, "Ode on a Grecian Urn"
- Charlotte Smith, "To Night"
- Allen Ginsberg, "A Supermarket in California"
- Margaret Avison, "July Man"
- Kenneth Koch, "To My Twenties"
- Margaret Christakos, "Late One Night"
- Molly Cross-Blanchard, "Winnipeg, you're so pretty"
- Robert Creeley, "America"
- Bernadette Mayer, "Ode on Periods"
- Pablo Neruda, "Ode to My Socks"

> *Write a meditative ode that uses apostrophe (direct address to an unhearing entity). You may use free verse or a fixed form, whichever you prefer. The ode should be at least 30 lines, in order to give yourself a chance to mimic the process of meditation on the topic you choose. Remember that your ode should be written about an abstraction, an object or an absent person in order to allow for apostrophe.*

The poem that students are tasked with writing here is not strictly an ode: the only formal requirement—apostrophe—is common in odes but not necessary, and all other formal restrictions are set aside. What students really must turn in is a poem that meditates on a specific theme, idea or object in a self-conscious manner. I explain that the purpose is to get them to play with thinking as a process, one where idea leads to idea, and where digressions and tangents are expected and productive. That is, they should play with the topic by letting their wandering thoughts lead them, and they should think of their ode as a transcript of how their brain forms connections between whatever thoughts come to mind in relation to their topic. Their odes, in that sense, should be a text where they let their minds play around with loosely connected thoughts. King, in his recent CW pedagogy chapter "On the Plurality of Practices," also tackles writing-as-thinking in poetry:

> Here anotoher truism, that a writer's material is language itself, also turns out to be revealing. For language is, depending on who you ask, either the matter or the instrument of conscious thought, or both. To be a student in a creative writing classroom is to be asked to make art with the very materials of thought and self-constitution—to use language without the guardrails of scholarly or even social convention. [...] Creative writing's materials are the very materials of thought—not, as with scholarship, a subset of those materials.
>
> (29)

To help them prepare for the ode, we do a quick in-class exercise where they each write down an object, emotion, text, or famous person, trade their paper with a nearby student, and then write down in one minute as many things that pop into their minds in relation to that prompt. We then go through three or four of these lists and brainstorm how we (not the lister) can generate connections between the disparate elements—and I finish by explaining that their meditative odes should aim for a content that mimics that loose connection between wildly various topics, periodically relating them all back to the poem's topic.

Crucially, this exercise of connections and associations introduces the argument that play is not all fun and games. While I encourage the students to let their thoughts run wild as a way of generating a rough roadmap for their ode, I explain that the difficult part is writing out the ode in such a way that the reader understands the way the various thoughts are connected. In that sense, they must start to exercise the discipline of making their play interesting and enjoyable for the reader. We discuss the old Creative Writing maxim "write what you want to read" by introducing the reader into the equation: "write what you want the reader to read," and we discuss the difference between writing for your own enjoyment and writing for the reader's enjoyment. Both types of writing involve play, but the latter reminds them that the point of a poem is usually to be read, not just to be written—so they are tasked with playing in such a way that the reader will find the result enjoyable (as Christakos's experimental ode works). We discuss how unexpected connections are playful but also possibly revelatory, as well as the importance of tone to guide the reader's responses (here, Koch's poem is exemplary). We also discuss how to make their odes feel unplanned, as though they were written extemporaneously in spite of the planning that needs to go into their odes (and we discuss how Ginsberg's narrator walks the reader through the poem in such a way that it feels like the narrator is commenting on a world presenting itself to him at the moment he is speaking, playfully leading the reader to see the world through his eyes).

By giving the students a focused form of address, apostrophe is a crucial element in this assignment. Forcing them to write as though they were speaking directly to their topic provides students with a relationship between speaker and addressee, one that I encourage them to play around with: what happens if that relationship is jocular, angry, distant, familial, etc.? We discuss this relationship by looking at Keats's poem (which discloses it addressee directly at the very beginning), Mayer's poem (which hides the addressee until the end) and Neruda's (which has an indirect addressee), and we think about how apostrophe presents the relationship with the reader as a site of play that the poet can manipulate to the poem's advantage.

Assignment Three: Animal Portrait Poem Exercise (Playing with your Own Opinions and Emotions)

Models read and discussed in class:

- William Blake, "The Tyger" and "The Lamb"
- John Donne, "The Flea"
- Emily Dickinson, "A narrow Fellow in the Grass"
- Gertrude Stein, "A DOG"
- E. J. Pratt, "The Shark"
- Marianne Moore, "Bird-Witted"
- Nasser Hussain, "THE ARK"
- Lawrence Ferlinghetti, "Dog"
- Christopher Smart, "On his cat Jeoffrey" from *Jubilate Agno*
- Denise Levertov, "The Cat as Cat"
- Elizabeth Bishop, "The Fish"

Write a portrait poem of an animal. Your poem can be of any length or form, but it must focus on description (rather than meditation). The animal you describe can be a specific individual (your dog Spot) or a type (octopuses), but the poem must focus on describing the animal and/or the opinion of the poem's speaker; for the purposes of this poem, the speaker must take a stance that conflicts with your own—i.e., if you are writing about dogs because you think they are terrific, the poem must describe them from a position of thinking dogs are terrible. Before you start to write, think about these issues:

- *how much of the poem's topic should you directly tell the reader, and how much should you try to imply;*
- *how much description of the subject do you need to include in order to make the reader care (and also try to think about how you can make your subject interesting to the reader);*
- *how can you make the subject seem new or unexpected to the reader;*
- *is it the subject that is interesting or the speaker's opinion of it—how much of either should you include, and in what order?*

This is where I used to start emphasizing imagery and a "show, don't tell" argument—but the more I thought about the examples I brought in at this point, the more I realized that each of them engages in a lot of telling. Each of the model poems starts off with a central topic (more than an image) and builds arguments around and through that topic. The models are not meditative, but they are certainly not image-based. In addition to the model poems, we look at a series of portrait paintings, ranging from self-portraits and still life paintings, to animal portraits and landscapes, and stylistically from realistic to abstract. In particular, we look at three paintings of cows: Rosa Bonheur's *Ploughing in Nevers* (a realistic piece from 1849), Van Gogh's *Lying Cow* (an impressionist piece from 1889), and Franz Marc's *Yellow Cow* (an expressionist piece from 1911). We discuss how the paintings wordlessly imply different attitudes, and then we move into a discussion of the model poems, particularly focusing on Pratt's and Levertov's as examples that attempt a degree of definition of their subjects, as opposed to Stein's and Moore's, which attempt to capture the speaker's experience of the subject.

Finally, we circle back to the first assignment and talk about how all these paintings and poems play with the action of taking a three-dimensional subject and translating it into paint or words. I emphasize that the main problem and opportunity of writing a portrait is in the play created by the absolute impossibility of taking a physical entity and translating it into a linguistic entity—that their poems do not just describe something; rather, they translate something fundamentally non-linguistic into words. This complexity of translation and invocation leads into a final discussion on diction and the extraordinary possibility for play when we choose our words. We end the class with a brief five-minute exercise, where they get into groups of three, choose the opening four lines of any of the week's model poems and swap out as many words as they can for words that mean roughly the same thing. We read out the results in class, which is usually very fun and also very eye-opening for the students: word choice matters.

A Break in the Action

At this point, we switch focus from weekly readings and assignments to two weeks of peer workshopping. This is the only full-class workshopping in the poetry section of the course, and I limit it to just two weeks (we look at one poem by each student; I keep strict timelines, which allow for ten minutes of group discussion on each poem, followed by three minutes for the poet to ask for clarifications or for thoughts from the group on aspects that were not discussed). Students are asked—but not required—to use one of their three assignments as their poem to be workshopped, and everyone passes out hard copies of their poem in class the week before we workshop.

The three assignments are then due as Poetry Set #1 in Week Seven, the week after the second workshop class. These revisions are graded in terms of the quality of the revised piece and also the amount of effort put into revising (students must pass in all of the drafts of each piece subsequent to my comments on their initial exercises).

Poetry Set 2: Assignments 4–6

The first half of my term with the students is the most crucial, since it sets the ground rule of play, play, play—and it gives students enough time to realize that I am quite serious when I tell them to play. The workshop classes at the mid-point of the term help to convince them that, as a group, they are creating worthwhile, "real" poetry. Play can be a hard sell, and it often takes the first half of term to make believers of the students—but most students are onboard by the time of the term's last three assignments. Because play still underpins this part of the course, but less directly so, I will spend less time discussing these exercises.

Assignment 4 is a sonnet, which tends to shock the students—after all, the sonnet's strict rules hardly seem like a place to play (and after I lecture for 30 minutes, explaining elementary scansion, it feels like no one will ever play again). However, I emphasize that the fun part of writing a sonnet is the enjoyment of working on a Rubik's Cube: the difficulty is what makes it fun, as play inevitably gives way to attention. Having said that, I explain that the secret to writing a sonnet is to focus on the content, not the form, by thinking of a sonnet as a tiny, intricately constructed argument: the first quatrain introduces the problem, the second quatrain offers a solution, the third quatrain either extends the solution or offers a counter-argument and the couplet sums up the takeaway for the reader. We do in-class writing, where students each choose a subject to which they have a strong affective relationship, then list what it is about the subject that makes them feel that way, and, finally, think of how those elements work together. Then I tell them that the play is to cram all of that argument into 14 lines with a fixed rhyme scheme (I let them choose the rhyme scheme, and I tell them not to worry about the meter). I ask them to write a free-verse or prose first draft, and then work to transpose that into the sonnet—with the result that the sonnet is a game played by three participants: writer, form and language. I tell them to let the form adjust their content, so that the sonnet's argument might not be their own, but rather the sonnet's.

Assignment 5 terrifies and thrills them in the opposite direction, as it asks them to create a visual or sound poem. By this point in the course, a good number of the students are usually enjoying what poetry allows them to express, but this exercise often inverts the pyramid and lets the less "poetic" writers shine, while the better writers sometime struggle to let go of their desire to express something in understandable linguistic patterns. I encourage students to move as far away as possible from sentences, phrases, even words, explaining that I want them to try to play without language's expected systems. I explain that the exercise will hopefully instil in them a sense of poetry as a stance towards play as ultimate possibility, one that can move even beyond intentional expression by moving outside of what we think of as normative language games.

Assignment 6 functions as a summative exercise by asking students to create a poem that uses intentionally heightened syntax and diction. I ask them to find a newspaper article, explaining that news reportage attempts to make writing as clear and transparent as possible; their task is to translate that article into a poem by playing with the diction and syntax. They must keep the same content, as much as possible, while changing the writing as much as possible. We discuss word choice, repetition, ordering of subject matter, etc., in terms of how the same subject matter can look radically different on the page. This last exercise, I explain, is quite literally playing with language to see what emerges.

Throughout the course, we do touch on basic poetic techniques and tools (line breaks, pacing, metaphor, imagery, tone, etc.) but never as a focal point. The emphasis always swirls around play in all of its poetic forms. I like to end the final class by reading out a quote from Ann Lauterbach's *The Night Sky: Writings on the Poetics of Experience*:

> You want to go somewhere away from what you know, this is a human instinct, the desire to discover some (-thing, -one, -place) else. Why else do we begin to crawl, noticing that to sit inside the perimeters of a scrap of cloth on the floor won't provide enough room to *find out more*? (155)

To truly "find out more," I suggest, they must continue to embrace poetry—and life—as a site of play, foregoing what they already know or have mastered in favour of playing around to both see anew and see the new.

Works Cited

Holbrook, Susan. *How to Read (and Write About) Poetry*, 2nd ed. Broadview, 2022.

King, Andrew David. "On the Plurality of Practices." *The Scholarship of Creative Writing Practice*, edited by Marshall Moore and Sam Meekings. Bloomsbury, 2024, pp. 23–34.

Lauterbach, Ann. *The Night Sky: Writings on the Poetics of Experience*. Viking, 2005.

Pound, Ezra. "A Few Don'ts by an Imagiste." *Poetry*, vol. 1, no. 6, 1913, pp. 200–06. *JSTOR*, https://www.jstor.org/stable/20569730.

Shockley, Evie. "Truth in Advertising." *Semiautomatic*, Wesleyan UP, 2017, p. 89.

Wah, Fred. "From *Pictograms from the Interior of B.C.*" *How to Read (and Write About) Poetry*, Susan Holbrook, 2nd ed. Broadview, 2022, p. 42.

Dr. Weaver's Recurrent Comments on Student Writing

1 Don't edit while you're writing—as they say in film, you can fix it in post!

2 Every ending can be a beginning! Try a draft where you move the last line of your poem to the very beginning—if you start there, do you need each of the other lines, or are some unnecessary? Does removing those lines make the poem more successful when you put the last line back? Is the poem more effective with that line at the beginning?

3 Don't give away the game before it starts! An effective title should help the reader by suggesting a tone or mental landscape they should inhabit, but it probably shouldn't just tell the reader what the poem is going to tell them.

4 Your reader probably wants to read poetry for some form of enjoyment or relaxation. Since you're the guide leading your reader through the poem, remember that people like to wander when they're on vacation. That is, linear thinking often isn't the most interesting pathway through a poem. Try a draft where you randomly reorder all of the stanzas (or rough sections) of the poem. Does that order suggest new pathways through the poem, or does it make some sections more effective or less necessary?

9 A Writer in Art School

Fostering Interdisciplinary Experiences in Postsecondary Art & Design Education

Catherine Black

Art and design practices and creative writing have long enjoyed a symbiotic, mutually inspiring relationship—as they do at OCAD University, the largest and most comprehensive art, design and media university in Canada—so it comes as no surprise that more and more post-secondary art and design institutions are seeing Creative Writing programs as a natural fit to educate creative problem-solvers. But beyond recognizing synergies of practice and process in a postsecondary arts context, how might we, as educators, foster true interdisciplinarity and an ongoing cross-pollination of creative modes of production between visual artists, designers and writers? How might these synergies be explored and expanded upon in the curriculum, the classroomand perhaps most importantly, in the community?

Since its inception in 2018, the Creative Writing program at OCADU that I have chaired since then has encouraged writing that seeks new spaces for language and engages with the precepts, materials and processes of art and design practices. We've fostered this way of writing, creating and collaborating in our students through curricular intersections, in-class experiences and exercises, public projects and by supporting student-led initiatives and publications. From the outset, our program's visionary, activist and dub poet Lillian Allen and I imagined a program with a studio-based approach to creative writing practice and pedagogy that welcomed hybridity, experimentation and play (Allen). But to get there, we first needed to be clear about what we meant when we spoke of an interdisciplinarity practice for writers in an art and design context.

Building the Program: Defining Interdisciplinarity

When we first proposed a BFA Creative Writing program in 2018, we encountered a handful of stakeholders who found OCADU a surprising fit for a program you might ordinarily find snuggled up (however awkwardly) with a Literatures department in a comprehensive university. We insisted we were different. We were creating a program with an interdisciplinary core, impulse and outcome; a program that emphasized the study and practice of writing as artistic process and production, encouraging students to traverse

DOI: 10.4324/9781032614144-12

genres and media and to explore the craft of spoken, written, visual, digital and experimental language forms. We wanted our students to develop a writing practice that might manifest in performances, recordings, text objects, image and text works, videos, installations and a variety of printed matter.

In proposing the program, we said the word "interdisciplinary" *a lot*. I knew what I meant when I used that word, as I'd experienced studio-based interdisciplinary learning in my own studies at the School of the Art Institute of Chicago [SAIC]. The UK's Ways of Writing in Art & Design research network is similarly interdisciplinary (Johnson). To me, interdisciplinarity had meant collaborating with photography majors, it had meant slicing and altering paper journals with a peer to produce a hybrid, frankensteined chapbook; it had meant conceptualizing language-based sculpture that might, someday, materialize in the context of the gallery; it had also meant getting messy. The new Bloomsbury anthology *The Scholarship of Creative Writing Practice* similarly questions, as Gregory Betts does here in Chapter 12, preconceptions about the reach of art-making and writing:

> Since poems (treated here as metonyms for works of creative writing) can happen in speech, on paper, on a screen, or elsewhere, neither ink nor paper nor the human voice are, by themselves, the poet's materials; nor can poetry be isolated by appeal to the physical book, just as painting can't be isolated as artistic activity on a two-dimensional surface. (King 29)

In my own postgraduate artist's education at SAIC I began to stop thinking of the book as the natural end-point of text. Text spilled off the page and into the world in unexpected ways at SAIC. And that's the spirit we would bring to OCADU's Creative Writing program.

When Lillian and I, both multi-genre writers and artists, spoke of an interdisciplinary practice, we meant

- A studio-based writing experience or project that draws upon the practices, materials and techniques of disciplines outside of traditional writing practices (e.g., fiction or print-based poetry)
- Language-based experiments including but not limited to sonic art, video, animation, printmaking, book making, zines, multiples, illustration, collage, painting, photography, typography, graphic design, game design, sculpture, installation, digital art, music and performance.

Core Curriculum: Creating Pathways for Interdisciplinary Explorations

To create pathways for experimentation, collaboration and (that word) interdisciplinarity, it was necessary to first establish a framework within the structure of the program that would encourage students to engage with studio art and design practices. We started by meeting and engaging with faculty from OCADU's other programs (e.g., Printmaking & Publications, Indigenous Visual Culture) and disciplines (e.g., graphic design, sculpture & installation, integrated media). This meant studio visits, meeting formally and informally with other faculty and attending curriculum meetings (curriculum meetings our counterparts at other comprehensive universities almost certainly do not attend). It was vital to know what our art-making, art-educating colleagues were doing in their practices if we were to create curricular intersections and fruitful collaborations. It was just as important to know what courses were being offered in our other faculties. Once we opened our worlds, our studios, our classrooms, our curriculum, it became easier for us to connect our students with faculty in other programs and disciplines. We also were able to determine those courses that would be central to establishing an introduction to interdisciplinary practices.

For the completion of the Creative Writing degree, we required core courses in the Faculty of Art's Art and Social Change stream—a program that emphasizes the value of art as activism—and Printmaking and Publications, as well as the Faculty of Arts and Science's Indigenous Visual Culture program. These courses and practices are non-negotiable. Not only do they provide students with an introduction to diverse epistemologies, including what Clarke calls "a very expanded idea of publishing, that I've come to call *Publishing as Process*" but they orient students to the culture and language of critique/workshop while introducing students to new hands-on practices (Janke).

The most natural space for students to enter the studio seemed through Printmaking and Publications classes. It was a first step, a foray into studio practice that was not wholly removed from the familiar world of books—after all, we might still see a spine, stitching, paper artefacts perfect bound and produced in multiples—but it helped students to begin to conceive of the book as something new: an object created by hand, not removed from their hands through some mysterious, outsourced publication process. There in studio with their peers in Printmaking and Publications, students encountered broadsides, guerrilla practices, the Risograph, foil stamping and lithography. They pulled levers on machinery they'd never dreamed of touching, sewed French Link stitches into small run chapbooks, and they were, in short, awakened to new possibilities. They began to reconsider how their writing might be distributed in the world, how it might reach the hands, eyes and ears of their audience through guerrilla distribution and public installation.

The tenets of social justice are central to our writing program, and so it was natural for us to collaborate with faculty in the Art and Social Change stream in the Faculty of Art. Together, with our film-maker colleague Min Sook Lee, we developed a course that would merge our disciplines while centring student agency for change. Our new course "Writer in Community," taught primarily by my colleague Ian Keteku, explores ways in which writing might engage with, critique and build community through public projects with a focus on orality, performance and verbal intervention. The students' exposure to and encounters with a wide range of works, performances and community projects by artists and activists inspired their own projects, which always manifested with a community-based element. In Ian Keteku's classes, student projects have included a series of poems addressing climate justice and indigenous rights written on large flags installed in front of City Hall, Queens Park and a Tent City in Toronto; a playable video game exploring the story of an autistic queer adult negotiating the trials and challenges of living authentically; and two hand-illustrated large scale posters with quotations created by a community of women in Peru to inspire change in the culture around sexual violence and abuse (these were installed on a public building in Peru).

Central to our curriculum and the wedded precepts of social justice and interdisciplinarity was the centring, the honouring of Indigenous epistemologies and teachings. Of the two core/required Indigenous Visual Culture courses, "Language and the Land" offered the greatest possibilities for interdisciplinary exploration and creation. In a course devoted to exploring Indigenous cosmologies and symbols as they are embedded in narratives of the land, students engaged with Indigenous narrative strategies, including the Wampum Belt, Pictographs, land works, as well as performances and interventions. Student projects have included sound works, artistic performance, documentation/archiving and writing experimentations involving, for instance, a deck of linocut cards inviting the reader to engage with non-linear storytelling relating to the student's Métis heritage.

Salon in the Classroom: Encounters with Practitioners

So, the curricular groundwork was in place—that is, a core curriculum established to prioritize language-based work that extends beyond the page and into other forms and artistic traditions. But before students actively engaged with studio concepts and practices, they needed to know what the interdisciplinary possibilities for writing were, or what they could be. Broad exposure to hybrid and interdisciplinary work is key; students can't do it and go beyond it if they don't know what it is and what's been done and what's on the horizon. Of course, many artist/writers' practices are inherently interdisciplinary. I'm thinking here of text-artists including Robert Montgomery, Jenny Holzer, Barbara Kruger, Lawrence Weiner, Erica Baum and contemporary Canadian practitioners like Chantal Gibson, Douglas Coupland, Derek Beaulieu, Kate Siklosi and Sasha Archer.

Through encounters with the work of these writer/artists, students learn to interrogate the interdisciplinary impulse: what's it about? What can be gained by interdisciplinary work in writing? How is engagement with audience affected? What is a measure of success? All of this is part of the orientation to language-based, interdisciplinary work. In fact, art-school interdisciplinarity requires a reconceptualization of the writing process, and who the writer is in the world.

First Marks: Allaying Fears

Making first marks comes with equal parts trepidation and excitement, whether those first marks are a brush stroke, a chisel mark in stone or ink on a fresh sheet of paper. It's necessary for students to lean into the exploration of a new discipline or skill, embracing the opportunity for play and happy accidents and outright messes. It's also important to remember that in interdisciplinary collaboration, it is not just Creative Writing students trying their (sometimes unsteady) hand at other disciplines, but also students in other disciplines trying their hand at writing. Citing James Elkins's *Why Art Cannot Be Taught: A Handbook for Art Students,* Andrew King considers whether

> methods of teaching art, as opposed to artistic technique, are 'irrational and largely unknown'—though art teachers 'continue to behave as if they were doing something more than providing *atmosphere*, *dialogue*, or *passion*'—studio art departments must claim to offer their students more tangible alternatives. (King 29)

Through this kind of vulnerable exchange, there is room for investigation.

We found it was best to start with small, contained, low-stakes or no-stakes exercises in the classroom: redacted poetry; collage; found poetry from magazines; using Instagram reels to write ekphrastically to animation or images; working ekphrastically to pieces in the collections of the Art Gallery of Ontario. These kinds of small projects, a dipping of toes in new waters, tends to allay fears. Writing students remember how to play. They remember the joy of getting messy. To further increase comfort, finding opportunities for student skill sharing through mini workshops with other students, where they get to be the 'experts', is an excellent way of building community, sharing knowledge and honouring the expertise many of our writing students already bring to the classroom. In first year, I engage in a simple exercise during our first class. In place of typical introductions, I have the students fill in the following blanks:

Hello, my name is X. My pronouns are X. I am an expert in X. I know a little about X. I am obsessed with X. I would like to know more about X.

Of course, the words 'expert' and 'obsessed' are left very open to interpretation. But the point is that students can reflect upon and communicate their 'outside' skills early in the course. What do you know how to do? What are your preoccupations? How might these merge in a project? Where is your skill gap? What do you want to know more about? The answers are as fascinating, surprising and hilarious as you might expect. Simple, yes. But it is a way to open the interdisciplinary conversation.

Later in the same foundational course, I ask my students to imagine their own work off the page, to audition various possibilities in their notebook.

Nothing needs to happen in three dimensions (just yet), as this is purely a theoretical activity taken to the page. In simply entertaining various notions of interdisciplinarity, the have begun to water a seed of experimentation, and they will continue to water it for the duration of their studies, hopefully culminating in the blooming of a thesis project for our Graduate Exhibition (GradEx) at the end of their four years ("OCAD University").

Without first establishing what skills in other media students might already have, and making interdisciplinary and hybrid options available to students in their classwork, we might have missed opportunities like those we encountered at Lillian Allen's end-of-semester reading at the AGO, where a first-year student schooled in modern dance wrote a tribute poem to her longtime instructor, read by another student while she performed through modern dance an interpretation of the sympathies and tensions of the poem and relationship in an exquisite melding of forms ("First Year").

Laying the Ground: In-Class Experiences and Exercises

Once students have experimented with low- and no-stakes exercises that incorporate other media into their writing practices, once they have been exposed to the work of cross- and interdisciplinary practitioners, seen what's possible, inquired into the nature of the interdisciplinary impulse and imagined their work off the page, they are ready for more hands-on studio based multi-disciplinary projects. One of the first projects involves creating a final portfolio—but not in the typical sense. The final portfolio, in this instance, addresses form as carefully as its content. This is the refrain: *all your aesthetic decisions must be intentional and accounted for as carefully as you choose each word, each line, each sentence, each image*. We ask our students to consider the form of their final portfolio in this way: it is a meaningful container for representative work. Past student projects have landed on our desks in the form of a pillow stuffed with crumpled poems to an ex and re-sewn, handed-in with a small pair of scissors; a box of recipes with each card pertaining to both the process of baking and family lore in flash fictions; a birdcage strung with origami poem birds; crocheted declarations in woollen banners.

In the same way, assigning a cine poem or video fiction or essay means students must give careful thought to the texture of the piece and its various layers: visual, oral and sonic. They must strive to balance visual and audio elements in their cine poems and video essays, creating a successful relationship between visual and written (audio) components so that the script, audio and images are all essential to the whole. With simple and intuitive programs, students can incorporate video and sonic elements to marry with their written scripts, experimenting with writing script first, then writing script to image.

Presently, our writing students are engaging in a collaborative assignment with my Faculty of Design colleague Nancy Snow's students to produce an animated typography poem, where Graphic Design students interpret text created by Creative Writing students in a way that is either literal or abstracted, "combining voiceover with video, animation, illustration, photography, and kinetic type" (Snow) based on the poem and interview conducted with the student poet. Ultimately, the project will be supported by a printed booklet to document the interview, and an informal screening of student works.

These forays are a first gesture towards longer, more sustained interdisciplinary projects that culminated, in 2022, in our first graduate thesis projects. A hallmark of OCADU's graduating experience is the longstanding tradition of the Graduate Exhibition, or GradEX, Toronto's largest free art and design exhibition, where upwards of 40 000 people pass through the studios and galleries of OCAD University's buildings for an inside look at the capstone year projects ("OCAD University"). In the thesis year, we worked over two semesters with our graduating students to support their independent projects with a public-facing element, with the Creative Writing thesis representing the culmination of work students had undertaken in their four years of study. They were expected to produce a substantive, publishable or performable work of creative writing and we encouraged projects that were an exploration of both concept and form, including hybrid experiments, performance, recording, digital works, multi-media and so on. Students were especially encouraged to include different aspects of any art practice they had engaged with in their studies to enrich and amplify their work (illustration, installation, photography, video etc.). For a recent summation of, and response to, the false binary of writing/art-making, see Jenny Rintoul's recent article "'I Came Here to do Art, not English': Antecedent Subject Subcultures Meet Current Practices of Writing in Art and Design Education."

Creative Writing contributions to The 108th GradEx included an eight-song album with accompanying video and 48-page illustrated lyric chapbook; a video-poetry installation exploring the perspective of a black woman's relationship to property; an interactive 'jukebox' musical on the life of a queer Jewish song leader; a slam-theatre style performance of a manuscript exploring experiences of being unsheltered and queer; and a series of screen printed, hand-beaded garments exploring the etymology of everyday terminology and words ("Exhibitors"). Where the public might have expected to see books on plinths, or to encounter traditional readings—both of which, of course, have their value—they were surprised to encounter interdisciplinary, hybrid and immersive works in a variety of media, and most importantly, our students discovered new ways for their language-based work to reach a wider and more diverse audience.

Finding New Spaces: Public Projects

Central to the development of the Creative Writing program in our unique art and design context was the concept of the permeability of the institution. Our aim was to ensure that our students were also connected to the physical possibilities of engaging community, not to train them away from community, but to prepare them to be in the world in a way that would make their lives important: to help them see that they can be a significant part of engaging and building in scholarly, social and creative contexts. As recounted in the *Journal of Writing in Creative Practice*, faculty and student artists around the world are similarly engaged in transposing art-viewing from dedicated galleries to public spaces *and* merging writing about art with writing as art. Ami Clarke, associate lecturer at University of the Arts, London, is also the "founder of Banner Repeater; a reading room with a public Archive of Artists' Publishing and project space, opening up an experimental space for others, on a working train station platform at Hackney Downs station, London" ("Ami"; Clarke) Through classes and projects that included designing, creating and leading interdisciplinary writing projects in various communities, we saw this goal realized.

It was important for us to not only showcase student work in the school community, but for that work to reach a broader audience through meaningful partnerships and exchanges with community partners. One of the hallmark experiences in showcasing interdisciplinary work in the community was in the development of a text project at Stackt Market—North America's largest shipping container market, situated in downtown Toronto. In 2020, my colleague Ian Keteku curated *Emergence from Emergency*, a cluster of poetic-artistic installations reflecting upon black experiences. There, several Black OCADU students were recruited to create poetic-artistic interventions in and around the Stackt environment. During our initial conversations, our partners at Stackt alerted us to the availability of a seven-foot-tall Stinson Owl-Lite traffic message board. This became a feature installation in an exhibition featuring the words of our student writers, addressing black experience. The traffic board, illuminated 24/7, was visible from one of Toronto's major commuter routes—the Gardiner Expressway—and was an imposing presence in the market greenspace. The installation featured rotating text written by our students, with declarations including: "His last breath, also mine" referencing the 2020 murder of George Floyd, "Black Joy, Radiance forever" and "Stain your tongue, say her name." In the same exhibition, *Black Realities* brought mural painting and the spirit of street art to the gallery in an interactive experience where students and Stackt attendees expressed in words and images on the walls and ceiling their reflections and meditations on black experiences and realities. Text became physical. The public became writers and artists, dissolving barriers and preconceptions about the written word and public space. The rarified space of the gallery was transformed into a place of welcome, a place for self-expression, conversation, reflection, storytelling and education. Ultimately the space was covered floor to ceiling in black, red and green text produced by many hands, the product of many conversations.

Again, our students were afforded the opportunity to reach into the community through our partnership with the Toronto International Festival of Authors (TIFA). In 2022, Ian Keteku produced layered, holographic-like projections of student readings that were visible during the night, illuminating space around the festival. We also engaged with the public in the very tactile experience of situating an installation of many writers typing on vintage typewriters, provided through Toronto Typewriters, interacting with the public ("OCADU Partners"). The intention was to create in-the-moment, bespoke writing: love notes, letters of apology, poems, flash fictions, descriptions, born of the conversations between writer and public. Is there anything necessarily interdisciplinary about the typewriter? In this context, yes—the installation of typewriters in a single room, creating a sonic landscape, providing an opportunity to interact with strangers in meaningful exchanges becomes one-part installation, one-part performance art. The act of typing on a vintage machine without the ability to delete, cut or paste, and the manual nature of the paper loading feature encouraged students to carefully consider design aspects, the visual presentation of their words upon the page.

In 2023, our projects at TIFA included a collaboration between OCADU's Experimental Animation program, Chaired by Phillippe Blanchard and our Creative Writing students. This co-curricular project was born of a small in-class exercise in my third-year poetry class upon discovering a treasure trove of short experimental animations—largely without audio—produced by EXAN students and posted on the program's Instagram page ("Experimental Animation"). After screening a selection of these animated shorts in class, my students chose a piece to write to—in essence, creating a language 'score' they would later record and combine with the videos. These brief animations were visually engaging, short, poignant, varied and inspiring. The exercise evolved into a conversation between faculty, a call for interest to students in our two programs, a proposal for TIFA, and, ultimately, a fruitful collaboration showcasing the work of seven Experimental Animation and Creative Writing partners, with text and moving images projected simultaneously on Harbourfront Centre's gallery walls. Most significantly, this created a conversation space (in person and online) between student collaborators in different faculties and programs, leading to further collaborations beyond the classroom.

They Take the Lead: Student Initiatives and Publications

One of the most rewarding, edifying experiences is to see students and recent alumni expand upon their interdisciplinary projects, taking experiences they've had in the classroom and writing community to branch outwards in bigger, bolder ways, independent of our instruction or intervention. One such example is the poetic-artistic installation *between starshine and clay (2022)* curated by OCADU alum and writer-artist Leaf Jerlefia, which featured five angled screens above Yonge and Dundas square, projecting words and images by OCADU student artists and writers. This striking installation was intended to create "a dreamspace for healing" and a space for the black community to reflect, rest, and recover, referencing "ancestors, abolitionists and activists who through mysticism looked to the sky for guidance" ("Digital Screens").

Despite our best efforts at producing a core curriculum that included key elements to foster interdisciplinary explorations, it became clear that students had their own ideas about how to branch out, how to experiment and what those experiments would look like. With all this emphasis on text-off-the-page, what about text on the page? What about publications? Was this too traditional for our rhizomatic program? Students answered this for us. They needed and wanted a signature publication to showcase the work of students in the program, and thus *Pulse* digital and literary journal was born. Our partner for this field placement course is OCADU Press, a burgeoning enterprise deeply embedded in the Printmaking and Publications stream. The first editorial board of *Pulse* was clear on their mission and mandate

> *Pulse* is a living, breathing archive, a gathering space to uplift OCADU writers and community. *Pulse* is made by students for students to explore and experiment with language and text without restrictions. We commit ourselves to accepting many modes of epistemic understanding and ways of contributing to knowledge. We welcome messiness and roughness and imperfection as an authentic record of creative process. This is a space for student experimentation: we are ever-growing, writing in the pulse. ("Living Archive")

It was a proud moment, to be sure, to see that the emphasis on creative process, messiness and experimentation were of value to the diverse members of the journal's editorial board and would be positioned at the core of their literary journal. Through the production of the journal, students gained vital industry experience in editorial process, formatting & design, budgeting, production, marketing & promotion and distribution. Of course, a print journal couldn't possibly house the integrated media, musical and performance work some of our students were creating, so the editorial board produced a website—an archive of language-based work that wouldn't fit on the page.

The process of creating the journal in-house was inherently wedded with studio and design practices, including the use of design software, Risograph printing, puncture binding and hand sewing. Students familiar with the printmaking and publications space took the lead, shared skills, learned to turn to studio staff and faculty for answers to questions I hadn't the expertise nor the experience to answer. In subsequent years, as the course became regularized, we could recruit students from Illustration to tackle the visual aspects of the journal, and students in Design to format and work closely with our editors.

Interdisciplinary intersections are often collaborative in the best ways. Recently, a student in the program undertook an independent study with me to create a massive interactive installation on the wall of our designated program space, affectionately known as "The Blue Room." Here, the student reworked source text, creating a homolinguistic translation of Brian Doyle's "Joyas Voladoras" creating 100+ pages hand-tinted/aged with natural dyes (in consultation with Art faculty, Nicole Collins), and workshopped, redacted, collaged and ink-stamped those pages in a workshop with her peers. The doctored copies were then wheat-pasted to cover an entire wall of the program space, incorporating Polaroid photos of the authors and leaving some sheets blank for future students to intervene and create. Student-led, collaborative projects like these are markers of success, in my opinion. Students see a possibility, a gap (or a blank wall) and address it, involving community, involving simple studio skills, play and exploration and an invitation to inclusion.

Expansions continue. Explorations continue. Students continue to push themselves and their interdisciplinary work in new directions beyond the curriculum. I've often remarked to recently on-boarded faculty that they should be prepared to be amazed by the depth, curiosity, creativity and dedication of our student writers. New projects are continually emerging, and my own understanding of the place of the writer in art and design school is ever evolving.

What's the Why: Interdisciplinarity as Tool of Empowerment

This may all sound impracticable to those outside of the art and design context. It's not. Sure, it's a privilege that we have access to this amazing equipment, these incredible faculty with diverse skills and expertise, and spaces for exhibition. But interdisciplinary work can be fostered in any student writer if we start small through low-stakes and no-stakes exercises, through exposure to contemporary interdisciplinary works and through giving a wide berth for play and exploration, with a focus on process rather than product.

But why does fostering interdisciplinary experiences (in any academic context) matter to the student writer? When we set about designing this program, our core mission was to empower students to become agile, skilled writers who understand their role as creators in community. Agility is born, I think, of brave experimentation, cultivating a beginner's mind, realizing and addressing skill gaps and conceiving of one's writing practice in broad terms. Interdisciplinarity shifts the focus and makes writing feel limitless. Practice and craft, community and outreach, as well as literary scholarship take on new values in the light of interdisciplinary practices. Through the cross-fertilization of ideas and practices, disciplinary porosity, writing students build confidence and increase capacity for critical perspective, compassionate reflection and of course, experimentation. Students have agency. They can weave their way through their studies, through disciplines, taking what they need from other disciplines as they progress and learn.

Creative Writing students at OCADU will undoubtedly push us and push our program to new and challenging areas as they continue to explore new media, theatre, hip hop poetics, sonic arts, partnering with their peers in

Integrated Media, Sculpture and Installation, Graphic Design, Experimental Animation, Printmaking and Publications and other programs. I envision our events and open-mics widening, becoming cabaret style, to include screenings, installations and interventions. Richly-textured work will be celebrated and encouraged along with visual and verbal texts and art that is innovative and interrogative. OCADU's students are envisioning the same, I think. At our latest weekly open-mic event, we had participation from Graphic Design students who rapped, Illustration students who took to the mic to read the work of other poets and one student who simply announced that she would like to form collaborations and friendships with students in our program. She was, she said, an illustrator who would like to know and work with more writers. One student's simple announcement meant everything to us.

Works Cited

"A Living, Breathing Archive." *Pulse Literary Journal*, OCADU Creative Writing Program, 1 May 2023, pulse.ocadu.ca/aboutpulse.html.

Allen, Lillian. "Home." *Lillian Allen*, 2017, https://lillianallen.ca.

"Ami Clarke." *University of the Arts London*, 2024, https://www.arts.ac.uk/colleges/central-saint-martins/people/ami-clarke.

"Black Students from OCADU's Creative Writing Program Interrupt Space at STACKT Market with Powerful Installation." *Shedoesthecity*, 20 July 2020, www.shedoesthecity.com/black-students-from-ocads-creative-writing-program-interrupt-space-at-stackt-market-with-powerful-installation/.

Clarke, Ami. "Artists' Publishing: Sites of Affective Experimentation." *Ways of Writing in Art and Design II: Part 2*, special issue of *Journal of Writing in Creative Practice*, vol. 17, Apr. 2024, pp. 51–76, *Intellect*, https://doi.org/10.1386/jwcp_00062_1.

"Digital Screens." *Yonge-Dundas Square*, Yonge-Dundas Square, www.ydsquare.ca/digital-screens.

Elkins, James. *Why Art Cannot Be Taught: A Handbook for Art Students*. U of Illinois P, 2001.

"Exhibitors - OCADU." *ePortfolio*, OCAD University, 1 May 2023, eportfolio.ocadu.ca/exhibitor/index/6e6febc2-6285-4207-9a72-3848f73712b1?fpid=6ea2b36e-358a-4e36-a8d8-022bfbff41b5.

"First Year Student Gala Reading." 5 Apr. 2023, Toronto, Art Gallery of Ontario.

Janke, Ahsley. "Banner Repeater: An Interview with Ami Clarke." *Temporary*, 9 May 2017, https://temporaryartreview.com/banner-repeater-an-interview-with-ami-clarke.

Johnson, Clare. "Editorial." *Ways of Writing in Art and Design*, special issue of *Journal of Writing in Creative Practice*, vol. 15, Sept. 2022, pp. 105–11, *Intellect*, https://doi.org/10.1386/jwcp_00032_2.

King, Andrew David. "On the Plurality of Practices." *The Scholarship of Creative Writing Practice*, edited by Marshall Moore and Sam Meekings. Bloomsbury, 2024, pp. 23–34.

OCADU Experimental Animation, Instagram, www.instagram.com/ocadu_experimental_animation/?hl=en. Accessed 12 Aug. 2023.

"OCADU Partners with Canada's Largest Literary Festival." *OCAD University*, OCAD University, 22 Sept. 2022, www.ocadu.ca/news/ocad-u-partners-canadas-largest-literary-festival.
"OCAD University GradEx 108." *OCAD University*, OCAD University, 2022, https://www.ocadu.ca/gradex2023/.
Rintoul, Jenny. "'I Came Here to do Art, not English': Antecedent Subject Subcultures Meet Current Practices of Writing in Art and Design Education." *Ways of Writing in Art and Design*, special issue of *Journal of Writing in Creative Practice*, vol. 15, Sept. 2022, pp. 140–56, *Intellect*, https://doi.org/10.1386/jwcp_00035_1.
Snow, Nancy. "Moving Poetry: Animated Typography Poem." GRPH-2004 Typography 2: Structures. September, 2023. OCAD University. Class Handout.

Catherine Black's Recurrent Comments on Student Writing

- This piece needs to be aerated. It needs to breathe. Build in some air, some breath, some holes.
- Locate where the piece clicks into gear (sometimes the second, third paragraph or stanza) and begin it there. Cut out any 'warm up' writing.
- Did you write past the natural ending?
- Modulate the pitch, energy and intensity.
- Don't explain the life out of the work. Remember to trust your reader—we can make the associative leaps.
- What changes from start to finish in this piece?
- Does the (poem, story) turn at any point? Does it twist to show the underside of the story or the thought or the character or the moment?
- We need these ideas (or abstractions) to be tethered to something in the concrete world. Start by looking for the 'things' and objects in this piece. What's there?
- Strive for compression. Crystallize this piece.

10 In Tranquillity

Writing through and beyond Ekphrasis

Stephanie Bolster

As I write this on a warm July Sunday in an eastern exurb of Montréal, I'm watching women and girls of all ages, shapes and sizes lower themselves into a deep pool of muddy water, after which they must climb a mountain of mud so slick that many of them slide back into the water. This ordeal is part of MudGirl, which markets itself as "an obstacle race dedicated to women" ("Carol") and sets up annually in various cities in Québec and Ontario. Last year, in 2022, my daughters and I were among the participants testing our endurance, confidence and tolerance for chill, grit and grime, but it didn't occur me to write about MudGirl until now: stationed here as a spectator/chauffeur/bag carrier while my older daughter and her best friend tackle the course. Standing at the entrance earlier, while a perpetually pumped animator embarked a new throng of participants every two minutes, I found myself tearing up. Why was this challenge so much more moving to watch than it had been to live?

"Because you're you," those who know me would say. I suspect many a writer—perhaps most writers—would feel the experience more fully as a relaxed spectator than a participant apprehensive about the big pink inflatable slide up ahead. When immersed in an activity, I'm too overwhelmed to articulate it, yet only once it's articulated can I begin to claim and understand it. Whether writers are "recollecting emotions in tranquillity" à la Wordsworth, reflecting upon someone else's thoughts or experiences, or contemplating another's artistic creation, distance is key.

***

My suburban Vancouver upbringing in the 1970s and '80s didn't involve much art unless one counts the book of unicorn paintings I bought as a preteen and looked through each day after school. (Yes, I was that kind of kid. I perused my sticker collection on a regular basis, too, finding sensory and imaginative inspiration in these little textured, sometimes scented, images.) I didn't visit the Vancouver Art Gallery until my late teens, with my cool art school friend. And it was only when I first travelled alone to the Maritimes and New York in the fall of 1994 that I experienced in art museums the transcendent connection—an intoxicating hover between proximity and

DOI: 10.4324/9781032614144-13

distance—that would come to characterize much of my writing. Observed in the moment, written at least a year later, my poem, "On the Steps of the Met" responds to that discovery. The final lines: "the folds of the woman's scarf / in Vermeer's portrait, their depth of shadow, / how the fabric came so close to itself without touching" (*Two Bowls* 24).

Two years later, living in Ottawa, homesick for Vancouver's Douglas firs, salal and mild winters, I found my greatest comfort at the National Gallery of Canada. Sometimes I went alone, and sometimes with fellow poet Diana Brebner.

When Diana and I first met, she'd already been introduced to my work through the then-editors of *The New Quarterly*, who had shared with her some of the poems about Alice (of Wonderland fame) that would later appear in my first book, *White Stone: The Alice Poems*. Those matchmaking editors had told her they sensed we would connect, and we did, despite her being 13 years my senior and a parent. She had already published three books, while I was still working on my first. Deeply serious and startlingly irreverent, she was just the guide I needed.

When Diana had approached me about working together through a new mentoring program the League of Canadian Poets had introduced, I readily accepted. She'd never thought much about teaching before, she told me, but she now believed she had a few things to impart. As a young adult newly living half-a-country away from home, I'd come to find my way through a landscape in which the vegetation, the geography and the climate differed profoundly from that in which I'd grown up, and in so doing I'd begun to write less about the natural world and more about the world of art. Diana, too, leaned towards ekphrasis, and we were both a little obsessed with Vermeer. There were no Vermeers in Ottawa, but the National Gallery was a 15-minute walk from my apartment and an easy bus ride from her house. We met once every week or two in the vast, sunlit café where we ate dry sandwiches or squares while she commented on my poems-in-progress. If she offered the line-by-line annotations I'd come to expect from workshops, I don't remember them. She looked at my poems as though stationed in a tower that surveyed the field of my work to date, a field I suddenly found small and monochromatic.

Diana set me the ekphrastic task of choosing three works in the Gallery's collection, with the additional constraint that they be ones I didn't like, perhaps even hated. We walked through the permanent collection galleries, generally peopled by only a handful of other visitors, and talked about the work we resisted. My picks: Lucas Cranach's half-a-millennium-old nude *Venus*, creepily coy, her diaphanous wrap barely concealing a crotch that might be a newborn girl's. Gustav Klimt's *Hope I* also naked, thrillingly, terrifyingly pregnant and surrounded by leering skulls and pained, contorted faces. I felt particularly uninspired by the only Canadian painting I chose, Jack Shadbolt's huge *Transformations No. 5* with its thick acrylics and swaths of butterfly wings.

A few years earlier, I'd spent a summer working in UBC Library's Special Collections, cataloguing a recent donation of Shadbolt's papers. I found a magazine-clipped photo of a disconsolate dog howling, only to later find sketches for Shadbolt's watercolour of the same image, transposed into a war context, *Dog among the Ruins*. Though it was exciting to find the forbear of Shadbolt's dog, the fact that he'd essentially copied the image didn't interest me. But the transposition opened up possibilities. At the very least, my work in writing about the paintings I chose-by-not-choosing would be an act of translation. But what thousand words would translate Shadbolt's enormous, unignorable *Transformations No. 5*? Maybe I needed to listen to the painting's title.

Diana had once asked me to consider the position of the speakers in my poems. I soon realized that they were usually standing in place, either implicitly (as I stood before the art about which I wrote) or explicitly (in a poem in which "the speaker" waded into a flooded path in rainboots and just stood there, contemplating all that water in the wrong place). How could I not have noticed this—about my writing, and about myself? How could I speak this painting of caterpillar, chrysalis and butterfly, in which even embodiment was broken open? Indigenous Canadian writer and U. Calgary CW prof Joshua Whitehead, in writing years later about his own work's evolution through ekphrasis, offers insight into mine, "And perhaps I cling to art that is in the rakes of destruction, the surreal of reality, which isn't so surreal when we are faced with the outcome that the earth is dying and our futures are maimed." Not surprisingly, the poem that emerged wasn't written in the gallery itself (few of my poems were), but after a slow process of letting go: of what the painting looked like, of what I thought my poetry should look and sound like (goodbye, left margin; hello, comma splices), of what I thought Diana would want me to do. The three poems became "Three Goddesses," the final poems in my second book, *Two Bowls of Milk*, and the poems of which I was until that point in my writing life most proud (*Two Bowls* 72–76).

* * *

As I write this, I'm sitting across the aisle from my family on a Boeing 777, nearly across the Atlantic, soon to land in Paris. The last time I was there, 19 years ago, I'd received a research grant to visit historic first-wave zoos and gardens, as well as more innovative sites. I wandered and pondered the *Jardin des Plantes* in Paris, one of the world's oldest known zoos. I visited zoos in Antwerp, Rotterdam, Amsterdam, on the Isle of Jersey, in London and the London suburbs; I visited the *Hortus botanicus* in Leiden and the Chelsea Physic Garden. I came, I saw, I wrote. What I mean is, I looked. There were cages, visible fences, textual plaques in English, French, Dutch. The poems became, eventually, *A Page from The Wonders of Life on Earth*, a title which harkened back to a favourite book from my childhood, in which some of my favourite illustrations were of extinct mammals.

I began this writing project about zoos and extinction, collection and representation, because I'd realized that as an adult I spent very little time thinking about animals and even less time interacting with them. Ultimately, the project became less about zoos and gardens than about collecting, arranging, looking. Through focussing on this one subject, I was coming to understand how I interacted with the world. Between these zoos and gardens, my partner and I took metros, tubes, trains of slow and *Grand Vitesse*. On the latter, we shot through the landscape at such speed I could focus only on objects in the distance.

* * *

As a Creative Writing professor who has spent her teaching career of more than two decades at Montréal's Concordia University, each year I take my students to the Montréal Museum of Fine Arts. Although it's just a block away from Concordia's downtown campus, many of them have, like my teen self in Vancouver, never been to a local but significant art gallery. (That begets some important conversations that exceed the scope of this essay, though they're relevant to the nature of the writing that may take place or the ease with which it does or doesn't take place.)

I avoid talking much in class about what we're about to experience, though I encourage the poets to be as attentive as possible to the experience. I suggest they avoid spending the 90 minutes speeding through the galleries in search of the perfect thing, but pick something after no more than 30 minutes of wandering, and stay with it regardless of their doubts—following Janée J. Baugher's guidance that, "To be a successful ekphrastic writer, one must be comfortable with uncertainty." For their generation—in fact for all of us these days—staying with it, whatever *it* is, can be difficult, but the museum, especially on a quiet winter weekday, which is when I schedule these visits, is blessedly free of distractions that don't take the form of other art.

What one tries to do in an ekphrastic poem is, ultimately, what one tries to do in any poem: to capture something (a painting, an experience of a painting, an experience generally) in a way that is faithful to one's experience of it (which doesn't mean being faithful to the perceived thing itself) and to what that experience sparks, and that addresses or at least alludes to both its known and unknown aspects. I remind students that choosing a work to write about has nothing to do with liking it.

For those who want more preparation, I offer these questions

What are you looking at?
What are you looking for?
How are you looking?
Who are you, looking?

I also offer suggestions of possible approaches:

Tell a narrative suggested by the work
Speak as a character in the work

Speak as the work as a whole
Explore the artist's role / process
Explore the social/historical context of the work
Put the writer/viewer into the poem
Explore the work's setting in a museum, gallery, public space, private space, book, on the Internet
Describe the act of looking (and perhaps of writing also)
Bring the work into relationship with others by the same artist or different artists
Bring the work into relationship with something outside it (e.g. another art work, a tree, current events)
Use the work and/or technique and/or artist relationship as a metaphor for something else

As I tell the students, each of these choices has implications

What role do you as a partaker of the art fulfil?
What role do you as a writer fulfil?
How visible do you want to be?

As always with writing/art-making, these questions lead to more questions

What do you in particular have to bring to this work in particular?
What do you in particular have to take from this work in particular?
Why is poetry the means by which to develop this exchange?
What is there for a reader/listener in this?

For those who want to get still more specific, I also suggest what to do in the museum, on a basic level:

> Look up close, look from far away, look at parts, look at wholes, look at the frame, look at the room, look at yourself. Look at (which may also mean "imagine") what the work suggests. Ultimately, the most vivid images in your poem may not even be in the work.
>
> Then write, if you're ready. Don't be afraid to write the obvious: describing what you see is sometimes the hardest part. Or don't describe: evoke. Or just freewrite, letting the work take you where only you can be taken.

* * *

As I write this I'm in a Thalys high-speed train, barrelling backwards through Belgium north towards Delft, where I haven't been in 20 years. I loved the city most when trying to find the spots from which Vermeer painted *A View of Delft* and *The Little Street*, though there has been much debate about whether the latter painting was representational in the first place (van Maarseveen). I'm anticipating seeking out those spots again, to reconnect with seeking-me-of-then who sought Vermeer as he sought.

* * *

In the winter of 2021, when classes were entirely remote due to the global COVID pandemic, I tried to turn the constraint of being unable to visit the museum into the liberty of "visiting" any museum we wished. (Ah, the days of Zoom and scare quotes. Nice to "meet" you.) I shared with the class a list of links, from museums in Montréal to such places as the National Gallery (in Ottawa, or in London), the Metropolitan Museum of Art, the Louvre, the Prado. I realized there was no reason not to consider Asia and the southern hemisphere. I added Intuit: The Center for Intuitive and Outsider Art (Chicago), a paradoxical site I hadn't known existed.

During our Zoom ekphrasis class, some student writers visited museums solo; others joined breakout rooms dedicated to a particular destination. In my introductory course, most of us ended up visiting MONA (Museum of Old and New Art) in Hobart, Tasmania, a spot not on my list, which one of the students had visited on a trip several years before and recommended for its remarkable architecture (Museum). Although I still haven't met some of those students in person, the experience we shared was very much a real one. When, in the months or years since, I have met some of those students I taught exclusively online, they haven't looked quite how I thought they looked, minus the frame of their Zoom box and the backdrop of the room in which they'd been willing—if they'd turned their cameras on at all—to be seen. That year, as we "looked" at "art," we were so aware of the unusual nature of our perspective that I didn't have to emphasize the importance of contextualizing what we see.

* * *

After our museum visit, none of the writing students is obliged to share their writing-in-progress unless they wish to, but everyone's encouraged to talk about their gallery experiences of perceiving art and trying to write from those experiences (or thinking about trying to write from those experiences). Some find a particular work immediately and devote their time to examining it in precise detail. Some wander, unsure what they're looking for. Some find what they weren't looking for. Some plan to go back.

If we later workshop material that began during the class's museum visit, the writer chooses whether or not they wish to discuss the work's origins and/or present the work as ekphrastic. I believe that a successful piece of ekphrastic writing can be read independently of its source of inspiration, although the reading experience will be richer for the reader who has seen the work in question. The writing adds to the artwork but doesn't require it, nor does the writing have the arrogance to try to make the artwork dependent on it. If the writer submits the piece to a journal, most readers will come to know the source image only if the writer names it and the reader is curious enough to enlist Google's help. Cole Swensen compellingly articulates the complex dynamics of this entwined independence:

> Word and image neither translate nor illustrate each other, but work inseparably as single compositions ... [W]ord and image are working at 'right angles.' They're conceptually perpendicular to each other, and thereby set up a conceptual three-dimensionality, which is to say that the mental and the physical worlds are not perfectly congruent; we find ourselves undergoing two different interpretive practices simultaneously, and their degree of off-set sets up a reverberation. Energy arcs over that gap, almost palpable. (73)

This particular exercise in ekphrastic writing inevitably raises more universal writing questions of appropriation: Do I as a writer have the right to imagine myself in the consciousness of the artist? I've written many poems in which I've tried to do just this, presuming that being a fellow creator is enough. I'm increasingly unsure of this chameleon approach, and decreasingly interested in such a direct relationship to the inspiring artwork. To take a line from Frank Bidart "The love I've known is the love of / two people staring, // not at each other, but in the same direction" (7). One can learn a lot from just trying to look where Vermeer has looked. Or maybe that's *how*.

***

As I write this during my first visit to Super Aqua Club, a water park northwest of Montréal, where I try to tunnel away from the blasting dance music while my daughters explore the waterslides, a gull stands on the towel a family left neatly folded on their picnic table. The gull chews on the lenses of a pair of sunglasses. It delights me that the wearer won't know this when they next put the glasses on. Every hour or so, my kids come back, dripping, with a tale of someone cutting in front of them in line, an adult called out for splashing kids. I'm still here at the picnic table on the sand, facing the lake, thinking about the advertising lining the underground stations I didn't have time to linger over two weeks ago in London.

***

Years after Diana's death from cancer at age 44, still more years after we looked at art alone together, I gave a talk called "Solitary Collaboration," referring to the opportunity ekphrastic writing affords to write autonomously while benefitting from another's creative energies and ideas.

In ekphrasis, as in all writing, writers may be more captivated by the process than the product. As Renate Brosch observes in "Ekphrasis in the Digital Age: Responses to Image,"

> Increasingly, what used to be a central aim of ekphrasis—the description of an artwork—has been replaced by modes of rewriting the artwork

> and in the process questioning accepted meanings, values, and beliefs, not just relating to the particular artwork in question but referencing the ways of seeing and the scopic regimes of the culture at large. (225)

Ultimately, writing ekphrastically makes us think more deeply and differently about what we do and why. Thinking about how we experience visual art helps us think about how we experience experience.

Many works of contemporary art in particular prompt us to notice habits of perception. How does duration play differently into our experience of a sculpture or a painting, as opposed to a poem? While most artworks can be apprehended (if not experienced) all at once, poems cannot. A reader may be able to *see* a poem, especially a short one, in its entirety immediately, but even a haiku can't be read in an instant or with the simultaneity with which we view Marcel Duchamp's *Nude Descending a Staircase (No. 2)* or Frida Kahlo's *The Two Fridas*. What does one make of this differential relationship to time across media, and how can it contribute to the process and/or product of ekphrastic writing? What obligation does an ekphrasis have to render the durational aspect of its source artwork; for example, how might one approach writing about a photograph versus writing about a video installation—and what if the video installation is of a still empty room? What if there's a tension between the movement and/or durational aspect of the artwork's inspiration, the artwork itself and the poem the artwork inspired? Inevitably, consideration of these questions involves not only the writing process and the viewer's imagined reading process but an attempt to reflect upon the visual artist's process and inspiration.

I've never been interested in answering questions with my writing, but I'm a big fan of asking.

The most exciting student work that arises from our visit to the museum and the thinking that follows transcends its sources while also transcending the writer's past work—the collaborative impetus hopefully frees the writer of whatever constraints they unconsciously bring to the act of writing. Not only can the experience open up a new, often more philosophical, awareness of process and intent, it can be emotionally urgent. Formally, the explosive quality of Jack Shadbolt's *Transformations No. 5* inspired me to use a jagged left margin; ethically, it made me question my urge to be good, by which I mean both the urge to be excellent and the urge to be nice. The attempt to be faithful to my experience of the work, both aesthetically and emotionally, made me get out of my own way for long enough to surprise myself.

* * *

This past year for my graduate poetry workshop, I created an assignment I called inside-out ekphrasis. The instructions

> Take a poem (by you or someone else) and adapt it into another medium. A poem for the page could become a performance piece, a wordless audio piece, a stop-motion animated film. Or an installation,

> a sculpture, or a dessert. A garden, a vinaigrette, a portrait in oils, an extended guitar solo, a video game, a contemporary dance choreography. (A looser way to interpret this instruction is: Make a work that is part of your thesis project but that is in a different genre/medium.)
>
> Submit, in whatever form is most interesting while also being feasible, the work you've created, and prepare either a presentation or a written commentary about the process and the impact of the experience.
>
> This assignment aims to push you beyond your comfort zone and prompt you to consider the essence of a work, however you define it. This could mean trying to create a new artwork, the process of making which feels like the process of making the original poem. It could mean trying to make a work that will have a similar impact on an audience as the original poem (if the source poem is by someone else, you are that audience). It could mean heeding the original impulse and seeing how it manifests itself in a new form and set of materials.
>
> Don't worry about expertise or lack thereof. This assignment is exploratory and will be graded accordingly—risks count! For the grade, the commentary is more important than the adaptation itself. What worked, what didn't; what was interesting, what wasn't; what have you learned about your project/the other poet's work/yourself?

The graduate students proved to be talented in many artistic disciplines (I don't know why this surprised me), but even if they hadn't been, what was most exhilarating was the range of approaches they tried, and how this process opened up their work. Poets photographed, knitted and clowned; they made videos, quilts, libretti, handbags, playlists. One outsourced their artwork to an AI, to which they fed ideas. One poet offered themself up as a model for a life drawing class; another created a series of yoga poses inspired by border security inspections. Just as the best writing moments make me feel I'm channelling creativity from an unknown source, while paradoxically being as deeply within myself as I can ever be, these writers lost themselves to find themselves.

* * *

The more time I've spent writing and thinking about writing ekphrastically, the more it seems like just plain writing. Just as erasure reminds us that we always work with a limited vocabulary, ekphrasis narrows the range of possible subjects enough to free us from the pressure of making an entirely new thing. To adapt a phrase from Margaret Atwood's *The Handmaid's Tale* (if not another writer behind her), *freedom from* is transformed into *freedom to*.

Works Cited

Baugher, Janée J. *The Ekphrastic Writer: Creating Art-Influenced Poetry, Fiction, and Nonfiction*. Kindle ed. McFarland and Company, 2020.

Bidart, Frank. *Half-light: Collected Poems 1965–2016*. Farrar, Straus and Giroux, 2017.

Bolster, Stephanie. "On the Steps of the Met." *Two Bowls of Milk*. McClelland and Stewart, 1999.
Bolster, Stephanie. "Solitary Collaboration: The Whys and Hows of Ekphrasis." Whitehorse Poetry Festival, 22 June 2013, The Old Fire Hall, Whitehorse, Yukon. Panel presenter.
Bolster, Stephanie. *White Stone: The Alice Poems*. Signal Editions/Véhicule Press, 1998.
Brosch, Renate. "Ekphrasis in the Digital Age: Responses to Image." *Poetics Today*, vol. 39, no. 2, June 2018, pp. 225–43.
"Carol Tanoush Shares Taking Part in the Mud Girl Obstacle Race in Ottawa." *CBC Video*. Canadian Broadcasting Corporation. Aug. 2023, https://www.cbc.ca/player/play/2250869827962.
Cranach, Lucas. *Venus*. 1518, National Gallery of Canada.
Duchamp, Marcel. *Nude Descending a Staircase (No. 2)*. 1912, Philadelphia Museum of Art.
Intuit: The Center for Intuitive and Outside Art. https://www.art.org.
Kahlo, Frida. *The Two Fridas*. 1939, Instituto Nacional de Bellas Artes, Mexico City.
Klimt, Gustav. *Hope I*. 1903, National Gallery of Canada.
Museum of Old and New Art. Museum of Old and New Art, 2023, https://mona.net.au/.
Shadbolt, Jack. *Dog among the Ruins*. Art Gallery of Greater Victoria, 1947
Shadbolt, Jack. *Transformations No. 5*. National Gallery of Canada, 1976.
Swensen, Cole. "To Writewithize." *Noise That Stays Noise: Essays*. U of Michigan P, 2011, pp. 69–73.
Van Maarseveen, Michel P. *Vermeer of Delft: His Life and Times*. Translated by M.E. Bennett. Stedelijk Museum Het Prinsenhof/Bekking Publishers, 1996.
Whitehead, Joshua. "On Ekphrasis and Emphasis." *Canadian Art*, 27 Aug. 2019, https://canadianart.ca/essays/on-ekphrasis-and-emphasis/.

Frequent Writing Comments from Prof. Bolster

I'd have been interested in hearing more about the *how*.

More specificity would have enriched this piece: spend time, look up close, do your best to articulate that which we normally skim past. Attention precedes, and is at the core of, writing.

An evocation is richer and more involving than an explanation. This may just be another way of saying the old, "Show, don't tell." A poem that is a transcript of an experience or a distillation of thoughts may be articulate and powerful, but a poem that is itself an experience—that enacts rather than describes—requires the reader to do something, and in so doing, heightens their chances of being transformed. And, from a selfish perspective, the act of writing it is likely to transform the writer.

That these poems are beautifully made is of course a strength, but also a potential weakness. I encourage you to distrust your facility. What is messy, confusing, unknown about your subject? A well-made poem demonstrates that the writer knows how to write a good poem; a broken, fragmented and/or ugly poem reflects, and prompts, questions that require the reader's involvement.

You know that expression: "Wherever you go, there you are"? Your ideas, imagination, vocabulary, way of thinking, distinguish all of these poems from anyone else's poems, and this contributes to making it hard to distinguish them from each other. You can work on that, but it's also important to realize that the distinctiveness of these poems is a strength.

The ending has that bang-on quality that can make an audience sigh during a reading, but I wonder if it comes too soon. It would be worth writing your way back into and through this poem again. Rewrite the poem (paraphrasing this draft or even copying it word for word) and then keep on going, writing your way past the ending.

11 Listening Out and In

Clem Martini

When writing for the theatre, one has only a few tools at one's disposal. Perhaps only three. There are the actions that characters can take, there is the scenography that evokes a setting and presents a visual picture, and perhaps most importantly, there are the words that the characters speak.

Those attempting to write theatrical dialogue for the first time, however, are prone to making a variety of related errors. The dialogue—all the dialogue—tends to suffer from an overwhelming sameness. The characters employ similar vocabularies, similar proclivities and similar cadences. They exchange similar jokes, reference similar cultural touchstones. These characters, in short, sound pretty much like the author. Sometimes, in an attempt to escape themselves, the beginning writer runs in the opposite direction and unconsciously imitates the stylings of a popular celebrity, comedian, television show or film, which only makes matters worse. Now, the dialogue, and the characters, feel thin and derivative.

But as one strives to create new and distinct characters, how is one to escape the tyranny of living within one's own body, attuned each day to one's own voice? How to create the unique speech patterns and sensibilities of others, when one is subject to one's own voice not only when one talks, but in the relentlessly churning current of one's own thoughts?

Writing good, distinct, effective dialogue is a difficult craft to master, yet an absolute necessity if one wishes to write compelling stage scripts. The only way that one can begin to develop writing vibrant, insightful, honest dialogue is to first listen attentively to others.

Attentive listening would seem like a normal, natural activity, but people generally race through the world and their lives so anxious and determined to advance their interests that they are only marginally aware of what others are saying, let alone how they are saying it. In "'They're Killing our Imaginations': Dialogue and Reflexive Writing Development in Historically Marginalized Students," Lucy Spence et al. note,

> Classroom opportunities for dialogue are necessary to expand students' perspectives as they grasp new ideas through multiple voices, which are essential for a diverse world view. In this way, a students' initial stance

DOI: 10.4324/9781032614144-14

> or ideology transforms through dialogue with others in essentially a constant renewal of the ideo- logical self (Halasek, 1999). (847)

And yet it is possible, in the theatre, in this most lifelike of all the art forms, in which live beings move and breathe directly in front of you, to create characters that are vivid and speak themselves into being in their very own, very singular ways. Consider these three examples:

> All the world's a stage, and all the men and women merely players. Jacques, from *As You Like It,* (Shakespeare, *As You Like It,* 2.7.146–47)
>
> Have you not done tormenting me with your accursed time! It's abominable! When! When! One day, is that not enough for you, one day he went dumb, one day I went blind, one day we'll go deaf, one day we were born, one day we shall die, the same day, the same second, is that not enough for you? Pozzo, from *Waiting for Godot* (Beckett 58)
>
> First thing you learn is what is. Next thing you learn is what ain't. Lincoln from *Top Dog Underdog* (Parks 77)

How differently the characters of these works express themselves. What different worlds they inhabit.

There are exercises I ask my students to perform as they first explore writing for the theatre—I offer the following two exercises as examples. None of these assignments guarantee success in their writing ambitions (indeed, nothing does), but each of the tasks holds the opportunity to waken the participant to a different way of approaching the craft.

Exercise I: Listening Out

One of the most important exercises is also one of the earliest I assign. I request that they venture out to listen in on some group of people engaged in conversation.

There are a number of different steps involved in this exercise.

Step 1. I ask students to listen.

The students must travel to some location where they can observe others speak without interfering in the conversation or disturbing the speakers.

There are many locations that prove ideal for this kind of activity: political forums, school lunchrooms, bars, churches, mosques, synagogues, temples, hospital waiting rooms, bus stops, subways, restaurants, cafes, sporting events and family reunions.

Step 2. I ask students to, discreetly, take notes.

I urge students to perform these exercises as an anthropologist might. They are to observe closely and record everything they hear and everything they see as precisely as they can.

Step 3. We reconvene as a group and apply analysis to the rough data.

Sometimes, students are surprised and impressed that a dramatic scene will unfold immediately in front of them. People are not as shy as is commonly supposed—that's a revelation. People overheard will argue, attempt to persuade, plead for forgiveness, demand compensation, pledge their love, chastise, challenge, soothe and seduce in the most public of venues. In the article "Fighting Talk," UK writer and CW lecturer Phil Emery overtly transposes "the techniques of drama and dramatic fight arranging to offer a methodology" for writing better dialogue (315). Sometimes, on the other hand, students return with notebooks filled with seemingly aimless, idle conversations. The actual diction they observe, and its level of dramatic intensity, only matter so much. In any case, we discuss the different ways that these strangers have expressed themselves. We consider how individually language is employed and investigate the different vocabularies that are revealed. What jargon is employed? What kind of phrasing—long and detailed, short and abrupt? What tone? Casual, formal, intense or relaxed? To whom do the participants defer to in the conversation? Whom do they talk over or ignore, and on the basis of what? We examine how dialogue is shared within a group—how permission is assigned to speak, and who assigns that permission. We study how status within the group is maintained or challenged. For my students who do not, for whatever reason, continue to write for decades after studying with me, or have their plays produced, I still think this is a crucial education, that their learning to map power, unity, inclusion, exclusion and more will be with them for the rest of their lives. Will be with them and should be with them.

Students are frequently surprised that conversations are not necessarily pursued sequentially or even in an orderly pattern. Individuals will interject abruptly with unrelated topics according to their own privately held agendas and regardless of what is being discussed at the time, or will loop back to doggedly pursue subjects already raised and dismissed.

Of course, many writers perform this kind of investigative activity as a matter of course. The journals of famous novelists and playwrights are littered with singular phrases that writers, having first heard, felt compelled to capture on the page. Anton Chekov kept a notebook in which he recorded his observations (Chekov), as did Arthur Miller (Miller) as did August Wilson (Lindstrom). Writing around observed dialogue and the need for believable, compelling, dramatic dialogue is also a major focus in the intersection of AI (Mirowski, Piotr, et al.; Terry; Stasaski).

In his article, "On the Journals of Famous Writers," Dustin Ingleworth notes,

> A writer's diary has often functioned as an archive for the overheard remark, the potent anecdote, the physical description that begs for inclusion in the next novel. James Salter wrote on napkins during dinner parties; Victor Hugo reportedly kept a journal on his knee beneath the table.

Step 4: The students write.

The students are asked to craft a scene inspired by what they have witnessed, employing some element of the rough material they have collected.

Sometimes, as I've said, a dramatic event will occur plainly and explicitly and may form that essential content of the newly written scene. Conflict and passions can after all erupt anywhere. I was once seated in a packed cinema when a man abruptly proposed to his girlfriend from the projection booth. Sadly for him, the proposal was rejected.

Sometimes, a story only emerges after considerable coaxing—one can speculate that a subject is being pursued, but it is only with some study that the desires of those involved may become exposed. But if a story isn't present in the original source material, I ask the students to take the rough clay and fashion a pot. I ask that they embrace an element from the observed conversation—a particular manner of speech, a dynamic of one of the relationships, a status transaction, whatever—and employ that element in their newly created scene.

It has been my observation over the years that scenes constructed after actively listening to others are quite different from the kind of material that students normally compose in isolation. The characters are more distinct in the way they speak and the way they behave. They approach matters in ways that feel fresh. Characters who begin from observed speech feel active and alive.

This kind of focused, purposeful attention is useful as a one-off exercise to prompt reflection upon the diverse ways dialogue can be constituted, but if practiced habitually, it holds the potential to change the way one conceives characters, and indeed, how one sees the world. Emery's "Fighting Talk" article borrows the stage combat lexicon of "William Hobbs's classic text on fight choreography *Fight Direction for Stage and Screen*" (315) and later notes "I've used 'attack' to denote aggression but 'lunge' to signal a more energised and direct attack. I interpreted these lunges as *heightened moments of emotion containing a degree of lack of control*" (317; emphasis added). Observed dialogue opens writers to the nascent drama in the quotidian.

One begins to see richness in everyday exchanges. One discerns how habitually subtext is employed. How swiftly passions can flare. One understands how closely connected language is to an individual's identity.

The activity of focused listening is a simple one, but it holds such great and long-lasting potential that, once embraced, it can be difficult to abandon.

However, the spoken word isn't only heard, it is also stored away; its echoes rattle about deep within us. There's a rich and elaborate vocal archive that each person possesses where the voices of all the characters ever encountered reside. The archive is established when we are young, but the pathway to that storage house is, in many cases, forgotten.

Those beginning to write for the theatre tend to resist accessing their memories. Sharing personal lessons can seem like a particularly threatening kind of exposure. Writing from personal experiences can feel like one is throwing one's past life, relationships and decisions—good and bad—open for commentary and censure. Afraid of accessing and employing these memories, many beginning playwrights, especially students juggling several other courses, switch them off, or at least mute them.

And yet, our past experiences are often unlocked by dialogue and/or other verbal memories. Individuals whose voices we are most familiar with, not just from the single observed instance, but from a lifetime of connection and observation, exist inside us, and those voices are particularized by the repeated exposures. Speech patterns, word choice and the power dynamics of dialogue are part of how we love and hate. Personal memory, then, is a second major tool for the apprentice playwright committed to improving dialogue to, really, writing character drama that comes alive.

Wanting to encourage students to also access their private lexicons, I ask them to listen in.

Exercise II: Listening In

Step 1. I begin by assigning a simple in-class exercise. Students are asked to recollect the voice of someone they feel they know, or have known, well, over an extended period of time. I provide them with this uncomplicated writing prompt, "I remember when X...." X being the individual they are asked to recollect.

They fill in the blank following a name with something that individual said or did. I ask that they describe that event or exchange as completely as they can, and when they have no more to add, nothing more to say, to begin once again with the same prompt, but a different memory of that individual. They are told they have ten minutes to recall everything they can about that that individual—everything they said, everything they did in as much detail as they can.

Because this exercise operates on compressed time—just ten minutes, and in class—the students can't overthink things. They start slowly, hesitantly noting a single phrase, but inevitably one memory leads to another and another and soon they are writing quickly, trying to keep pace with the recollections as they cascade one upon the other.

When I announce that ten minutes have lapsed and they must stop, it's clear that that they could profitably—and effortlessly—have continued writing for a much longer time.

Step 2. I ask them to review what they have written and choose one or two lines that they feel comfortable sharing. They make their selections. We go around from student to student, usually in classes ranging 12–20 students.

The memories tend to be very precise, the voices captured, distinct and resonant. Because the quotes never emerge out of nothing, there is almost always a telling incident or event described that accompanies the memory. So, a clearly voiced character emerges from the exercise attached to this quote, coupled with a contextualizing story.

The participants tend to be astonished at how painless the writing feels, how quickly one memory triggers the next, how much writing they have generated in so short a time, how sensuous and vivid these tiny postcards from the past are.

Step 3. We transition to the next portion of the assignment, which is to seize another voice/memory of an individual that they know well. This memory should be charged with strong emotion. It doesn't really matter what the emotion is—it could be one in which they felt outraged, embarrassed, amused, aroused, afraid, jealous, joyful, surprised or saddened.

I request this unearthing because a memory is more likely to be honed sharp when scoured and abraded by emotion, and because it permits the students to contend with writing that deals with strong feelings, something that the students tend to avoid. Dealing with powerful emotions can be uncomfortable, in real life and in fiction. There is, perhaps, the anxiety that in writing the memory, it will be mishandled in some way, or that the writer will be viewed as embellishing or exaggerating. On the rare occasion that emotion is confronted and/or unpacked, it tends also to be dispensed with swiftly. A character who is hurt by someone quickly recovers. A character gripped by a passionate impulse promptly suppresses it. This exercise in recreating the memory of a second, different character not only permits the students to reflect on how individuals speak, but how *differently* they speak as feelings escalate to a place beyond normal banter.

I caution participants to only draw upon events they feel capable of exploring and then sharing. They go home excited, but apprehensive.

When they return with their written assignment of observed character, it is with a particular sense of investment. It's interesting how this exercise conjures scenes that resist standard tropes and clichés. While most of the written material emerges from everyday activities, there is a vein of individuality that nourishes the text. An unexpected late-night exchange of hidden truths between siblings. An abrupt and surprising realization that a marriage is broken occurs while making a bed for visiting guests. There are no gunfights or car chases in these scenes. It's a revelation to students that drama can be conjured from the everyday, rather than imitated, copied and pasted from the extraordinary events they view in films and television episodes.

We exchange these stories within an attentive and supportive environment. Nervous that their writing will be found strange, embarrassing, or even worse, boring, students are pleasantly surprised to learn that, instead, their peers find them arresting. Again, the reflections tend to reveal characters whose voices are conspicuously individual, possessing their own particular idiom, their own particular interests, emerging equipped with a history, with objectives and extraordinary strategies for attaining those objectives.

Step 4. This composite series of assignments culminates in an exercise in which the students are tasked with crafting a scene inspired by an emotionally charged memory, the described memory from Step 3 or another. This final stage permits students to select a memory and then shift, alter or amend things. This revision permits the students to access the memory, recollect it fully and then free themselves of its borders and boundaries, and construct as they wish. They may reconstruct the ending, amend the beginning, embellish, add or subtract characters as they wish.

Rewriting memory is liberating. Liberating both to learn that one can handle super-heated memories without being incinerated, liberating to understand that once one elects to work from memory, one is still not bound to conform to it.

To see how other writers have handled autobiographical material, the workshop students and I read from various dramatic works based upon the author's recollection of lived events. We might invoke the opening stage directions cum production notes of Tennessee Williams's *The Glass Menagerie:* "The scene is memory and is therefore non-realistic. Memory takes a lot of poetic license. It omits some details; others are exaggerated, according to the emotional value of the articles it touches, for memory is seated predominantly in the heart" (1). Larry Kramer's *The Normal Heart* is similarly aware of how in part we need to listen to memory, listen to the memories that should be retained but also those that might be dropped or even, well, revised:

BEN: Me agreeing you were born just like I was born is not going to help save your dying friends.

NED: Funny—that's exactly what I think will help save my dying friends. (54)

David Henry Hwang's *Yellow Face* warns of self-narration becoming a double-edged sword (or mask): "Years ago, I discovered a face—one I could live better and more fully than anything I'd ever tried. But as the years went by, my face became my mask. And I became just another actor—running around in yellow face" (62)

Taken together, these two projects—Listening Out and Listening In—permit early-stage writers to reach beyond their usual writing habits and writing limitations. Students are constantly advised that they must be "creative" and "inventive" and they understand this to mean that they must create and invent the world, the situation, the characters, the voices, in the manner that a kind of omnipotent God, might—from nothing at all. From dust.

These exercises, taken together, provide them with another set of processes and protocols for reflecting on voice, and a productive mechanism for constructing aspects of character. As a playwright, it isn't necessary that one invent everything. Sometimes, it's sufficient just to listen.

Works Cited

Beckett, Samuel. *Waiting for Godot*. Grove, 1954.

Chekov, Anton. *The Personal Papers of Anton Chekhov: His Notebook Diary and Letters on Writing*. Forest Grove. UP of the Pacific, 2002.

Emery, Phil. "Fighting Talk." *New Writing: The International Journal for the Theory and Practice of Creative Writing*, vol. 17, no. 3, 2020, pp. 315–23, https://doi.org/10.1080/14790726.2019.1629963.

Hwang, David Henry. *Yellow Face*. Dramatists Play Service, 2008.

Illingworth, Dustin. "On The Journals of Famous Writers." *Literary Hub*, 19 Jul. 2016. https://lithub.com/on-the-journals-of-famous-writers/.

Kramer, Larry. *The Normal Heart*. Samuel French, 1985.

Lindstrom, Natasha. "August Wilson's Early Life, Writing Process to Anchor Pittsburgh Center's 1st Permanent Exhibit." *Trib Live*, 18 Feb., 2020. https://triblive.com/local/pittsburgh-allegheny/august-wilsons-early-life-writing-process-to-anchor-downtown-pittsburgh-centers-1st-permanent-exhibit/.

Miller, Arthur. c.1910s–2013. *An Inventory of His papers at the Harry Ransom Center. Manuscript Collection MS-02831*. University of Texas at Austin, Austin, TX. https://norman.hrc.utexas.edu/fasearch/findingAid.cfm?eadid=00786.

Mirowski, Piotr, et al. "Co-Writing Screenplays and Theatre Scripts with Language Models: Evaluation by Industry Professionals." *Proceedings of the 2023 CHI Conference on Human Factors in Computing Systems*. 2023.

Parks, Suzi Lori. *Top Dog Underdog*. Dramatists Play Service Inc., 2002.

Shakespeare, William. *As You Like It*. Folger Shakespeare Library. https://www.folger.edu/explore/shakespeares-works/as-you-like-it/read/.

Spence, Lucy "'They're Killing our Imaginations': Dialogue and Reflexive Writing Development in Historically Marginalized Students." *Reading Research Quarterly*, vol. 57, no. 3, 2022, pp. 847–62.

Stasaski, Katherine, and Marti A. Hearst. "Pragmatically Appropriate Diversity for Dialogue Evaluation." *arXiv preprint arXiv:2304.02812* (2023).

Terry, Robert, and Lisa Dusenberry. "Serious Interactive Fiction: Constraints, Interfaces, and Creative Writing: Pedagogy." *Journal of Creative Writing Studies*, vol. 3, no. 1, 2018, pp. 1–25.

Williams, Tennessee. *The Glass Menagerie*. 1945. *Heinemann Plays* Ser., Heinemann Educational, 1996.

Prof. Martini's Advice to Students

Remember this. While there is an immense body of good and useful advice that extends back thousands of years, there are no rules governing the writing of plays. No rules, and, even if there were, no police to enforce them.

12 Generous Writing

Teaching the Avant-Garde

Gregory Betts

> Let's face it: Too many humanities scholars are alienating students and the public with their opacity, triviality, and irrelevance. —Bruce Cole, "What's Wrong with the Humanities?"

If you are reading this essay, despite the cajoling of conservative critics like the Bruce Cole of this ironic epigraph, you may be curious about the possibility of teaching weird literature and textual methods that embrace "opacity, triviality, and irrelevance." Brace yourself. Students may resist. Colleagues may will chide. Inside and outside the campus writing workshop, formally and ideologically disruptive texts work in shocking defiance of productivity and efficiency and present a challenge on multiple levels—where the challenge is itself often the reward, and where our training as readers and writers falters. If poetry slows a reader down from the linear rush of prose, then weird writing, sometimes called the difficult text, and otherwise known as the domain of the avant-garde, asks something more troubling. Weird writing provides both a text but also an arduous process that often requires new strategies for understanding meaning making. What possible value could teaching avant-garde writing, which is rarely embraced by Canadian publishers, have in the contemporary Canadian (or global) university classroom? Who has time to attend exclusively to the sound of letters? Why should we slow down our reading to the point of listening to the punctuation of a text, the strategic ambiguity of parataxis or the delicate suggestiveness of a neologism?

Why has efficiency become such a dominant valence for university life? Notice, for example, that Matthew Salesses's cherished critique of the CW workshop teaching model primarily concerns the teaching and writing of student fiction. From his title—*Craft in the Real World: Rethinking Fiction Writing and Workshopping*—to his opening paragraphs, Salesses calls for a redress of how fiction writing is taught but not, notably, of redressing the centrality of fiction teaching in CW educations. His second and third sentences explicitly seek a redesign of the fiction workshop, not of CW programs that favour fiction: "as if meaning in fiction is separate from meaning in life" and "Race, gender, sexuality, etc. affect our lives and so must affect our fiction" (xiii). In contrast to so-called realistic fiction, Digital Humanities

DOI: 10.4324/9781032614144-15

scholar Kathleen Fitzpatrick notes that "the building of relationships and the cultivation of care are slow and difficult and of necessity inefficient" (10). Calls for making the tertiary CW workshop more inclusive, from Salesses to Janelle Adsit to Felicia Rose Chavez to Junot Díaz, might, as his chapter advocates, include more inclusion of diverse genres and definitions of the writer-reader relationship. When we are compelled by difficult texts to question our critical reading strategies, to resist the coercive ideologies of our habits, we take the time to recognize the relationships and unique patterns between all the elements of a text. When we write even non-avant-garde works, we take on the burden of care to map out the network of significance and potential of these elements in our own writing, crafting them such that the parts and the whole contribute to the meaning making we intend. Most writers discover that the more care they put into each element of their text, the more potent the overall text becomes. Thus, this work is slow and difficult and necessarily inefficient. Every deleted word and scrapped draft attests to this burden of care. To put it bluntly, as Hemingway does, "Don't get discouraged because there's a lot of mechanical work to writing. There is, and you can't get out of it. [...] The first draft of anything is shit. When you first start to write you get all the kick and the reader gets none" (qtd. in Samuelson 11). This difficult process to produce polished work is true of all writing, but things get even more complicated in the realm of the avant-garde where the habits of linguistic convention are called into question, upset and reinvented in the hopes of a different, better future.

Consider the work of Canadian poet and essayist M. NourbeSe Philip who, across nine volumes of poetry and prose, has struggled to write through the long, colonially inflected history of the English language, her mother tongue, back to the initial displacement of her ancestors through the brutal violence of slavery. She explains her particular burden of care for this legacy:

> The exquisite challenge every writer faces is that language always stands in for the experience, the thought or feeling. The struggle is to reduce the gap between the experience and the expression of that experience. In my case, there is a double burden, if you will, because of the history of the language in relation to me and my history. Essentially, language represents a wound for me. (*Blank* 55)

With language de-naturalized, NourbeSe Philip's experimental writing requires new forms to embody the alienation she feels from the English language: "it would have been very difficult, if not impossible, to find a [traditional] poetic language for what cannot be told yet must be told" (15). In her acclaimed book *Zong!*, Philip addresses this problem directly by writing against the story of enslaved Africans murdered for an insurance claim in order to recover or at least honour and acknowledge the intrinsic value of those lives. As the details of their lives has been cut from history, she makes use of the cut-up technique in order to smash a colonial-era record of the insurance claim on the lives of African men and women murdered by the crew of the *Zong*. By writing through that harrowing record, she thereby expands upon its glimpse of the tragic truth of the lives lost. It is in such a work, indeed across her works, that the difficult text can be recognized as engaging with a difficult necessity.

Like many avant-garde writers before her, in Canada and beyond, Philip's cutting into language that papers over such horror is a profound act of resistance. If we start our approach to writing and language from Dionne Brand's apposite epigram that "no language is neutral," and with the institutional critiques of Chavez et al., we can begin to integrate into our classrooms the inevitability, or, to soften things a bit, *the possibility*, that writing become strange and even awkward. In the parlance of the avant-garde, via Russian theorist Viktor Shklovsky, we would call such language acts defamiliarized ["ostranenie"] (see "Art as Device"), and we would praise and encourage the estrangement from entrenched perspectives and language use. In almost every historical case, the avant-garde begins with just such an interrogation of the neutrality of language, ultimately rejecting the coercive ideology presumed by the consciousness of a text. Whether the cause is revolutionary disruption of Western white supremacy in NourbeSe Philip's and Brand's work, or the violence and repression of rationalism in the case of Surrealism, defamiliarized language still serves as a primary site of revolt in the contemporary Canadian avant-garde. In the case of Surrealism, its founder André Breton describes the incredulity of last century's artists:

> We were beginning to distrust words; we were suddenly noticing that they had to be treated other than as the little auxiliaries for which they had always been taken. Some thought that they had become worn down from having served too much; others, that by their essence they could legitimately aspire to a condition other than the one they had — in short, we had to free them. ("Words without Wrinkles" 100)

How does a Creative Writing professor, or student, free the words a full century after Breton's scepticism? To begin, it is now a recognized mistake to teach from a presumption of language's possible translucence (cf. Chaves, Junot Díaz). Instead, the American poet Evie Shockley celebrates "how the poet can take a word and hold it up to the light to see what it obscures" (ix). This careful, slow attention to the obscurantism of language might not liberate immediately, but the care by which the writer interrogates and reimagines their language determines its liberational potential. Despite the heavy baggage of North America's colonial languages, in Shockley's estimation, the poet can yet "blow air into it to hear its song, its call, its howl; can crack it open, can use it to open us." The Canadian avant-garde stalwart bpNichol encouraged something very similar in an unpublished essay from 1968: "turn print back on itself! destroy language with language!" ("Further" 26). Across all of its various and wildly incompatible manifestations, from the 1850s to the present, the consistent primary antagonist of the avant-garde has been an orthodoxy that language helps to sustain. That the arts fall prey to orthodoxy is the truism that proves the need for an avant-garde jolt to perpetually break it out of deadening habits; a problem I continue to encounter as a CanLit professor, scholar, editor and author.

Cracking open all habits in the CW classroom and in professional practice is one way to revitalize language use, for, in Charles Bernstein's words, "disjunction is a means to more intense connections" ("Up Against Storytelling"). Orthodoxies, others observe, creep into even the most liberal classrooms, including the once revolutionary CW workshop, bearing the seeds of most often unintended ideologies. When we teach to rule, for instance, insisting that students perform our own aesthetic valences, from "Show; don't tell" to fiction's transformed protagonist, we end up in the same trap: preaching an orthodoxy that is desperately in need of an avant-garde disruption. Even our models of efficiency in the classroom, demanding that students churn out a regular, steady output of goods to be product-tested in a workshop, is a model that more befits the assembly line than an unfettered imagination. *Finnegans Wake*, perhaps the most exquisite book-length example of well-wrought language, took Joyce 17 years to write. He would have flunked out of every one of Canada's CW programs, undergraduate or graduate, for that indulgence. What does this incompatibility demonstrate about our Creative Writing programs?

Building from Kathleen Fitzpatrick's notion of "generous thinking" in her book *Generous Thinking: A Radical Approach to Saving the University* (2019), I want to propose the possibility of a generous Creative Writing pedagogy—a recognition that creative writing, the activity or the popular academic field, is ill served by both efficiency and orthodoxy. Generous thinking is Fitzpatrick's attempt to re-orient the classroom away from a default negativity, a mode of enquiry that pulls classroom discussion away from the internal logic of texts prematurely to critique them vigorously. Such an approach fails to meet the texts on their own terms and leads students, in her estimation—and I concur—to misunderstand basic elements of the works they are critiquing. Generosity is not the antithesis of critique, but a call for a more grounded, patient, less foreclosed ergo less efficient mode of critique. Instead, Fitzpatrick proposes a pedagogical stance "of paying attention, of listening, of *reading with* rather than *reading against*" (2, emphasis mine). Similarly, I imagine a Creative Writing pedagogy that does not begin with orthodoxies (including the most limiting concept of *publishability*), nor with workshopped critique, but with a concerted effort to inhabit the aesthetic impetus of each student's project. This generosity asks a lot of teachers, including a humility that is anathema to our training as scholars, but this is where the avant-garde can be a useful interruption of normal patterns and habits. Expanding the possible modes of textual production, even inventing new modes, requires more of the teacher and, ultimately, more of the student. Generous teaching requires an encounter with and even an embrace of the difference between texts, which is akin to the difference between the teacher and the student. The radical methodological openness of the avant-garde is a useful tool for denaturalizing hierarchies and orthodoxies, including all literary conventions. Instead of convention (another word for prevailing tastes), students and their work might be met on their own terms, might be encouraged to move by their own inner necessity, discovering something vital—art—in the alignment of form and content. In teaching the works of others, this might lead to exercises such as producing imitation works in the manner of another author, cutting-up existing texts, or even uncreatively re-typing another author's text to help inhabit its idiosyncrasies. In mentoring the production of new works by students, this preference for organic meaning-making over adherence to a convention (e.g., rising action) might also mean recognizing that the student has embarked on a 17-year project, and refashioning assignments to help serve them in their ultimate pursuit beyond our classrooms and degrees.

The avant-garde is instructive for both its consistent insistence on expanded practice, creating a more open frame of mind, but also for supplying a series of innovative tools and techniques for producing new literature; this latter project is surely part of our mandate as CW instructors. It is important not to overlook the contexts in which writing technologies were created, for each bears a trace of the initial disruption in their subsequent redeployment. For instance, the prototypical Canadian avant-gardist Brion Gysin, the first Canadian member of Breton's Surrealist group, was not necessarily thinking about resistance to chattel slavery in his development of the cut-up technique deployed so effectively by NourbeSe Philip. He was, however, thinking about methods to get beyond the violence of Western rationalism. He developed the technique just over a decade after producing the first study of slavery in the Canadian context, called *To Master A Long Goodnight: The History of Slavery in Canada* (1946), highlighting abuses and obscenities here. He went back to Europe in search of the source and origins of slavery, but was diverted from the academic life by the lure of avant-garde art (Gysin 152). The cut-up method emerged from his desire to get beyond himself, his ego, and to find a cultural path beyond the colonial violence he had witnessed, particularly in Algeria: in his words, "I thought I was going to rebuild the world" (153). Gysin's cut-up technique, then, while ostensibly politically neutral, still carries a radically disruptive lineage that subsequent writers can tap into. Canadian writers have (Gysin, mid-twentieth century) and do (NourbeSe Philip, early twenty-first century) disrupt language and more; Canadian CW profs can, and should, teach disruption.

Some students may resist such efforts. In fact, it has been my experience that writers who deploy avant-garde methodologies in pursuit of contemporary ideologies are enormously well-received by students. Such students collect new tools with a refreshing hunger. Indeed, while Philips' and Brand's experimental works are challenging, they are amongst the most taught and most popular works in the country right now. I have had great success introducing found poetry by Souvankham Thammavongsa or visual poetry and plunderverse by Nisaga'a poet Jordan Abel. Such writers tailor their methods to their project, showcasing the flexibility and importance of moving beyond conventional verse forms—or even beyond what we sometimes describe as poems that look like poems. Thammavongsa's *Found* interacts with a found scrapbook of her birth in a refugee camp that her father had thrown out. She includes a long series of pages with no words, only a single handwritten line reflecting his notation for the passing of time in the refugee camp. Abel's *The Place of Scraps* carves up a colonial text documenting the carved totems of his ancestral Nisga'a village as they were confiscated by the Canadian government. He gives pages over to the detritus of the carved up colonial text, where stray letters and punctuation (the scraps) are collected. Both texts deploy disjunctive methods to realize more intense connections. The most materially-oriented pages of these texts come to embody the turmoil of their path to self-discovery.

Yet still, some students, and colleagues, will resist. In one of my first CW classes, we did a section on sound poetry. I will never forget the anger of one brilliant student, well trained in mastering texts, who stormed into my office with shouts of frustration that "It's not poetry! It's not anything!" A professor in the hallway murmured, "She's got a point." Of course, I had not properly prepared her for the disjunction and the intensity of such texts (side question: is it still disjunctive if you can anticipate it?). For every future writer who resists the radical openness of the avant-garde, though, there are others who relish the expansion of the field. In the next class (which she did not attend), a group of students interrupted a conversation on Cubist poetry and Gertrude Stein by standing on their desks, intoning strange improvisational sounds, hijacking the class as if for a Dadaist happening. They thought sound poetry was "funny" until they started doing it, at which point the sensual experience of letters became palpable and the world of tone revealed itself to them. We were able to take that material experience of language into our discussion of Stein's poetry and beyond.

So, here is an exercise for your class: give your students a text—any text, it doesn't matter which: a newspaper article, the Canadian Bill of Rights, something found in the trash, *this essay*—and invite them to cut it up, re-arrange the words, and thereby create a new poem. They might assemble it randomly, the way David Bowie and Laurie Anderson wrote their lyrics, or by careful design, the way NourbeSe Philip and Abel produced their books. They will bristle, not because it isn't fun to cut and paste in a serious way in a university class, but because the words aren't theirs. This sense of ownership over our language, and the need to dominate it, though, is one of the sources of the problems I've been talking about throughout this essay. As Gysin once wrote,

> The poets are supposed to liberate the words—not chain them in phrases. Who told poets they were supposed to think? Poets are meant to sing and to make words sing. Writers don't own their words.

> Since when do words belong to anybody? 'Your very own words,' indeed! And who are you?
>
> (*Let the Mice In* 12)

They may also bristle at Gysin's claim that they will never own the words they use, but ask them earnestly, without any hint of come-uppance, who *do* you think you are? Let them write from whatever they glimpse. In response to a similar prompt, Gysin once wrote the lovely palindrome, "I am that am I?" For a follow-up to the cut-up exercise, let writing students revisit the assignment and choose a source text of their own, perhaps a text that somehow prevents them (or symbolizes that prevention) from becoming the person they aspire to be. Cut it up, then, and liberate the words. Liberate yourselves!

The Jamaican-Canadian Dub poet Lillian Allen, an avant-gardist as much as anybody already mentioned in this essay, asks a series of pertinent questions in her poem "Whose voice is in your head?"

> whose head is in your voice
> whose land is in your voice
> whose body is in your voice
> whose words whose power
> whose song
> whose money
> whose memory
> whose hope
> whose anger
> whose love (46)

Each of these questions asks an important question about the coherence of the voice, how—left unexamined—the self we think we possess might well be more integrated or even subordinated to influences from outside us. Each of these elements becomes the coordinates for self-identity (place, body, vocation, affect, etc.), but Allen questions our claim on each. How can a writer, let alone a citizen, write or speak with integrity if their own voice is composite? This is not a statement of fear of influence, nor is it a rejection of community, but a question of how present and self-aware one is within oneself. Allen invites her readers to consider the composition of their own composite self, to make its determination conscious. For, as bpNichol confesses, "we do not know the edges of our own head's spaces" ("Review" 37).

Living as we do in a settler-colonial, capitalist, heteronormative patriarchy, students in Canada, if not elsewhere, will almost inevitably discover some niggling voice inside their head that is not their own (what Sigmund Freud would have characterized as the "superego," the collection of internalized ideals from our parents and society). How did it get in there? How to get it out? It can be disturbing to discover that you disagree with the voice inside your head. This is where we encounter the question of alienation that Bruce Cole was apparently so concerned about in the epigraph to this essay. Historically, alienation was a term developed to describe our separation from God. The philosopher G.W.F. Hegel developed it to describe the process by which individuals come to self-consciousness (a process, in his estimation, that still relied upon religious precepts). Karl Marx refined alienation away from religion to describe the process by which a worker is separated from the value of their labour which their employers claim as their own, as profit. Cole, meanwhile, a former Chairman of the American National Endowment for the Humanities (NEH), breaks with the philosophical tradition by feigning sympathy for Humanities students while rejecting the disciplinarity of the Humanities as a legitimate space of enquiry. For Cole, alienation is the result of students being invited to read Humanities texts that are theoretically-rich, specialized, or informed by the lens of race, class, gender, or theory—approaches that are *explicitly barred* from funding by the NEH ("What's Wrong"). These he dismisses as "trivial aspects of popular culture." He invites Humanities scholars to see beyond "the weaponization of the academic humanities for the promotion of social or political agendas, something I'm sure we all frown upon," and imagine the usefulness of our teaching to future doctors and lawyers, to the writing of more populist bestsellers, and to stop serving the "cultural elites."

This applied-value approach conveniently ignores the true nature of alienation in our contemporary society, which is not from overzealous Humanities scholars, but from economic, political and judicial systems that marginalize and disenfranchise the voices of their subjects. Thus, Sociologists like John Bellamy Foster, Hannah Holleman and Brett Clark have pushed beyond Marx's approach to alienation, "going beyond general political economy and including explorations in capitalism, colonialism, and slavery" (Foster et al. 98). When we talk about barriers to Humanities, including in the Creative Writing classroom (avant-garde or not), we need to include financial pressures, historical cultural barriers and the wider market-driven pressures to maximize the outputs, outcomes and economic value of the lives of our students. These are the forces that make our students alienated from their true, eventual, creative selves. Ironically, Cole's sense of alienation calls for an increase of Marx's sense of alienation, where students are valued for their potential value to future employers. He asks, what can we as a society extract from these students, and how might they be developed into future extractors themselves?

The avant-garde, like generous thinking, sits diametrically opposed to such models of efficiency. Avant-garde writing is slow, requiring extraordinary efforts to conceptualize the particular nature and direction of its eruption from established practice. There is a reason that most avant-garde movements produce manifestoes and extensive theoretical examinations and explanations of their effort. This contextualization of their projects, often revolutionary, is a feature not a defect! Avant-gardists take the necessary time to carve out a space to make something entirely new. This is not to say that avant-garde works exist outside the economy, or other social hegemonies—Joyce died in poverty, but a first edition copy of his novel *Ulysses* now sells for $1.2 million while tourists line up to take photos beside his statues; Marcel Duchamp died without significant recognition but has since been reclaimed as the most important artist of the twentieth century, whose works are now worth gargantuan sums of money. One art critic estimates the value of the original urinal used for his rejected prank piece *The Fountain* at around $100 million (Ellsberg). Obviously, value accrues around the avant-garde act of disruption, and many scholars and writers have wrestled with the almost inevitable co-option of avant-garde work by the mainstream. This co-opting is a different problem, though, from the restrictive pressures facing emerging writers today. Another related and more pressing question is how we ultimately imagine our students, as artists, relating to the wider world in which they will work.

As a Renaissance Art History professor, Bruce Cole rejects the idea of artists "as people with a vision and a calling" ("The Artist in Society" 12) and places them firmly within the surrounding economy: in those days, "They had no special title which implied that, either by vocation or inspiration, they were different from any other group of craftsmen." Masterpieces, the subject of Cole's many books, were but the exceptional products of exceptional commissions: "and he [the artist, masculinized intentionally in Cole's books] most definitely would have considered it a *product*" (14, emphasis in original). From such a vantage, the artist is a worker firmly locked within an economic system that they serve. Cole betrays no interest in or sympathy for the anachronistic value of avant-garde works and their delayed contribution to the market economy, nor for the possibility of art being a venue for advancing thought and leading society forward. His call for efficiency in the Faculty of Humanities, then, can be understood as an insistence on vastly outdated orthodox role of the artist as a passive vessel for their society and a rejection of the need for the freedom of the artist in society.

A much better sense of the role of the artist in their society is offered by Canadian English professor Marshall McLuhan, who writes, "Without an anti-environment, all environments are invisible. The role of the artist is to create anti-environments as a means of perception and adjustment" (36). McLuhan's anti-environment is an imaginative place of freedom, akin to the loftiest goals of the avant-garde. Only by that act of dislocation can a writer truly perceive the world around them. The role of the Creative Writing teacher, I would hasten to add, is to create just such an anti-environment. Studying, teaching and producing avant-garde texts becomes useful in this capacity for the encounter with an anti-environment. Only through recurring attempts to establish just such a perch might one perceive their social context—and what might lie in the next valley beyond. Creating an alternate space of perception is not easy work, though: it requires inhabiting an anti-environment enough to establish a new kind of perception, which means, by definition, leaving one's comfort zone, and of course temporarily leaving the economy in which we are mired. This, I would propose, is a task well suited to the university Creative Writing classroom. We might not have time to oversee (and, dear god, grade) the works that emerge from an entirely new perspective on the world, but we can provide the freedom of space and time of an anti-environment for our students—or at least provide them with as diverse a set of tools as possible that might, one day, give them the leverage they need to secure a ledge of their own. Generous writing takes up the possibility of the anti-environment by working against the models of efficiency and taking the time necessary for the full recognition of the relationships between the elements of a work.

Works Cited

Abel, Jordan. *The Place of Scraps*. TalonBooks, 2013.

Adsit, Janelle. *Toward an Inclusive Creative Writing: Threshold Concepts to Guide the Literary Writing Curriculum*. Bloomsbury, 2017.

Bernstein, Charles. "Up against Storytelling, for David Antin." *Literary Activism*. 2018, https://www.literaryactivism.com/up-against-storytelling-for-david-antin/.

Brand, Dionne. *No Language Is Neutral*. McClelland & Stewart, 1998.

Breton, André. "Words without Wrinkles." *The Lost Steps*. 1924. Trans. Mark Polizzotti. U Nebraska P, 1996, pp. 100–102.

Chavez, Felicia Rose. *The Anti-Racist Writing Workshop: How to Decolonize the Creative Classroom*. Haymarket Books, 2021.

Cole, Bruce. "The Artist in Society." *The Renaissance Artist at Work: From Pisano to Titian*. 1983. Routledge, 2018.

Cole, Bruce. "What's Wrong with the Humanities?" *Public Discourse*, 1 Feb. 2016, https://www.thepublicdiscourse.com/2016/02/16248/.

Ellsberg, Michael. "The Story of the 100 million dollar Urinal." 28 Nov. 2017, https://www.ellsberg.com/100-million-urinal.

Fitzpatrick, Kathleen. *Generous Thinking: A Radical Approach to Saving the University*. Johns Hopkins UP, 2019.

Gysin, Brion. *His Name Was Master: Texts and Interviews*. Trapart Books, 2018.

Gysin, Brion. *Let the Mice In*. Something Else Press, 1973.

McLuhan, Marshall. *Essential McLuhan*. Taylor & Francis Group, 1997.

Nichol, bp. "Further (An Unpublished Preface to an Abandoned Book of Saints)." *Meanwhile: The Critical Writings of bpNichol*. edited by Roy Miki. Talonbooks, 2002, pp. 26–27.

Nichol, bp. "Review of *Notations*, by John Cage." *Meanwhile: The Critical Writings of bpNichol*. Edited by Roy Miki. Talonbooks, 2002, pp. 36–37.

Philip, Marlene NourbeSe. *Blank: Essays & Interviews*. First edition. BookThug, 2017.

Philip, Marlene NourbeSe. *Zong!*. Middletown: Wesleyan UP, 2008.

Salesses, Matthew. *Craft in the Real World: Rethinking Fiction Writing and Workshopping*. Catapult, 2021.

Samuelson, Arnold. *With Hemingway: A Year in Key West and Cuba*. Random House, 1984.

Shklovsky, Viktor. "Art as Device." 1917. *Theory of Prose*. Trans. Benjamin Sher. Dalkey Archive Press, 1991, pp. 1–14.

Shockley, Evie. "Her Tongue Tries She (or How NourbeSe Philip Breaks English to Fit Her Mouth)." *She Tries Her Tongue, Her Silence Softly Breaks*. Wesleyan UP, 2014, pp. Ix–xiv.

Thammavongsa, Souvankham. *Found*. Pedlar Press, 2008.

Professor Betts's Recurrent Comments on Student Writing

1 Your first line is the VISTA for your entire poem. Use it to set the Voice, Imagery, Style, Tone and Arrangement of the work that follows.
2 Surprise! To make the poem pop (and crackle), there has to be at least one element in your VISTA that surprises the reader. Think of those opening lines to William Carlos Williams's wheelbarrow—"so much depends," that stress of a normal tool's importance is a surprising tone. T.S. Eliot's night spread out like a patient etherized is a surprising image, Margaret Atwood's fish hook, and so on. Start with a surprise!
3 The poem is so polished it doesn't leave any place for purchase in the imagination. Break things up a bit, make it jagged, avail yourself of the power of ambiguity. Ugliness is a form of beauty.
4 Something isn't working in this section. Cut up the words, rearrange them randomly, rearrange them from last to front—see if we can't revive the corpse with a little violent electricity.

Part III

Letters Home

13 MFA vs. NYC vs. MBA

Timothy Taylor

Campus Botanica

It's one of my favourite sights on a UBC campus walk, right up there among the many brilliant visuals to be found on this famously pretty coastal campus. You have your famous Rose Garden up there to the north end of Main Mall, with its vistas of the North Shore mountains. And you have your renowned Reconciliation Pole to the south end, with its deeply convicting story of historical injustice. Those two campus sights are both worth considering to be sure, both worth thinking about. But you also can't miss them, the one being as wide as the horizon, the other as deep as North American history and carved out of an 800-year-old cedar tree by James Hart, Haida master carver and hereditary chief.

What you might miss, and surely gets a lot less Instagram play, is a number of small signs in the turf at the base of trees and shrubs along the mall. They read oddly, not your typical botanical garden signs, or not merely. They inform you that the words "Yew" and "bow" are the same in Nisga'a and 11 other First Nation languages. Or that the Incense Cedar tree smells like pencils because that's the stuff of which wooden pencils have long been made.

Or this one:

> Westernsnowberry
> *Symphoricarpos accidentalis*
> **Snowberries,** associated with snakes, corpses, and ghosts,
> are the saskatoon berries in the land of the dead.
> (Stl'atl'imx)
> North America CAPRIFOLIACEAE

I like these half-cryptic signs for being a wrinkle in the reading day, text in the wrong place with not quite the expected content. I like them even more for being the creative output of a student with the UBC School of Creative Writing, working on a course we developed in partnership with the SEEDS

DOI: 10.4324/9781032614144-17

Sustainability Program in which students worked with a wood engineer and the campus arborist in designing text-based campus installations.

The course—which internally we just called "the SEEDS course"—was run in 2014, just a year after I arrived at UBC. As creative writing pedagogy, it wasn't typical. But the output of the course was the more surprising, including poems in trees, a *cento* written on stones that stood in a circle around the Ladner Clock Tower, birdhouses with the engraved stories of refugee students and these little signs, a blending of science and poetry and ancient story, combined in a way that caught your glance and paused your day.

Campus Botanica was the name of the sign project. Saskia Wolsak was the Creative Writing student who conceived it, who braided together her interest in botany and science communications, who consulted the *Musqueam* and other First Nation elders on the various stories and details. And while the 120 original signs might have been culled by natural forces since—chewed up by lawnmowers or "borrowed" for dorm room souvenirs—Wolsak's text is largely intact. It is un-remaindered.

Surely that's part of what satisfies me, seeing a student "publication" still in active use after so many years. But as ten years have now passed since I arrived, from an unexpected path, to be a Creative Writing professor at UBC, I see these signs also as an indication of what may be the most important lesson I've learned about teaching Creative Writing. And I learned that lesson from students.

Boom Time in Program Land

A ten-year active lifespan is long for published words these days, though not so much for academics (published or otherwise). Academics, for the most part, hope to be on a track to become academics from about the moment they start grad school. This does not describe my path into the profession, however. I'm just ten years into my life as a Creative Writing professor and not young. A glance at our departmental faculty page reveals that I studied business and economics, arriving here by a late and non-standard route. All this to say that I didn't follow the route as laid out in Chad Harbach's Famous Essay.

You remember the Famous Essay, of course. It ran in *n+1* magazine Issue #10 back in 2010. Then it ran again in 2014 as the eponymous introduction to the FSG/n+1 published anthology (same year as my SEEDS course, as it happens). But even if you didn't pick up either the magazine or the anthology, you heard about it later. There was chatter. There was perturbation. Sides were taken.

MFA vs. NYC, Harbach writes. These were the two lodestars in the contemporary writing life: the Program and the Metropolis, roughly. But not—as I mistakenly thought picking up *n+1* those few fateful years before I entered Program Land myself—because these were the two alternative and mutually exclusive ways in which one might be *guided in the process of becoming a writer*. Instead, I discovered actually reading him, Harbach was arguing that these were the two dominating ways to *live as a writer after getting your MFA*.

You streamed up into the booming Creative Writing pedagogy sector, ran this argument. Or you left the leafy confines of whatever campus had been your incubator and flew off to where the really tall buildings were in your area, you found some scribbler's job or other, and commenced a whirlwind of attendance at publishing parties.

Those were the emblematic options. Either way, let's be real, you started with an MFA.

"Of the Conspicuously Young writers I've mentioned above," writes David Foster Wallace in his posthumously published contribution to the anthology, written way back in 1988, "I know of none who've not had some training in either a graduate or undergraduate writing department" (74).

More succinctly, from Harbach himself: "We are all MFA's now" (11).

Setting aside the oddly arch phrasing—and whether or not I felt excluded or enticed by this framing at the time of original reading, when I was still several years shy of even *thinking* about academia—what I hear now is a lot of Miranda Priestly in both comments. A lot of: *Everybody wants to be us*. And what comes with that (with unswerving human certainty, I submit) is a nervous eye cast into the future. Where does this tide carry us?

This sort of questioning is what smart people do when booms are underway, clearly. (Ask Michael Burry. Or Bill Ackman. Or Jesse Livermore, for that matter, though he's long dead.) But it's the questioning that pretty much *everybody* does in the wake of booms that have already busted. Creative Writing wasn't busting anytime soon in either 1988 or 2010 or 2014, as it turns out. And it isn't busting now, on the evidence. But it's notable to me that both Wallace and Harbach were indeed writing in the wake of *other* busted booms, in fact, *uber busted booms*. Wallace's essay came just a year after 1987's Black Monday, when the Dow Jones dropped almost 23% (Maley). Harbach first published "MFA vs. NYC" a year following the 2009 financial meltdown when for several days it was even money whether the global banking system would survive. If you hear the MBA of my title creeping in here, you aren't imagining things. Still, set that financial thought aside for now. *Put a pin in it. We'll circle back*.

The point being: the future was considered both by Wallace at the very beginning of the Program Boom, and again by Harbach as it reached a point of maturity some 20 years later. And what the long Program Boom seemed to mean for both writers was that there was a lot more Program to come. The Metropolises of the publishing industry were by 2014 already striking Harbach as "cautious and embattled, devoted to hanging on" (27). And Program Land, with its reliable money and its flood of new students, was going to look a lot more attractive to MFA grads as a place to ply the writing trade as a direct result.

This is the money we're talking about here. And 20 years earlier, Wallace saw the same thing in all those proliferating professorships and lecturing positions, teaching assistant jobs and editing positions at university lit mags that grew along with the rise in CW enrolment. "Programs," Wallace wrote, having just emerged from his own, "tend to be a sweet deal" (73).

Excuse My Gap Analysis

So, this MBA business. It's time to confess. I have one.

Indeed, when the Dow Jones dropped 23% that fateful day in 1987—right about when David Foster Wallace was graduating from the University of Arizona's MFA Program (Cruz), as it happens—I was a freshly minted MBA, just out of the Smith School of Business at Canada's Queen's University, a couple months into training for my first ever real job at the Toronto Dominion Bank, one of the "Big Five" in Canada's banking sector.

Imagine the mood that day. Or better, imagine the mood the next day when the *Globe and Mail* was able to crystalize exactly what had gone down the day before with its front page, above-the-fold headline

Panic Sweeps Financial Markets Smashing Records of 1929 Crash (Lem)

We financiers-in-the-wings were all thinking about the future that moment, I assure you. And yes, we survived. Financial markets themselves survived only to crash in the late 90s (biotech), then crash once more before Harbach's Famous Essay came out (real estate). By that point, I'd long quit banking and was almost 20 years deep into a freelance magazine career which I had not yet accepted was itself crashing. (Which it was, because print magazines were crashing, and I'd eventually come to accept that too though not until a fateful UBC job posting got me thinking. But that is a whole other story.)

What I'm pointing out is that I'm still enough of a Smith MBA grad (and after ten years probably just enough of a Creative Writing prof) to wonder where we are now relative to where Harbach and Wallace thought we might by now end up in MFAland.

In addressing that gap, it needs to be acknowledged what these two prognostications got quite right. And in that regard, Harbach says it best in the anthology in his own eponymous "MFA vs. NYC" essay, sounding quite a lot like someone who might have graduated from a business school (not Harbach's Harvard) (Foley)

> A business model that relies on tuition and tax revenue …; the continued unemployability of twentysomethings; and the continued hunger of undergraduates for undemanding classes, does seem more forward-looking than one that relies on overflow income from superfluous books by celebrities, politicians, and their former lovers. (28)

On the pure economics of this point, Harbach has been overwhelmingly right. Were these matching trades possible, no hedge fund betting on literary publishers and betting against universities over the past ten years would have survived. Program Land has continued to flourish and grow, if at a bit more stately a pace than previously. Literary publishing meanwhile ... well, nothing measurable has "flourished" on that side of things for writers over the same timeframe in Canada or the United States: not advances, not publicity budgets, not column inches devoted to book coverage, not editing jobs.

Of course, Harbach didn't nail everything. That's the nature of estimates. But even where his own "MFA vs. NYC" essay seems quaint or anachronistic, it has guided us to crucial evolutions in Program Land over the years since its writing.

His quip about "undemanding classes" is an example (28). Maybe this was true in those early years when Creative Writing saw itself as the cool kid smoking outside the English department, *keeping it real.* We wanted to be writers in Program Land, after all, not scholars. And ranking artwork—the true value of which we understand to be ineffable—could not possibly be more scholarly and *bourgeois.*

Maybe for mid-century prose writers and readers. Today, any program growing rapidly within the overall academy—the UBC School of Creative Writing within the UBC Faculty of Arts over the past 12 years, for example—will find itself standardizing practices including grade consistency. If you have 12 MFA students and a few sections of fiction and poetry, that's one thing. At 85 sections of everything from podcasting to climate writing to video game scripts, serving a population of 5,000 undergrads and 150 ongoing MFA candidates in any given year—UBC numbers, but the idea transposes—you're trading on the Big Board and all the regular institutional scrutiny will apply.

That said, the more crucial and telling gap between Harbach's projections in 2014 and what has manifested in Program Land today lies in the actual substance of what's being taught in these various classrooms. With a particular focus on the MFA programs here, you can assess this shift in what students are now reading. Harbach in 2014 described two competing canons. Program Land had the short story writers, the minimalist brush strokes of Raymond Carver, Ann Beattie, Richard Ford, Joyce Carol Oates, Denis Johnson and the like. Over in the Metropolis, you had your novelists: Philip Roth, Don DeLillo, Thomas Pynchon, Paul Auster et al. (Harbach 18–20). "Maximalists all," via Mark McGurl (375).

Excuse me, "canon"? I hear you ask.

Well, yes. Exactly. If you did a coffee spit take reading "canon," it merely indicates that you live in some proximity to Program Land today, where if you declared a canonical war between two notional sides—minimalists versus maximalists, or something else entirely—neither would show up.

The canon is dead, and we have killed it, you and I.

The Editorial Board Simulation

I use a workshop device now in almost all MFA workshops. I call it the editorial board simulation. It works like this. When you write a piece for submission, you are asked also to identify a real world publication where you would ideally like to see the piece run. You're also asked to describe the publication to the workshop in a short preamble to your story. During the workshop itself, the group then plays the role of the editorial board of that publication, treating the submission as a story that they had themselves assigned, and working on it the way editors and writers do in such cases, which is jointly trying to get something ready for publication.

It's a conceit. Nobody has to actually place their work in the chosen publication, although many do, which is a significant bonus. It levels up the whole classroom experience for the students in question. It also gives me several moments a year to privately do an endzone dance upon seeing some measurable publishing success in the world.

I use this technique for both fiction and nonfiction, as I teach both. It works better for nonfiction in the sense that literary short fiction is only rarely assigned and mostly submitted on spec. But I find a willingness to suspend belief for the purpose.

But something else too. The approach meshes well with another ongoing project of mine at UBC, which is to develop ways that students can engage in interdisciplinary projects. The SEEDS course was just the first instance, a project that put our MFA students into contact with experts from a range of other fields: sustainability, engineering, landscape architecture, as well as Campus and Community Planning. Since then I've pursued other projects including collaborations involving doctors, historians, physicists and art curators. But the idea here is that having pushed students out of their comfort zones, it is reassuring to sketch into place a publication end point, and a specific implied audience. Even in simulation, it's liberating to work as if the piece in question is *already assigned*. You have the gig—be it for *The Atlantic, Electric Lit, Nature, Paris Review*, you name it—now relax and write the piece. This simulated editorial board really works.

As for seeking interdisciplinary opportunities, I don't mind acknowledging that the habit carries over from my pre-university freelance years, when I was constantly nosing around in other people's lives and spaces: researching, interviewing, observing. Originally, I thought academia would be all about this kind of thing, botanists and economists and historians of Japanese political history all in happy conversation over the watercooler. It wasn't. (And I should have known. Organizational silos are just as real in academia as they are in business, maybe worse given peer colleagues determine everything from our course load to our merit pay, our service assignments to the timing of our coveted study leaves.)

But motivating the combination—interdisciplinary work for students, an editorial board simulation to handle output—is really my response to what I see as an evolution in our student body. And that evolution has everything to do with those collapsing canons.

Any Creative Writing professor could write a lot on this topic of *why* the canon faded, why the very idea of a list of sacred texts is impossibly outdated.

But in my brutal summary it just has to do with trust. *These are the greatest writers in the English language? These are the people I'm supposed to read?* A decade of social awakening later—a decade since many white people first learned of #BLM, a decade since #MeToo, since the discovery of unmarked Indigenous graves at residential schools (Austen), since the 45th President of the freaking United States (whose name I will not utter)—the response to these questions for many people is going to be: *says who?*

We are no longer "ingloriously" labouring, as Wallace has it, in "countless obscure graduate writing workshops" in a pursuit of a realism defined by "Field Marshal Lish (who ought to know)" (*Girl* 265). We couldn't do that if we wanted to (and nobody wants to) because the era of submitting to someone else's vision of what our writing should be has disappeared behind us in a mist of scepticism and disillusionment. Gordon Lish, whom *MFA vs. NYC* depicts as a notoriously abusive Creative Writing prof (Spanbauer 208; Blumenkranz 210–14, 216, 220), is no longer the agreed authority on depicting reality in prose any more than Raymond Carver or Amy Hempel, or Shakespeare, or Wallace himself for that matter

This is not to say that students don't read anymore, or read recommended books or even ask for recommendations. But from one faculty member to the next, from one student to the next, you wouldn't anticipate agreement on any one set of books that must be read as exemplary. The common recommendation would be pedagogy books instead, circulated to faculty by anxious program leadership instructing on the topic of how to support the emergent canonless state that results. And if there is a *sacred* remaining, it's the student's own views as expressed in workshop and in their own writing, which will only on the rarest of occasions reflect a debt to the mid-century contemporary masters such that the consensus might be offended.

So yes, reading lists will be tweaked and tuned to correct their bias towards dominant groups. And yes, those with power, including professors, will be asked to listen. And students will stand to accept their new authority in these affairs, not because we gave them permission, but because they assumed it from the cultural moment, awakened to the *reality* that the police do not always serve and protect, men do indeed abuse their authority over women on occasion, and some politicians lie with every breath. So does a professor know everything there is to know about writing? Of course not. They might not know *anything* relevant to the student themselves, not their experience, not their real identity, not the truest of truths about what the world is *to* them.

This is an ontological and not an epistemic issue. In a climate where distrust is omnidirectional, and in a broad way justifiable, only the student can ever say what is sacred. And in that framing of the student self—disembedded from the hierarchies of power and taste that might otherwise have gated their progress one way or the other, the self who is empowered to ask *Cui bono?*—what canon could remain but the student themselves? What topic remains?

I had an instructive experience before introducing the Editorial Board Simulation workshop model. It was in a fiction class. The piece in workshop that day was an excerpt from a science fiction novel, in which a race of alien people struggle with oppression at the hands of a different alien race. There is a war going on. There is suffering. There is resistance. And here a hand is raised followed by difficult questions. *Had the submitting writer been through a war, faced oppression, confronted the risks of resistance?*

The student who raised their hand did so precisely because they could answer "yes" to each of these and estimated the submitting writer could not. And they were right. Still, the submitted writer protested. And a brittle exchange ensued.

I wondered afterwards: should the submitting student *not* have allowed their imagination to tend in this direction? Given they were working in a speculative framework, talking about imaginary beings, was appropriation even possible under the circumstances? Were they restricted in such entirety to writing only about themselves and their direct experience?

Then I wondered what would have happened if the student who raised the questions had agreed to the assignment in advance. Simulated or otherwise, would that agreement between an imaginary editorial board and a writer on imaginary assignment have been enough? Which is to say: would a simulated handshake between the editor with war experience and the writer with a speculative imagination have been enough to give the work the *sacrality* the moment demanded?

On Heroism

"The novelist who converts heroic effort into effortless prose has been a standard figure since Flaubert," Harbach wrote, in 2014 ("MFA" 25–26). No arguing with that. Of Jonathan Franzen, though, Harbach continues: "this project comes to seem like … the willed effort of the entire culture to create for itself a novel that it still wants to read" (26).

Here Harbach and I part ways. The novelistic project from Flaubert to Franzen was always about the author exerting the willed effort, estimating what the culture wanted to read. And the culture had all along reserved the right to change its mind.

Plus, Harbach clearly hadn't read his Flaubert all the way to the end, to *Bouvard et Pécuchet*. Flaubert who—like Wallace, literary critic Christopher Mooney points out in his brilliant blog *Hexagon*—grappled with a sprawling and heroic novel until the text wrapped itself around his throat and throttled him:

> And then, on 8 May, while writing the final chapter at his desk in the garden shed, under the etching by Callot and the glass eyes of Loulou, his brain, overloaded with the contents of the 1,500 titles he had by then stuffed into it while researching the novel—books on agronomy, arboriculture,

> gardening, canning, distillery, chemistry, anatomy, physiology, medicine, nutrition, astronomy, zoology, geology, archaeology, architecture, museology, Celtic religion, antiquities, history, biography, politics, love, philosophy, theatre, literary criticism, grammar, aesthetics, gymnastics, spiritualism, magnetism, mesmerism, logic, religion, education, phrenology, drawing, natural history, morality, music and town planning—after ingesting all that, plus a stack of insipid historical fiction, his brain burst an artery, and he died on the spot.

A "heroic effort" in service of what? Even if we accept that all Flaubert's voracious curiosity was in search of masterful depiction, it clearly wasn't effortless. And the subject of depiction remains an open question: brilliance, foolishness?

Delusion, one must agree, is a distinct possibility. Because that whole depiction business has long been going the way of the buggy whip. And the automobile passing at speed, kicking up a great cloud of silky, choking dust: that's everybody else's opinion on everything, every thought and non-thought, every Insta, every Snap, every Tweet.

Sure that final novel killed Flaubert. But that's only because we didn't get to him first.

The QMI Course & Conclusions

I loved the SEEDS course that sent our UBC writers out into and onto campus. I've already said that, but it bears repeating. I look back and I remember how generally positive those workshops ended up being. One feature in particular stands out: the writing was all so energetically directed *outwards*.

We sat in a workshop just like any fiction or nonfiction MFA workshop. We talked to each other about text composition. But we talked to other people too. We talked to an engineer about how to build installations to carry the text. We talked to the campus arborist about how the text installations could then be sited in the environment around us.

And all the while, the reader hovered at the edge of the room, notional, but real enough to be sensed there waiting. The reader was *everyone else on campus*.

That course wasn't picked up the following year, though there was interest. There were administrative reasons, the less addressed the better. Only last year did something really just as promising come along, something with all the features of a course that I'd been looking for to both accommodate and capitalize on the contemporary learning moment that we've been sketching here, a time of complicated sacreds and delicate strictures.

And so emerged a new collaboration, as stretched a cross-disciplinary undertaking as any I've attempted previously, all the way from my creative world at the north edge of campus, near the Rose Garden, all the way south to the rigorous and at times inscrutable scientific undertakings of the Blusson Quantum Matter Institute, itself not terribly far from the Reconciliation Pole.

I'll try to avoid the Flaubertian outcome in the book I've agreed to write about what they do at the Blusson Quantum Matter Institute. Every nonfiction magazine assignment I've ever experienced could be plotted in the two dimensions of comprehension difficulty and my own degree of fascination. Suffice it to say that on this assignment—in simultaneously trying to get my head around quantum uncertainty, wave functions, one-dimensional materials and quantum entanglement—I'm pushed up to the vanishing upper right corner of my own chart of experience.

But we ran a class too. And here is where the SEEDS course finally passed the baton. We put an equal number of Creative Writing MFAs and QMI PhD candidates into the same class. And we tasked them with writing a popular article about a quantum physics topic.

Some observations:

1 There was easy agreement that in a time of scepticism—amid anti-vax sentiment, climate change denial, and when estimates of the number of flat-earthers ranges from 30 to 120 *million*—that writing well about science was not just a calling but a social and societal urgency.
2 When Science and Creative Writing students gather in the same room with a common goal to write the same kind of material, they see advantages in the skill set of the discipline *other* than their own.
3 When the target publication is one never previously considered—the popular science magazine never typically having been on radar for either an aspiring research scientist or literary writers—the attentiveness of students to their audience is greatly heightened.

We all sat nervously in that workshop on the first day. We all thought about what we did not know. We talked about scepticism, about storytelling, about persuasion. And then we traipsed off to the Quantum Matter Institute to talk to the scientists there, to be amazed, to be intimidated, to choose the area of wonder that we would explore and try to explain.

We simulated the editorial board for these workshops too. We sat as the editors of *Nautilus, WIRED, Nature, Science News, Popular Science* and others. We read pieces together on exponential growth and laser-induced breakdown spectroscopy, profiles of scientists working at QMI in such areas as crystal growth or magnetism. And here's a beautiful and counterintuitive thing to realize as an instructor: nobody in that room ever knew *entirely* what was going on at any given moment. For every person in that room—every MFA and PhD candidate, the auditing faculty members from the Belkin Gallery and the QMI itself—some part of the communications or the technical picture was missing. But the project was common. And all the while, that notional reader hovered at the edge of the room, real enough to be sensed there waiting.

Our attention bent to that reader. And we brought ourselves vigorously to the project of addressing them. We attended to that task with dedication and calling.

We're running the QMI course again next year. If you ask me in five years and it's still going strong, I'll count it the one out-of-the-park home run of my UBC career. And I'll walk out into the mall after the final day of that semester, out there along the grass verge, north from the Reconciliation Pole past Earth Sciences, the Beatty Biodiversity Museum, the Rose Garden distant, the mountains beyond.

I'll look for snowberries as I walk. Or *ghostberries* as I now know to call them, *Symphoricarpos accidentalis*. I'll look for those small white beaded fruit, inedible, but on the fingers, smelling faintly of wintergreen.

Works Cited

Austen, Ian. "'Horrible History': Mass Grave of Indigenous Children Reported in Canada." *The New York Times*, 28 May 2021, https://www.nytimes.com/2021/05/28/world/canada/kamloops-mass-grave-residential-schools.html.

Blumenkranz, Carla. "Seduce the Whole World." *MFA vs NYC: The Two Cultures of American Fiction*, edited by Chad Harbach. n+1/Faber, 2014, pp. 209–21.

Cruz, Johnny. "University to Host Memorial Tribute to Alumnus David Foster Wallace." *University Marketing & Communications*, 24 Apr. 2009, University of Arizona, https://news.arizona.edu/story/university-to-host-memorial-tribute-to-alumnus-david-foster-wallace.

Harbach, Chad. "MFA vs. NYC." *MFA vs NYC: The Two Cultures of American Fiction*, edited by Chad Harbach. n+1/Faber, 2014, pp. 9–28.

Foley, Ciaran. "Harbach on Inspiration, Writing, and 'Dudes'." *The Harvard Crimson*, 17 Apr. 2012, https://www.thecrimson.com/article/2012/4/17/chad_harbach_fielding_feature/.

Lem, Gail. "Panic Sweeps Financial Markets Smashing Records of 1929 Crash." *Globe and Mail*, 20 Oct. 1987, pp. 1+.

Maley, Matt. "The Real Reason for the 1987 Crash, as Told by a Salomon Brothers Veteran." *CNBC*, Trading Nation, 3 Nov. 2017, https://www.cnbc.com/2017/10/16/cause-of-black-monday-in-1987-as-told-by-a-trader-who-lived-through-it.html.

McGurl, Mark. *The Program Era: Postwar Fiction and the Rise of Creative Writing*. Harvard UP, 2009.

Mooney, Christopher. "Reading Contempt: Why Books Are for Schnooks." *Hexagon*, 3 Sept. 2023, https://thehexagonstack.substack.com/p/reading-contempt.

Spanbauer, Tom. "Untitled Interlude." *MFA vs NYC: The Two Cultures of American Fiction*, edited by Chad Harbach. n+1/Faber, 2014, pp. 208–08.

Voce, Antonio, Leyland Cecco, and Chris Michael. "'Cultural Genocide': The Shameful History of Canada's Residential Schools—Mapped." *The Guardian*, 6 Sept. 2021, https://www.theguardian.com/world/ng-interactive/2021/sep/06/canada-residential-schools-Indigenous-children-cultural-genocide-map.

Wallce, David Foster. "The Fictional Future." *MFA vs NYC: The Two Cultures of American Fiction*, edited by Chad Harbach. n+1/Faber, 2014. pp. 73–80.
Wallce, David Foster. *Girl with Curious Hair*. Norton, 1989.
Ward, Kevin. "What Is the Reconciliation Pole?" *Student Services*, University of British Columbia, 3 Mar. 2020, https://students.ubc.ca/ubclife/what-reconciliation-pole.

Professor Taylor's Recurrent Writing Comments

1 Specify. The room is messy. With what? Close your eyes, visualize, then tell us exactly what you see. Specific descriptive details give you authority in the material and allows the reader to attach to the story more surely.
2 Understand the critical function of scenes, over exposition and narrative summary. Scenes are where readers attach to our characters emotionally. When the reader senses a character in a single moment, with choices to make that will affect the future, the reader begins to calculate stakes. Upsides and downsides. Outcomes they might prefer. And that's when you have them.
3 Don't default to the present tense because it feels more "active." It might be. It isn't always. And the past tense implies a narrator who is on the far side of the narrative arc in question, with perspective and new understanding that they might share.

14 From the Pool to the Page

What Coaching Swimming Taught Me about Teaching Creative Writing

Angie Abdou

After over 20 years teaching Creative Writing, and publishing eight books of fiction and creative nonfiction myself, I experienced a crisis of faith. I could no longer articulate the value of my teaching. I worried my income, and, consequently, raising my own children, relied on selling students a bag of impossible dreams and false promises. Every year, aspiring writers came to me sure they had a book in their future, maybe even several books. These keen writers seemed equally convinced that the experience of publishing would improve their lives, bringing them buckets of money, widespread attention, and even the ever-elusive self-validation. With a sizeable stack of published books myself, I doubted that publication (for any of my students lucky enough to achieve it) would improve finances, fame or self-worth.

I succumbed to cynicism. I worried that we mislead students, granting them Creative Writing degrees and encouraging dreams of publishing when we know the challenges (financial, psychic, even professional). Worse yet, I struggled with guilt, wondering if we Creative Writing teachers–and our whole programs–engage in intentional deceit. Our livelihood does after all count on these students believing in the pot of gold at the end of the Creative Writing degree rainbow. A commonly cited statistic is that one to 2% of submitted manuscripts get accepted for publication: for years, the "Submissions" page at *The Fiddlehead*, Canada's oldest anglophone literary journal still in print (and one centred at the University of New Brunswick's robust Creative Writing program), stated "acceptance is around 2%" (*Fiddlehead*). None of my former students makes a living as a writer. About a dozen have published books. Most–maybe all–were, understandably, disappointed by that experience. A typical print run at a Canadian literary press is a thousand books. If a writer makes 10% of the cover price and sells out a first print run, that *successful* writer will earn about two thousand dollars, for years of work. Moreover, independent literary presses have notoriously low budgets for promotion, and writers often find themselves pedaling their books to their own friends and families. Plus, after about six months (or less), the publishing cycle ends, and reviewers move onto the next round of new books. I have students who have published good novels and never received a single review. To witness the heartbreak of an aspiring artist, thrilled to

DOI: 10.4324/9781032614144-18

be accepted for publication, release a book to absolute silence made me question my own mentorship role. A key irony is that I, like most writers I know in Canada, could not live without a second income beyond the volatile, and low, income I receive selling and speaking about my well-received novels and memoirs. My professorial salary pays me both to write and to teach writing, yet stable professorial jobs in Canada are as rare as publishing contracts. In a double exclusivity, very, very few of the student-writers I teach are likely to publish books or to have stable teaching incomes for an expertise in book publishing.

During this dip in my passion for my Creative Writing profession, I fell into a new role–swim coach. Though I'd been away from the pool deck for about 20 years, I did grow up swimming with the Thunder Bay Thunderbolts, the Moose Jaw Kinsmen Flying Fins, the Regina Optimist Dolphins and finally the varsity team at the University of Western Ontario. As a teenager, I trained for two hours every day before school and put in two more hours in the pool after school. I loved everything about the sport: the thrill of finally making an impossible set, the endorphin high of pushing the body to its limits, the lifelong friendships founded on shared sacrifice and commitment, the pride of getting in a grueling predawn workout before most of my classmates got out of bed, the connection to other athletes around the country and world, the travel with a purpose, the extended group of pseudo-parents found in coaches and chaperones, and even the ubiquitous smell of chlorine. Many of my non-athletic accomplishments in life—from completing my doctorate to writing book after book to winning a coveted tenure-track faculty position, even to being a multi-tasking parent, I credit to my foundational experience as a young swimmer. Recent neurological studies confirm that when children have the experience of setting and completing goals, as young athletes may do in a more programmatic way than those lacking the calibrated structure of sport, that pattern hardwires in the brain, and they carry that work ethic and drive to completion into adulthood (Berkman 2018). I am very good at goals and hard work–swimming made me that way before I even hit high school.

I'm not, then, surprised at how quickly I fell in love with coaching swimmers. The shift in focus and energy was, though, an odd choice: starting a new "career" right at the height of my professorial career, after over 20 years of teaching and right when I needed to focus on getting promoted to full Professor. While others may have been confused by my decision, I felt no surprise at how comfortable I felt on deck, how naturally I adopted the coaching role, how little anxiety I had about swimming taking energy and time away from my "real work," or how much meaning I found in guiding young swimmers. What does surprise me, however, is what coaching swimming teaches me about teaching Creative Writing. I did not expect the new job to change the old, yet it did: rekindling my enthusiasm, increasing my commitment and–most of all–changing the way I find meaning in the writing and learning processes, for myself and for my students.

Noticing my enthusiasm for the pool, and my anxiety around the page, I started to explore the difference in my approach to mentoring swimmers and mentoring writers. Though I fret about my writers' limited publishing opportunities, I have never experienced a moment's worry that none of my swimmers has ever made–and none likely ever will make–the Olympics. I'm not in the least concerned that I mislead my swimmers by asking them to devote hours every day to an activity that will never make them wealthy or famous or even provide a livable income.

Why not? Because I am absolutely convinced of the value of the training process, the benefits of belonging to the club's community and the importance of striving for striving's sake. I see the way swim club adds joy to the athletes' lives and the way daily training gives a sense of purpose, which staves off depression, boredom and existential angst—as well as diverting these swimmers from the many less productive pastimes in the obstacle course of teen life. Of *any* life. I know that finding activities I love to do and then pushing myself toward excellence makes me feel more alive. Every day at the pool, I see this same spark of life igniting in my swimmers.

And here's the thing: writing can work in the *exact same way*. An aspiring writer need not sign a six-figure book deal in order for writing to add value to his or her life. In fact, a book contract might not even be a reliable marker for the worth of a writing life (anymore than making the Olympics will indicate how much happiness swimming has brought to an athlete's life). This little epiphany, though it took its sweet time coming, caused me to think about how I could bring my coach's conviction in the value of process from the pool to the page. How could my writing courses be explicit about the challenges of the business of publishing, while also foregrounding the many ways writing–and working to get good at writing–*can* improve lives?

To answer this question, and to develop a pedagogical philosophy of Creative Writing founded on the answer, I turned to lessons I learned in my training with Canada's National Coaching Certification Program [NCCP]. Here are the five main tips that grew out of that exploration:

Emphasize Process, being Explicit, Specific and Detailed about the Stages that Come before Publication

NCCP is explicit and specific about the stages of athlete development, even providing slide shows and handouts that calibrate progress. Swim Canada follows the NCCP training philosophy, breaking the swimmer's life into five parts: "fundamentals, learn to train, train to train, train to compete, compete to win" (National 2). Those parts are also book-ended with "active start" and "active for life." In "active start," Swim Canada stresses the importance of multisport at a young age. In "active for life," Swim Canada has a well-developed program that keeps swimmers training, and even competing, into their 90s and beyond. These swimming stages—from birth to death—highlight elite competition as one small part of a lifelong commitment to the sport. The program makes clear that only a small fraction of athletes will achieve the elite stage ("compete to win"), but that the other stages have value, not only as steppingstones but in and of themselves. Because each training/learning stage includes detailed definitions, clear expectations of level of commitment and the average number of years required to reach the next stage, athletes (and their parents) are dissuaded from false expectations or even delusions of grandeur, a reality-check one doesn't always see in writing students, some of whom are choosing their author photo part way through their second, or even first, writing course. Anyone can see that getting to the "train to compete" level involves a long, arduous climb, before even contemplating the final "compete to win" stage. The detailed description of the program makes the process—and the intense combination of commitment, talent and luck needed to achieve the final stage—fully explicit. Swim Canada's detailed information sheets also clearly outline the rewards of—and skills achieved in—each individual stage.

I am currently working with a similar progression diagram, at the draft stage, in my writing program. I have book-ended the chart with inspiring a love of reading ("early literacy") at the start and lifelong engagement with books and journaling ("literacy for life") at the end. The middle five stages parallel those of Swim Canada with fundamentals (learning grammar and working toward clear and effective communication and then being introduced to characterization, plot, setting, dialogue and other basic elements of fiction), learn to write (building a daily writing practice while working toward mastery of the fundamental skills), write to write (living the writer's life, engaging with writing communities, participating in literary culture, building craft), write to publish (advancing craft with a focus on rigorous revision while beginning to interact with publishing communities and learning business aspects such as cover letters, query letters, proposals and public presentation), writing as a career (beginning to submit work for publication while also exploring other work available in the publishing industry as well as jobs outside of the publishing industry but suitable to those with a writer's skill set). With a detailed infographic explaining these stages, I am ready to respond to those students who arrive at the first class asking about agents and publishers or the student who gets an A on a 200-level short story and immediately wants to submit to the lit mags. I am also building into the infographic a list of marketable skills acquired at each level, so the students (and their parents) know that students who never make it to the writers' Olympics will leave the program with communication skills valued in the workplace.

Teach Students about Smart Goals

All NCCP certified coaches learn about "S.M.A.R.T goals" (Coach 1). To be useful, goals must be "Specific, Measurable, Achievable, Relevant, and Timebound" (Coach 1). The coaching team starts every season by having the athletes write out their goals, as well as the commitment they make to achieving those goals, detailing the exact steps they will take daily, weekly and monthly to work toward their desired outcomes. We teach the swimmers about short-term goals and long-term goals, and have them articulate weekly goals, monthly goals and season goals. We then meet with them regularly throughout each season to assess their progress and re-evaluate what they need to do to succeed.

I've learned that having aspiring writers complete similar goal sheets allows me to individualize each student's program (because each writer, like each athlete, has unique dreams and will be motivated in unique ways). This process also helps me ask my students important questions that familiarize them with the long, arduous publishing process. For example, is it *specific* to say you want to publish? *Where* do you want to publish? *Why* there? Have you familiarized yourself with the publishing market? What publishers are looking for submissions in your specific genre and style? Who's your audience and what publishing house has best access to that audience? In these questions, we find many students' first specific goal–i.e., to familiarize themselves with the market by reading five books a month and keeping a reading journal, making notes about publishers that appeal to them as well as lessons they can learn from each book. That is a *specific* goal as well as being measurable, achievable, relevant and timebound.

I am also a fan of daily morning pages (as advocated in Julia Cameron's *The Artist's Way*) and regular freewrites (as in *Wild Mind: Living the Writer's Life* by Natalie Goldberg). *Write three pages every morning:* that is a specific, measurable, achievable, relevant and timebound goal for starting writers. I remind the students that just as athletes train, putting in a lot of non-competition lengths before they hit the pool for a big race, so too must writers put in their practice pages. I encourage all students to build those training sessions into their S.M.A.R.T. goal program.

Build Community

The main reason I never have any doubts about the value the swim club adds to our athletes' lives is the importance the other coaches and I put on creating a positive culture and building community. We teach the athletes to support each other through failure, cheer each other through success, help each other through the tough parts of training and share their joy of the sport. Many literary communities include equally supportive writers, but, unfortunately, the less supportive as well. Our swimmers become each other's social security net away from the pool and through those socially trying high-school years. Even when they're not best friends, fellow swim athletes count on each other as a kind of extended family and achieve that warmth and happiness associated with a group of people who truly "get" each other (weird goals, constant eating, chlorine hair and all).

I've realized I can also build community overtly with every class, reminding them, and me, that, for the duration of our time together, we can transform our shared knowledge of what each other is doing, our similar goals and our comparable skills into a support system. Ideally, these connections will extend into other classes and into post-degree life. I challenge my students to sign a contract that not only details appropriate behaviour and helpful contributions during peer critique (standard in many classes), but also outlines other ways the class members will build community. Each class creates an original contract (for large classes, I have students break into smaller community groups). Here are examples of community-building activities different groups might agree to: host monthly potlucks, participate in weekly activity nights, attend public readings together, encourage each other to present work at open mics, establish an annual literary event at the student union, print an end-of-class chapbook, start a book club to support the class journaling project, encourage younger writers by inviting them to open mics and literary events and commit to reading each other's work and providing honest and constructive feedback.

Foster and Value Connection

I mentioned that one of the reasons I'm grateful for my involvement in youth sport is the pseudo-parents swimming provides via coaches, managers and chaperones. When I stepped into a coaching role, I found that sort of connection with young people very meaningful. My time on the pool deck meant giving up a lot of writing hours which led to a decline in my publishing productivity. Before I switched from lifetime swimmer to swim coach, I had just published four books in five years, including a genre shift from novels to memoir, with *Home Ice: Reflections of a Reluctant Hockey Mom in 2018* and *This One Wild Life: A Mother-Daughter Hiking Memoir* in 2021. Colleagues questioned my shifting priorities. I couldn't quite articulate my defence. Then at the end of the season, one of my most improved swimmers approached me with a thank you card. In September, Abbi couldn't even do butterfly; by June she was competing in 100 fly at big city swim meets. She'd not even raced a 200 free and could now swim a perfectly paced 1500 free. That summer, she represented our region at the BC Summer Games (traveling there with her team on a charted airplane!). More important than the many ways Abbi's swimming had progressed, the sport had also boosted her confidence and happiness. These changes in Abbi alone made my time on deck worthwhile. At season's end, Abbi gave me a piece of orange construction paper with block letters in purple crayon reading THANK YOU ANGIE. I reprint the card's contents with Abbi's permission

> Dear Angie, I want to thank you for being the best coach any swimmer could ever ask for. Every single day, you inspire me to be the best I can be. I thank you for being patient while I recite the entire set back to you 500 times to make sure I have it right. I strive to be a coach like you one day in the near future. You, Angie, encourage me so much! You pick me

> up when I feel down, thank you. You could be anywhere in the world, like sitting on a beach in Mexico, but instead you are at the pool coaching me. You by far are the BEST coach I've ever had. I'm very excited for next season! Thank you very much Angie Abdou for being the best swim coach ever. -ABBI WANNAMAKER

I like to show this card to my writing friends and say "This! This means more to me than publishing a book." I think they understand. In an ideal world, I write simply to connect. In the process of developing a career, the reasons for writing grow more complicated, my motivation and goals muddied. Coaching swimming brings me back to that basic appreciation of human connection and reminds me of its importance. There are many ways to connect, and being single-minded helps no writer. With these acute pool-deck reminders of the value of connection, I have also been able to bring that simple pure goal back to the page.

I now try to think of my connection with my writing students in a similar way, as coaching, as unlocking, not career-making. I am not just a university writing instructor doling out skills but also a mentor, a cheerleader, a positive presence and a friendly peer. Aidan Chudleigh, the Australian who currently works as Head Coach at the club where I am Assistant Coach, told me that his coaching mentor taught him that his best feeling as a coach is not having his swimmers qualify for–or even win–nationals but *getting invited to their weddings*. "When you're at a swimmer's wedding, that's when you know you've accomplished something important." Now, I make note of those ways I have a meaningful connection with aspiring writers–maybe even *especially* when those ways have nothing to do with writing.

Prioritize Your Own Writing Practice

My crisis of faith in *teaching* Creative Writing coincided with a crisis of faith in my own writing career. In response to a personal setback, I'd taken a break from writing. Without the reminders of the regular rewards of a writing practice (such as increased empathy, gratitude and awareness), I tended to focus instead on perceived failures on the professional side of my writing life. Who knows what these were? It doesn't really matter. Let's say I'd never won a Giller Prize. I'd never made the *New York Times* bestseller list. I'd never been invited to the Ubud Festival of Writers and Readers in Bali. Whatever. This sense of despair and failure as a writer couldn't help but infect my attitude toward teaching Creative Writing. I know my experience is not unique: too often the demands of the teaching life leave no time and energy for our own writing life.

My re-entry into coaching swimming, on the other hand, followed shortly after an enthusiastic re-entry into training and competition. I *know* my love of the latter bred my conviction in the importance of the former. My passion for doing the sport made me passionate about coaching the sport. Plus, every time I get in the water, I learn something about coaching. Maybe a drill I thought as great is actually stupid. Maybe the way I tell my swimmers to execute a movement is not at all the way it feels when I execute that movement. Maybe some sets are too easy, and others are too hard. Maybe I'm simply reminded how much I love the activity and how much it makes my life better. I only learn how to coach by doing.

Write. Find a way. Writing is crucial to being a good writing teacher.

***

Reflecting on my time at the pool helped me reframe my role as Creative Writing professor with an emphasis on the relationship between goals and happiness, the importance of an individual approach to each athlete/artist and the role of human connection in coaching/teaching. Yes, neither swimming nor writing will likely ever make my athletes and artists rich or famous. But now I tell both: if swimming brings you joy and a sense of purpose, swim; and if writing brings you joy and a sense of purpose, write. Know that neither owes you fame nor fortune as a reward for your commitment and hard work, but also be alert to the specific and multitudinous ways that devotion to an activity you love improves your life.

Works Cited

Abdou, Angie. *Home Ice: Reflections of a Reluctant Hockey Mom*. ECW Press, 2018.

Abdou, Angie. *This One Wild Life: A Mother-Daughter Hiking Memoir*. ECW Press, 2021.

Berkman, Elliot T. "The Neuroscience of Goals and Behavior Change." *Consulting Psychology Journal*, vol. 70, no. 1, Mar. 2018, pp. 28–44.

Cameron, Julia. *The Artist's Way: A Spiritual Path to Higher Creativity*. Penguin, 1992.

Coach Foundation. "Coaching Techniques: SMART." 2023, https://coachfoundation.com/blog/smart-coaching-model/.

Fiddlehead. "Submissions." *The Fiddlehead*. 14 Apr. 2009. Internet Archive. https://web.archive.org/web/20090414080413/http://www.thefiddlehead.ca/submission.html.

Goldberg, Natalie. *Wild Mind: Living the Writer's Life*. Bantam, 1990.

National Coaching Certification Program. "Long-Term Athlete Development Information for Parents." n.d., https://coach.ca/sites/default/files/2020-02/CAC_7516A_11_LTAD_English_Brochure_FINAL.pdf.

Professor Abdou's Recurrent Comments on Student Writing

As with swimming, I tend to focus on basic technique and getting the small details right. I give tips to help prose writers improve their sentences knowing that when good sentences add up, they can turn into good stories.

1. Avoid weak verbs. Every time you finish a story, circle every *is/was/were* and then do whatever you can to get rid of as many as possible. Strong verbs make for more powerful sentences which make for better writing.
2. Follow Orwell's famous advice: if you can cut a word, do.
3. While you're at it, follow Orwell's other famous advice: any time you see a combination of words you're accustomed to seeing in print, strike out the phrase and find a new combination of words.

15 The Climate Crisis in the Creative Writing Classroom

Catherine Bush

I'm writing this as climate scientists declare the recent, unprecedented temperatures of 2023 "absolutely gobsmackingly bananas"—after a Canadian, and global, summer of wildfires, heat domes and floods (Carrington). As if anyone needed reminding, although it often appears we do, climate disruption is not a future threat but a present reality. Given this immediacy, it seems crucial to figure out how to bring the climate crisis into the Creative Writing classroom. If as writers we aim to respond to the complexities of our individual and societal worlds through imaginative practices while teaching students how to do the same, how can we fail to contend with the fire burning in the middle of the room?

The question is how—how to address our climate crisis without thoroughly depressing students and depriving them of agency and hope? Rather, I've searched for ways to offer students a sense of imaginative possibility and new ways of engaging with the world. I will outline some of my strategies for what I might call "climate-responsive" writing in three different contexts: a graduate Creative Writing MFA program; an e-learning module for provincial undergraduates; and in two undergraduate Creative Writing workshops.

To be clear, I'm not arguing that all Creative Writing students should be compelled to write *about* the climate crisis—to make it the primary focus of their work. I am inviting students to consider how they can bring an awareness of this crucial driver of our existential condition into the imaginative worlds they create, particularly when these worlds endeavour to represent our own with some degree of realism. The climate crisis isn't an 'environmental' or a 'scientific' problem that exists somewhere over there: it is seamed into the matter and manner of all our lives. Imaginative realism that consistently ignores this reality creates a false realism. Of landscape art, Neil Evernden knows, "The artist makes the world personal—known, loved, feared or whatever, but *not neutral*" (100). More pointedly, in *The Ecocriticism Reader: Landmarks in Literary Ecology*, Scott Sanders notes,

> All fiction is a drawing of charmed circles, since we can write about only a piece of the world. [...] Much contemporary fiction seems to

DOI: 10.4324/9781032614144-19

> be barren in part because it draws such tiny, cautious circles, in part because it pretends that nothing lies beyond its timid boundaries. (183)

In her article "Climate Change and the Struggle for Genre," which appears in the anthology *Anthropocene Reading*, Stephanie Lemenager writes, "The question of what it means to be human in this ecological moment and how to narrate the problem of 'being human' lies at the center of Anthropocene thinking" (Chapter 12). While the term Anthropocene may be a contested one and our impact may remain small over geological timespans of billions of years, Lemenager's words can serve as a useful guide for thinking about contemporary literary realism. What follows are some of my attempts to respond to her call and overcome the lost opportunities if CW teaching does *not* address the climate crisis.

For 14 years, from two years after the program's founding by original Director Constance Rooke in 2006, I was the Coordinator of the University of Guelph's Creative Writing MFA, a satellite graduate program located in Toronto, an hour from Guelph, housed on the north campus of Humber College. As Coordinator, I taught the MFA's core Plenary courses, two distinctive reading courses, Writers on Writing and Writers in the World, offered in alternate years. The Plenaries, which bring together all students in the program—two cohorts of 13 students writing in a diversity of genres—once a week during the fall semester, function as a colloquium, combining short lectures, student presentations, discussions and professional visitors. Every year, I adapted and updated course reading material, a mixture of primary texts and essays by writers broadly on the aesthetics and ethics of writing, on craft and the varied, complex issues of constructing a writing life. One of the questions that fuelled my conception of these courses, which, while distinct, I endeavoured to have speak to each other, was: How do we write now? And, relatedly: What do we write now? It was never my pedagogical place to provide answers, only to open up for students expanded realms of possibility and engagement. My pedagogical framework for both Plenaries welled from this core question: How do we pay attention as writers—on the page and in the world? Entwined with that 'how' is necessarily a 'what': what are the presences we bring to the page, the absences (historical, political, cultural as well as personal) that we gesture to, and those that we fail to acknowledge?

I often began the semester by referring to a crucial lesson taught to me when, as a fellow at the Bread Loaf Writers' Conference in the summer of 2000, assisting the esteemed naturalist and writer Barry Lopez in the classroom, I listened as Lopez pointed out how the words 'tender' and 'attention' share an etymological root in the Latin verb *tendere*—'to reach towards, to stretch.' Reaching need not be just as one grabs an object but as one extends towards another in a relationship where there's a possibility of response or reciprocity. Lopez then asked students to write about the landscape they'd just walked through on the way class, to describe it tenderly without using the word. What resulted from this exercise were acts of specific, lively noticing, this being the lesson that Lopez was imparting to us. Tenderness focuses our attention.

In 2021, the first year we gathered in person after pandemic closures, I asked my MFA students what the term "climate fiction" meant to them. What I heard most emphatically was that they considered it a genre, a dystopic one, rooted in post-apocalyptic survivalist narratives set after some kind of global disaster—not a strand in realistic narratives or part of the texture of the world they might summon on the page. Examples might range from Margaret Atwood's speculative MaddAddam trilogy to Jeff Vandermeer's *Borne* to, closer to home, the novel *Moon of the Crusted Snow* by indigenous writer Waubgeshig Rice. I wanted to shift these post-apocalyptic assumptions, not because I felt students should be writing something they or I considered "climate fiction" but because a realism that completely ignored the impact of our amplifying fossil fuel use and the climate disruptions caused by this—unpredictable and extreme weather, magnified storms, which are not just backdrop or 'setting' but shaping, even curtailing, forces in our collective lives—seems, once again, a false realism. How could we bring an awareness of climate disruption to the page not necessarily as subject matter but as presence seamed into the world our characters or subjectivities inhabit? As Sanders observes, "The gospel of ecology has become an *intellectual* commonplace. But it is not yet an *emotional* one" (194). And how might we expand our range of awareness beyond the wholly human to the rest of the biosphere also severely impacted by human behaviour? As advocated by Indigo Perry, art and writing might "speak the Anthropocene" (251).

When teaching our CW MFA plenary course "Writers in the World," I began by asking students to consider their relationship to place, spurred by an exercise that Mississauga Nishnaabeg writer Leanne Betasamosake Simpson had brought to the MFA classroom during an earlier visit: what did students know about the land that they were on in Etobicoke (a name that derives from the Mississauga First Nation word used to describe the Etobicoke creek and environs, *Adobigok*, meaning 'where the alders grow') and its history, including geological history (Harris). What was the land like 20,000 years ago? 10,000? 1,000? 500? Students had difficulty placing themselves in deep time frames: 20,000 years ago, the land was under a kilometre of ice, which began to melt about 14,000 years ago as the Wisconsin glaciers retreated, leaving behind a subarctic, then boreal landscape where mammoth and mastodon roamed (Nickerson and Smith-Belghaba), and the first humans arrived around 12,000 years ago ("Toronto"). After these gestures towards situating ourselves spatially and temporally, we read Jeannette Armstrong's iconic essay "Land Speaking," in which Armstrong articulates how her Indigenous relationship to land enters her writing, and "Landsensing," a paper written in response to Armstrong by Métis writer Warren Cariou, who gave me permission to use a draft version in the classroom. Cariou identifies one of the fundamental brutalities suffered by Indigenous children in residential school as a form of "percepticide," the intentional destruction of the children's intimate, sensory relationship with the land, a term he takes from the work of Diana Taylor. Taylor uses percepticide to describe the "state-sponsored perceptual warfare" of Argentina's dirty war, in which people self-inflict a censorship of their senses in order not to take in the violence of disappearances publicly happening all around them (124).

Through additional readings and class discussion, the Guelph CW MFA students and I grappled with how to address our own complicated relationship to land or lands, including immigrant, settler and diasporic relationships, how to search for reciprocity by uncentring ourselves, how to develop a specific land vocabulary that is not taxonomy but grows from vital attention to specifics: flora, fauna, weather phenomena. As British nature writer Robert Macfarlane points out "to identify" is both to name and, if we say "identify with," to find empathetic connection with another ("April 15").

This course discussion in turn provided the context in which we turned to climate-specific readings: Rob Nixon's summary of his argument about the problems of making narrative out of climate and ecological shifts that until recently manifested as "slow violence" and thus were often resistant to storying (200); Amitav Ghosh's urgent call for literary writers to turn their attention to the climate crisis, as challenging a subject as it might seem. To ignore our existential condition becomes, to use the title of his influential book, a "great derangement."

In tandem, we read Ted Chiang's brief story, "The Great Silence," narrated by a parrot on the verge of their kind's extinction, calmly wondering why humans, while searching for alien intelligence in the universe, cannot see the alien intelligences, such as parrots, in their midst. In an excerpt from *Undrowned: Black Feminist Lessons from Marine Mammals*, Black queer writer Alexis Pauline Gumbs describes her self-identification as mammal alongside "as a Black woman ascending with and shaped by a whole group of people [who] were transubstantiated into property and kidnapped across an ocean" (5) and offers a "subversive and transformative" (7) guide, based on practices of "identifying with … [t]o see what happens when I rethink and re-feel my own relations, possibilities, and practices inspired by the relations, possibilities, and practices of advanced marine mammal life" (9). Neither text is obviously climate writing, yet each situates itself within the context of ecological threat and asks a reader to reframe their relationship with the world beyond the human, to engage with ardour and love in a new animism, in imaginative acts that bring non-human others into focus, inviting us into reciprocal relations and responsiveness that enlarge possibilities for both realism and imaginative world-building. In the MFA plenary course Writers on Writing, we read ecologist and phenomenological philosopher David Abram and Potawatomi writer/botanist Robin Wall Kimmerer to consider and debate how the construction of language itself—the abstractions of alphabet, the way we use the pronoun 'it' in English to refer to the nonhuman—can reinforce a structural un-animacy.

Over my many years teaching in the MFA, I saw shifts in the temperament of student cohorts; in the early years, many students, the cohorts themselves mostly but not entirely white, resisted or compartmentalized writing that they saw as 'political.' In more recent years, as the student body has become ever more diversified and inclusive of traditionally marginalized bodies and voices, the nature of student engagement has radically altered. Yet, 'environmental' writing is often still seen taxonomically as a genre that can be boundaried, rather than of collective concern, the so-called 'environment' including and entangling us at every moment. This boundaried attitude was one that I hoped at least to unsettle.

In late 2021, I was asked by a University of Guelph colleague, Emmanuelle Arnaud, a glaciologist in the School of Environmental Sciences, to create a module as part of an ECampus Ontario course, "Perspectives in Climate Change and Sustainability" funded by an ECampus Ontario grant awarded to a team of instructors from the universities of Guelph and McMaster. Combining modules from 12 instructors in different disciplines, the course would allow students to explore these issues from social, cultural, economic and scientific perspectives, and was designed to appeal to students from various disciplines while emphasizing the inherent interdisciplinarity of the subject matter. The interdisciplinary nature of the project spoke to me: when addressing the climate crisis in the classroom, getting outside of our academic siloes feels crucial—and structurally challenging. Beyond this disciplinary mobility, the climate crisis demands a multi-pronged response: both students and faculty need to be speaking to each other across disciplines.

For this rare course available to undergraduates at various Ontario universities in various degree programs, I conceived a unit that focused on climate storytelling, emphasizing how the stories we tell about the crisis shape not only our understanding but the nature of our response. For instance: corporations heavily invested in the fossil fuel industry prefer to promote stories that make climate response a matter of changing individual behaviour rather than requiring an industrial-scale decarbonization as part of an overhaul of business and economic systems. For example, the fossil fuel company BP intensively promoted the phrase "carbon footprint" to shift responsibility onto individuals in what *The Guardian* calls "a $100m-plus a year BP marketing campaign" (Supran and Oreskes). A narrative of energy transformation allows us to imagine a very different future than stories of climate collapse. I wanted students to be able to approach and understand storytelling as a social and cultural practice, a way of creating meaning and agency relevant across disciplines, from sciences and social sciences to humanities; I also wanted to engage them as storytellers in practices that might offer them personal engagement, even mental health benefits, noting the importance of using the imagination like a muscle that would atrophy if not worked out regularly.

Within the "Perspectives in Climate Change and Sustainability" online unit, I outlined two metaphoric scenarios, pointing out that analogy can be a useful way of allowing us to see a real-world problem newly. Since part of the problem of drawing attention to atmospheric greenhouse gas accumulation is its invisibility, I asked students to imagine a world in which carbon dioxide particles were red and, as human fossil fuel use intensifies, the sky grows a deeper red, intensifying towards scarlet. In a second scenario, anything made from plastic or any petroleum-based product, which plastics are, emits a low hum. Despite their convenience, plastics bring this downside, which seems small at first, only the hum keeps growing louder as plastic particulates penetrate the far corners of the planet's land and oceans, are ingested by the fish and animals that we eat, microplastics entering soil and water. Plastics, too, take hundreds of years to break down so that our descendants will hear this hum growing louder and louder. As an evaluative component, students were asked to develop a story using one scenario or the other: create a fictional character and decide what, faced with skies growing a darker red or an unstoppable hum, their character wants, what their character's desire makes them do, what obstacles they encounter, put them in motion and see what happens.

I linked students to a project I'd been developing through funding from the Guelph Institute of Environmental Research (GIER), an interdisciplinary research Collaboratory at the University of Guelph (University, "U of G Builds"). Within "Imagining Climates," an online GIER site devoted to the role of imagination in climate-crisis response which I co-lead, one subproject, "Micro-Climate Stories," features brief, 150-word pieces focused on a specific element of climate or ecological disruption written by scientists and creative writers to create a cross-disciplinary conversation (University, "Micro-Climate"). Each student had to write their own 150-word micro-climate story, responding to a personal experience of climate change; they were asked to focus their attention on specific details that engaged all their senses. The point wasn't to go dystopic but to notice keenly the world around them.

My climate storytelling module also emphasized the need to make space for wonder and awe; I asked why it's easier to imagine dystopic stories than utopic ones. In an interview about his recent novel, *The Ministry for the Future*, American speculative fiction writer Kim Stanley Robinson says: "the story of getting to a new and better social system, that's almost an empty niche in our mental ecology" (O'Keefe). Prompted by writer Rebecca Solnit, I queried why it's easier to imagine hero narratives than stories of people coming together collectively to solve problems, while noting how such writers as Waubgeshig Rice and Premee Mohamed do attempt to imagine communities responding to climate breakdown in their recent novels. All these questions offered students potential storytelling prompts. I cited a study out of the University of Colorado in Boulder, which paired students with comedians to create stand-up climate comedy, and whose organizers "found that 90 percent of students felt more hopeful about climate change when engaging with the subject in a fun or joyful manner, and that 83 percent felt that their commitment to climate change action was consequently more sustainable"

(Yeo). I noted that being able to access humour was a beneficial life skill in times of extremity or high stress—not humour that attacked others but the kind that lanced to the contradictions of a predicament.

Writing a comic climate monologue or scene, or creating one as a group exercise, was the module's final evaluative component. Throughout the module, I endeavoured, once again, to move students away from the generic climate disaster narrative, which seems so depressingly self-reinforcing. Comedy sticks to the skin in ways that dystopia doesn't. Because the module was created for online delivery, I've never had the opportunity to engage with the students who've taken the course or learn from their responses.

For the past two years, since 2022, I have been teaching in the University of Guelph's new and burgeoning undergraduate Creative Writing Major, introduced in the fall of 2022, approved with a thematic focus, our main program page notes, "on writing that explores issues of social justice and the environment" (University "Creative"). Currently, Carrianne Leung, Lawrence Hill and I are the three core Creative Writing faculty members teaching in the undergraduate program. Each of us seeds these thematic concerns into our overall pedagogy; the program also offers courses that address these foci directly, including "Fiction: Writing the Anthropocene," "Ecopoetics" and "Writing for the Inclusive Screen/Inclusive Stage." In this context, I've been responsible for developing two new courses, "Speculative Fiction" and "Creative Nonfiction: Writing Nature," both of which weave in climate content.

In the second-year workshop, "Speculative Fiction," we address the topic of climate fiction directly; like my graduate students, the undergraduates immediately identify climate fiction as a dystopic and post-apocalyptic genre, one that offers dire visions of how to survive after a global disaster has wracked life on the planet. They're lively in this discussion, angry and frustrated at the bleak narratives thrown at them culturally—and in their high school classrooms—that all is lost, we're headed for ruin, their generation will inherit a wrecked world, which makes them feel as if they might as well give up. Yes, our condition may be perilous, I say, but they don't need to tell themselves or others the nihilistic, all-is-lost story. Much of the corporate and industrial world may seem intransigent to necessary change—yet the use of renewable energy sources continues to rise, these days at astonishing speed (Thompson). That's another story. One of them offers up the story of technological responses—carbon capture, still experimental, not yet feasible on a large scale, potentially a tech hack for continuing to burn fossil fuels—yet we're already moving away from the disaster narrative.

I've framed our climate fiction discussion with a class in which we consider the speculative possibilities of entering the Umwelt of other creatures (nineteenth-century scientist Jakob von Uexküll's term for every living organism's unique perceptual interface with the world) (Schroer). After reading an excerpt from Barbara Gowdy's classic novel, *The White Bone*, which takes a reader deep into an imagined elephant culture and bodily experiences, we use the introduction to science journalist Ed Yong's *An Immense World*, a recent investigation into the extraordinary realms of creaturely sense perception, as a prompt to write our own way into a non-human consciousness. Yes, I say, for this exercise, it needs to be a creature living on this planet—not an alien. Yong himself urges his readers to do just this imaginatively (Yong, "Introduction"). We acknowledge what we cannot know, I say, but we're attempting an act of *unselfing*, to perceive a world that extends beyond us. I want our climate discussion to springboard from this place—not disaster but our embedded relationship with the rest of the biosphere.

In our next class, the one devoted specifically to climate fiction, we read the Canadian speculative fiction writer Thomas Wharton's essay, "Cat, Fox, Neutrino," in which he calls for stories that matter now, that confront wonder as well as dread, "place humans and their inwardly focused lives within something larger, a wider and wilder universe … stories that would take me further out of my own skin." Wharton decries the way that the rest of the living world has been banished to children's literature or non-realism and offers a series of suggestions for writers, including that we write as if "everything is alive"—the final line of Québécoise writer Christiane Vadnais's climate story collection *Fauna*, from which I offer the class an excerpt. I set Wharton's essay and suggestions alongside an essay by British YA climate fiction writer, Lauren James, founder of the international Climate Fiction Writers League, who argues that our climate narrative needs to focus on solutions and fiction should reflect that; James, originally a physicist, who writes science-driven stories, offers a series of tips for writers as well as pragmatic pointers on her own approach to writing climate fiction featuring younger protagonists who have agency and enact change. Students respond enthusiastically to the practicality of both essays and the tips offered, which provide them with ways to recentre their approach to climate issues and climate fiction. More than one declared Wharton's essay their favourite reading of the course, generating both excitement and new ways of engaging with the world. The stories they tell themselves matter, I say, in addition to the stories they write. Both essays provide useful prompts for class assignments.

In "Writing Nature," a second-year creative nonfiction workshop, I've pushed my pedagogy further by consistently taking my students outside the walls of the classroom. I did not see how I could teach a course called Writing Nature, in which I ask students to write in relation to the rest of the living world, without having students encounter it. Since the course's introduction, I've become aware of others engaged in similar activities. At the University of Toronto, writer Sharon English, who teaches a course called Writing the Territory, and scholar Andrea Most, who teaches environmental literature and whose pedagogy involves a strong experiential and community-engaged component—have each moved much of their teaching outdoors, a pandemic practice transformed into a teaching philosophy. For better or worse, my "Writing Nature" course has been scheduled in the winter semester, not ideal for outdoor Canadian learning but, as often in a university context, you work with what you've got, and, in its first year, we were able to take advantage of both outdoor and indoor settings, including the university's expansive Arboretum and a university teaching greenhouse (University, "Plant").

Again, my pedagogical focus in the CNF course "Writing Nature" invites students to expand their realm of sensory, embodied attention, to bring it beyond the human, then find ways to translate this into writing. Some students expressed initial reservations, fearing that they needed to bring scientific knowledge to the course; I affirmed that they did not, that the course is about encountering and responding to the world around them, about considering the porousness between themselves, their bodies and what we deem "nature"—a line of thinking that has particular resonance in the afterhaze of the COVID-19 pandemic. We discuss the climate crisis in the context of this relationship-building.

While most of the students in the workshop's first iteration were Creative Writing majors or minors, "Writing Nature" also drew students from other disciplines including the natural sciences: students brought a range of disciplinary and place-based knowledge to the class. We began the semester by situating ourselves in relation to the places where we live now, the places we come from, and by attempting to 'story' some of the objects around us, including our phones, imaginatively tracing all those who might have touched our phones in their creation, attempting to time-travel back to when their component parts originated as earth elements. In our second class, I told students to bundle up for a walk through the Arboretum, using the cues of an auditory piece accessible via their indispensable phones. *How to Draw a Tree*, created by sound artist Dawn Matheson, brings listeners into a practice of sensory noticing during a walk in the Arboretum. In the Bovey Greenhouse, where we spent two three-hour classes, we were welcomed by Rodger Tschanz, the technician who oversees the greenhouse and who introduced students to the plants that surrounded them (orchids, cacti, a fig tree with aerial roots). Inspired by a prompt from writer Robert Macfarlane, students were asked to create and share words for specific natural phenomena for which, as far as they knew, no actual word exists. In a unit focused on touch and the thematic issue of being and feeling in and out of touch, they were asked to touch the plants—gently, with permission—and write about how this changed their relationship to a specific plant. After reading an interview with biologist David Haskell (Vaughan-Lee) on the loss of sounds as an ecological threat and encountering an excerpt from soundscape ecologist Bernie Krause's *The Great Animal Orchestra*, I sent students outdoors to listen and note what they could hear of the world beyond the human (challenging on a university campus, even one with a broad, central green). These and other practices remind students of the reciprocity between what Shannon Sandford et al. mark in their article "Green Encounters: Critically Creative Inter/Actions with-and-in Ecologies of Crisis," as "writing the environment and the writing environment" (6). Afterwards, a couple of students said that the practice encouraged them to take out their earbuds more often as they walked.

Philosophy professor Stefan Lindquist, who has worked with octopuses, spoke to the class about octopus behaviour and theories of octopus intelligence, sharing videos of his own underwater encounters; another week, volunteers from Wild Ontario, an educational program based in the university's department of Integrative Biology, which rehabilitates injured raptors and uses those that cannot be re-released to the wild in its programming, brought some of the raptors (a red-tailed hawk, a saw whet owl, a merlin) into our classroom (University, "Wild"). In future course iterations, I hope to access the university's Hagen Aqualab, an aquatic research facility (University, "Aqualab"). In addition to specific prompts and assignments, including a flash memoir, a short, researched piece, students were asked to respond to these experiential encounters in their writers' notebooks. Course assignments culminated in a braided essay that had to weave together at least two strands (personal and research), a form that feels ecological in its very nature given the way it brings disparate elements into relationship.

In their end-of-the-semester self-reflections, some students commented on the mental-health benefits of the course, even as course reading material did not shy away from difficult subjects such as the global pervasiveness of plastic or ongoing ecological loss; one student noted that the braided essay form gave her a new way to conceptualize and articulate her racial justice concerns within a broader context. Despite the winter-into-early spring Canadian weather, students affirmed that they would have been happy to spend more time outdoors in the Arboretum, to which we returned at the end of the semester, after the snow had melted and the weather slowly warmed. There, while following the Mtigwaaki Trail, a series of signposts highlighting Indigenous knowledge created by Indigenous environmental science grad student Brad Howie (University, "U of G Graduate"), students asked questions about our land relations. Not only did these creative nonfiction students work with a series of sensory prompts that I provided, but, when asked to come up with their own prompts, the students set off once more in small groups into the early-spring woods where I found them lying on the ground, touching trees, scribbling in notebooks and staring at the sky. Finally, we came together under a grove of pine, attempting to feel our own mycelial threads reaching towards each other beneath the earth. I thought students might balk at this exercise, at being asked to raise their arms in the air like tree branches. But they didn't—any more than my MFA students did when, during the pandemic, we met outdoors in Toronto's High Park for movement sessions with choreographer Julia Aplin, who has a degree in Environmental Studies. Since we were unable to come close to each other, Aplin encouraged students to lean their bodies against the trunks of trees and balance fallen branches on their limbs, which they did with playful whimsy. In the Arboretum, each of the undergrads read aloud a sentence or two they had written, often with surprising linguistic details, creating, as I relayed to them, a small forest of words that summoned the sky and woods around us.

We were a long way in those moments from a narrative of climate dystopia—while never denying realities of climate breakdown. Within the Creative Writing classroom as outside of it, I don't want my intergenerational legacy to be one of hopeless nihilism. Instead, I hope to seed generative practices through which students can enmesh themselves in stories of biospheric connection and attention, reimagine a living world, conceptualize change and bring such practices to the task of reimagining a future for themselves and the world around them.

Works Cited

"April 15, 2022 Episode Transcript." *As It Happens: Canadian Broadcasting Corporation*. Canadian Broadcasting Corporation, 17 Apr. 2022, https://www.cbc.ca/radio/asithappens/april-15-2022-episode-transcript-1.6422360.

Armstrong, Jeannette C. "Land Speaking." *Speaking for the Generations: Native Writers on Writing*, edited by Simon J. Ortiz, U Arizona P, 1998, pp. 174–95. *JSTOR*, https://doi.org/10.2307/j.ctv27jsm69.11.

Cariou, Warren. "Landsensing: Body, Territory, Relation." *Land/Relations: Possibilities of Justice in Canadian Literatures*, edited by Smaro Kamboureli and Larissa Lai, Wilfred Laurier UP, pp. 307–20.

Carrington, Damian, [Environment Ed]. *The Guardian*, 5 Oct. 2023, https://www.theguardian.com/environment/2023/oct/05/gobsmackingly-bananas-scientists-stunned-by-planets-record-september-heat.

Chiang, Ted. "The Great Silence." *Exhalation: Stories*. Kindle ed. Vintage, 2019.

Ghosh, Amitav. *The Great Derangement*. U of Chicago P, 2016.

Gowdy, Barbara. *The White Bone*. HarperCollins, 1999.

Gumbs, Alexis Pauline. *Undrowned: Black Feminist Lessons from Marine Mammals*. Emergent Strategies Ser., AK Press, 2020.

Harris, Denise. "A Brief History of Etobicoke: From Township to Amalgamation." *Etobicoke Historical Society*, 2014–2023. https://www.etobicokehistorical.com/brief-history-of-etobicoke.html.

Howarth, William. "Some Principles of Ecocriticism." *The Ecocriticism Reader: Landmarks in Literary Ecology*, edited by Cheryll Glotfelty and Harold Fromm. U of Georgia P, 1996, pp. 69–91.

James, Lauren. "Can a Climate Fiction Novel Be Uplifting?" *Lauren James*, 27 Sept. 2021, https://laurenejames.co.uk/2021/09/27/positivity-in-the-apocalypse-can-a-climate-fiction-novel-be-uplifting/.

Lemenager, Stephanie. *Anthropocene Reading: Literary History in Geologic Times*, edited by Tobias Menely and Jesse Oak Taylor, Kindle ed., Penn State UP, 2017.

Matheson, Dawn. *How to Draw a Tree*. 2022. University of Guelph Arboretum. Culture Days. https://culturedays.ca/en/events/e0263939-da92-4c2d-ac2e-ae0c56348e5e.

Mohamed, Premee. *The Annual Migration of Clouds*. ECW Press, 2021.

Nickerson, Cara, and Aicha Smith-Belghaba. "Early Indigenous People Hunted Mammoth in Hamilton Area, 'Unprecedented' Study Suggests." *CBC News*, 22 Dec. 2022, https://www.cbc.ca/news/canada/hamilton/evidence-mammoth-butcher-in-ontario-1.6693736.

Nixon, Rob. *Slow Violence and the Environmentalism of the Poor*. Harvard UP, 2011.

O'Keefe, Derrick. "Imagining the End of Capitalism with Kim Stanley Robinson: An Interview with Kim Stanley Robinson." *Jacobin*, 22 Oct. 2020, https://jacobin.com/2020/10/kim-stanley-robinson-ministry-future-science-fiction.

Perry, Indigo. "Speaking the Anthropocene: Slow Writing in Collaborative Performance Art." *New Writing: The International Journal for the Practice and Theory of Creative Writing*, 28 Sept. 2018, pp. 251–62, https://doi.org/10.1080/14790726.2018.1520892.

Rice, Waubgeshig. *Moon of the Crusted Snow*. ECW Press, 2018.

Sanders, Scott. "Speaking a Word for Nature." *The Ecocriticism Reader: Landmarks in Literary Ecology*, edited by Cheryll Glotfelty and Harold Fromm. U of Georgia P, 1996, pp. 182–95.

Sandford, Shannon et al. "Green Encounters: Critically Creative Inter/Actions with-and-in Ecologies of Crisis." *New Writing: The International Journal for the Practice and Theory of Creative Writing*, vol. 21, no. 1, 11 Jul. 2023, https://doi.org/10.1080/14790726.2023.2223188.

Schroer, Sara Asu. "Jakob von Uexküll: The Concept of *Umwelt* and Its Potentials for an Anthropology Beyond the Human." *Ethnos*, vol. 86, no. 1, 2021, pp. 132–52, https://doi.org/10.1080/00141844.2019.1606841.

Solnit, Rebecca. "When the Hero is the Problem." *LitHub*, 2 Apr., 2019, https://lithub.com/rebecca-solnit-when-the-hero-is-the-problem/.

Supran, Geoffrey and Naomi Oreskes. "The Forgotten Oil Ads That Told Us Climate Change Was Nothing." *The Guardian*, 18 Nov. 2021, https://www.theguardian.com/environment/2021/nov/18/the-forgotten-oil-ads-that-told-us-climate-change-was-nothing.

Taylor, Diana. *Disappearing Acts: Spectacles of Gender and Nationalism in Argentina's "Dirty War."* Duke UP, 1997.

Thompson, Andrea. "Renewable Energy Is Charging Ahead." *Scientific American*, 21 Apr. 2023, Springer Nature America. https://www.scientificamerican.com/article/renewable-energy-is-charging-ahead/.

"Toronto." *The Canadian Encyclopedia*, Mar. 2022, https://www.thecanadianencyclopedia.ca/en/article/toronto.

University of Guelph. "Aqualab Facilities." *Department of Integrative Biology: University of Guelph*, n.d., https://www.uoguelph.ca/ib/infrastructure_and_facilities/aqualab/rooms.

University of Guelph. "Creative Writing." *College of Arts: University of Guelph*, n.d., https://www.uoguelph.ca/arts/sets/programs/cw.

University of Guelph. "Micro-Climate Stories." *Guelph Institute for Environmental Research: University of Guelph*, n.d., https://sites.uoguelph.ca/gier/micro-climate-stories/.

University of Guelph. "Plant Agriculture Growth Facilities." *Plant Agriculture: University of Guelph*, n.d., https://www.plant.uoguelph.ca/people-and-places/research-sites/plant-agriculture-growth-facilities.

University of Guelph. "U of G Builds On Environmental Expertise with New Institute." *News Release: University of Guelph*, 23 Oct. 2019, https://news.uoguelph.ca/2019/10/u-of-g-builds-on-environmental-expertise-with-new-institute/.

University of Guelph. "U of G Graduate Student Shares Anishinaabe Forest Knowledge." *News: University of Guelph*, 1 Nov. 2021, https://news.uoguelph.ca/2021/09/u-of-g-graduate-student-shares-anishinaabe-forest-knowledge/.

University of Guelph. "Wild Ontario." *College of Biological Science: University of Guelph*, 2023, https://wildontario.ca.

Vadnais, Christiane. *Fauna*. Translated by Pablo Strauss, Coach House, 2020.

Vaughan-Lee, Emmanuel. "Listening and the Crisis of Inattention: An Interview with David G. Haskell." *Emergence Magazine*, 21 Apr. 2022, https://emergencemagazine.org/interview/listening-and-the-crisis-of-inattention/.

Wharton, Thomas. "Cat, Fox Neutrino." *Hazlitt Magazine*, 26 Jul. 2023, Penguin Random House. https://hazlitt.net/longreads/cat-fox-neutrino.

Yeo, Sophie. "Jokes Are a Surprisingly Effective Way To Talk about Climate Change." *Changing America*, 29 Jan. 2020, https://thehill.com/changing-america/sustainability/climate-change/480364-the-most-effective-jokes-on-climate-change/.

Yong, Ed. *Introduction. An Immense World*. Knopf Canada, 2022.

Recurrent Student Writing Comments from Catherine Bush

Can you create more polarity, more push-pull energy, from positive state (or desire) to negative state (or desire)—or the reverse? This will create movement and ultimately more energy in your story.

Go deeper into your chosen point-of-view. How does your specific character perceive the world? How does their mood, state of mind, background, predicament, desire, shape what they notice about the world? Be specific in your noticings. Choose key details. Use all your senses.

Start us in scene not summary. Ask yourself: Do we have what we need to orient ourselves in this world? Are we clearly rooted in POV, know where we are, when? How are we in motion from the get-go? How soon do we encounter a character's desire?

16 Shaggy Dog Queer Comedies, Handshake Deals and Speaking Back to Power

An Interview with Multi-Genre, LBGTIQA+ Writer Prof. Natalie Meisner

Natalie Meisner and Darryl Whetter

DARRYL WHETTER: I'd like to ask a couple of questions about genre, ideally queerness and genre (though not yet, unless you're interested, genres *of* queerness).

NATALIE MEISNER: Fascinating! This could be a topic of a book or an article for another time, but to dive in briefly: While examples of what we term "queer lit" might have nothing in common in terms of style or form, they have historically been grouped together by content. The content of queer lives often having a degree of struggle has meant that the literature can lean into tragedy and be under-represented in comedy. Works of literature that articulate queer joy and open the door to laughter are under-represented, yet can do a great deal of good in the world.

DW: Genre also has me wondering about an origin-story question. Between my spending 20 years of summers in the rural Nova Scotia fishing village of Advocate Harbour—in a house, by the way, that was once owned by Canadian actor Meagan Follows, in the village where Sam Shepard sat out the US draft and one named after the first credited playwright in North America, lawyer or, *en français, 'avocat,'* Marc Lescarbot—and my teaching at Université Sainte-Anne in another rural Nova Scotia fishing village, I've spent plenty of time this century in rural coastal Nova Scotia. While one of 'my' municipal government buildings now flies the pride flag in June, am I right in thinking that your 80sish tweenhood or adolescence in a rural NS fishing village occurred before essentially a Canadian paradigm shift in queer acceptance? Or perhaps that phrase should be "queer safety."

DOI: 10.4324/9781032614144-20

NM: From where I sit now, several decades into a dual career as a writer and professor of writing, I can see that being an LBGTIQA+/gender-diverse person is a boon, but it wasn't always so. As a rural working-class person, a first-generation university attendee, a member of two mom bi-racial and bi-national family, I've learned to speak from the margins, to re-hearse history and to question the canon. Things that felt like barriers to entry for any kind of writing life have made me a more flexible and versatile mentor to the diverse group of students and writers that I work with, but stepping out of the closet was never without risk. In the East Coast fishing town that I grew up in, it was decidedly unsafe to be out. Homosexuality, while no longer criminalized, was pathologized, stigmatized and an open invitation to violence. The burgeoning exploration of identities that our communities now enjoy were still unheard of then. Marriage equality, the right to adopt and the formal apology by the Canadian Government to those who were "purged" from the civil service, RCMP and Canadian Armed Forces for being gay were far in the future (Harris).

DW: While, as we'll get to, you're now a multi-genre writer of plays, memoirs, poetry and children's books, you began, I believe, as a playwright. Back in another paradigm shift we didn't see coming, of life before the Web—to what degree was the theatre a queer haven for you, and an urban one, growing up where and when you did?

NM: Yes, indeed, when I went to "the city" (as Nova Scotians call Halifax) to study literature and journalism, I was immediately drawn to theatre. We had very basic schooling where I grew up, so not a lot of arts and culture, but I somehow had a sense that theatre artists were open-minded about gender and sexuality. I was not wrong. I saw a poster for the King's Theatrical Society's upcoming production of Jean Paul Sartre's *No Exit* and auditioned. The team liked the monologue I'd prepared and wanted to cast me in the role of Inez, the lesbian. As I headed for the door, they mentioned in an offhand way that the role would require me to kiss another woman on stage. "That wouldn't bother you, would it?" asked one of the team. And I thought: "*Bother me?* I didn't even think this was a possibility in real life, let alone in the theatre." This casual comment did more than they ever knew in terms of allowing me to come out and to find my footing as an artist and a gay person. I built community and friendships and came out to family and friends and colleagues. While I figuratively lost some bio family who could not accept me as an out LGBTIQA+ person, I gained a network of chosen family in theatre who continue to be a key part of my pod ever since. Gender and sexuality on the stage, while often recuperated to cis/white/het norms by curtain time, is still a matter for rehearsal and play. No surprise then, that theatre has remained central for me and that my Creative Writing pedagogy continues to be informed by liveness/theatre and improvisation techniques.

DW: To address those early years of secrecy and danger one more time, what lessons or attitudes do you feel those experiences make you want to impart to your writing students today—not all of whom, we have to recognize, are necessarily going to become professional or even lifelong writers: I always like to remind everyone that a Creative Writing education is also a great education, not just or exclusively preparation for a writing life.

NM: I feel that being able to be an out and proud professor, and a member of a two-mom, bi-racial, and immigrant family has been a benefit to the students who might be finding their own footing as differently gendered or LGBTIQA+. I also think having someone with big visible "differences" facilitating the workshop and teaching the class makes sharing space, questioning the canon and having difficult conversations a kind of given. First- or second-generation immigrants, neuro-diverse students, Indigenous students, first-gen university students, queer students and others with differences receive the message that our voices matter, and that's the first step to writing bravely. You are right that Creative Writing can be professionalizing, but it's not always about teaching students how to write work to publish. It is also a workshop for some of the most human and irreplaceable live communication skills that I think students will need in the future; everyone deserves this learning.

DW: I think I recall you having studied at Canada's National Theatre School, as an actor, and when you Skyped into my master's playwriting class in Singapore you spoke of the contrast between the queer lives of your fellow actors and theatre folk offstage versus the predominantly ingénue roles you were offered as a young female actor. To what degree was your becoming a playwright a version of Toni Morrison's advice about writing to create the books or stories you weren't finding? I should let readers know that one of your latest plays, *Legislating Love*—written and produced maybe 20 years after your bright-lights-big-city move to acting/the stage—tells the story of Everett Klippert, the last Canadian jailed for homosexuality. If the Canadian theatre world you'd met around 1995 had more queer stories, would you still have become a playwright?

NM: Great question. I loved the bare-knuckle challenge of memorizing and embodying ninety pages of text, of going on stage with my compatriots and helping to carry a show. As an actor, you get to love text and take risks with texts in a way that perhaps no one else does. My leap to writing was likely due to the lack of complex queer and gender-diverse characters available, in tandem with the pressure to be "universal" in acting training (which was strongly coded to conventional femininity) at NTS at that time. I remember being told that I read as "frigid" on stage by a much-lauded star visiting director/acting coach which, as far as I could tell, meant that I did not code as hot/submissive to him.

A very troubling way to speak to developing actors, this, and it thankfully would not pass now, but it was totally normal at the time. This casual violence might have been some of what lit a fire under my ass to write a more diverse range of characters who spoke back to power, but I think that I also love text so much that I might have found my way to writing, it just might have taken a bit longer.

DW: Back to genre again. Around 2018, you were a perfect online guest writer for my Singaporean grad students when they had just transitioned from one semester writing creative nonfiction to a new one writing scripts for stage then screen. You told the *very* personal story of you and your wife trying to not just get pregnant as lesbians but also to get pregnant without the anonymity of a sperm bank. You've written that story both in the play *Speed Dating for Sperm Donors* and also in the memoir *Double Pregnant: Two Lesbians Make a Family*. More recently, you're currently the Poet Laureate of Calgary. Big, open question on Natalie Meisner and genre. What makes Genre X right, for you, for Story Y?

NM: I often encourage students to try an idea in more than one format. An idea and/or life experience that is yours can be realized as a poem, a story, a piece of creative nonfiction, or a play, provided you have the skills in your repertoire to realize it. What matters to me is the handshake deal that you have with the audience or reader. If you commit to creative nonfiction, as I did in *Double Pregnant*, I believe you must strive for the highest possible degree of fidelity and honesty to events as they transpired. This in and of itself is a risky endeavour given the vagaries of the self and the fact that humans are so rarely fully transparent to ourselves. If we write something "inspired" by or with characters based on people like ourselves, readers understand that that leaps of invention have been taken. In the play version, *Speed Dating for Sperm Donors*, I really wanted to up the ante in terms of the comedy and challenge myself to write a big, warm, fuzzy, shaggy dog of a queer comedy, as I felt this to be an underrepresented mode for LBGTIQA+ art. In order to do this, I needed to take some distance from my family's "real" story, which had many more elements of heartbreak and bumps in the road that just would not fit into a 90-minute comedy.

DW: And of course you told our class how you'd spent some version of a year writing a memoir you wouldn't publish if your wife found it too revealing.

NM: I am not sure if it is about being too revealing; the book takes the reader as close as I can into my telling of our lives as we asked near strangers for the most intimate kind of favour. Creative nonfiction, in my view, *is about the reveal*, but what I wanted to be sure of is that what I had written did not infringe on her version, on our future maybe babies' stories. This is done by puncturing the myth of objectivity. My version is only my version, but it is interlocking with those stories of my loved ones. Even those who are not writers have their own stories, and I am not about to trample those. So, I tried to make the book as revealing as possible of my view of our journey, but I would have left it forever in a bureau drawer if she'd read the draft and not given it her blessing. I gave her the draft to read and then went to the next room. The moment I heard her laughing out loud was when I first thought it would be okay to publish and could even do some good in the world. In this way, I do subscribe to some writer's version of the Hippocratic oath: "first, do no harm." Unless of course what you are writing is telling a hard truth and/or aimed at an oppressor or oppressive power structure, then I concur with the wonderful Anne Lamott, who writes in *Almost Everything:* "You own everything that happened to you. If people wanted you to write warmly about them, they should have behaved better" (92).

DW: Follow-up: working in all these different genres, what skills and/or lessons for her students does Professor Meisner the multi-genre writer have now that a younger Natalie Meisner didn't have? What teaching superpowers has your multi-genre writing given you?

NM: As a queer writer, I have had to develop what some folx would call a thick skin, but what to me is more an acknowledgement that taste is a huge part of any given selection process. I send the message to developing writers that we must make our writing exquisitely crafted, relevant and suited to the intended audiences/markets for which we make it. However, that exquisitely crafted work may still be rejected due to the tastes of an editor, a panel or artistic director. This is often discussed as the gatekeeper effect and of course unconscious bias and overt racism/sexism/homophobia play a part in this, and those structures must be dismantled. It is also valuable to find ways to take your work directly to audiences at the same time by reading at open mics, making zines, staging your own shows. I recommend doing both to make a life in the arts. My super power is keeping lots of lines on the water and encouraging my students to do the same. Find ways to move your craft forward by reaching out to audiences in both conventional and self-starting ways. I can now find great titles for other people's work and help them find the heart of it. Somehow, the most compelling line of a given work seems to reach out to me and "ring in the air" just like a line of great dialogue.

DW: Now, finally, Calgary. To non-Canadians, I should spell that out as *Calgary, the financial epicentre of our planet-scorching tar-sands industry*. I'm still touched that you and I swapped in-progress manuscripts with your play *Boom Baby* and my tar-sands novel *Our Sands*. While now, with Kate Beaton's deservedly celebrated graphic memoir

Ducks: Two Years in the Oil Sands, CanLit finally has some tar-sands stories, I think it almost collusive that landscape-obsessed CanLit went so long without stories in what is, for better or worse, such a defining Canadian landscape.

Calgary, like the Nova Scotia where you were born, goes through similar boom-and-bust cycles, presumably with deep public subsidies as well, comparable to what we all see in our truly mad national tar-sands industry where, for example, nearly 2.5 barrels of natural gas are burnt to liquify one barrel of oil (oil that actually begins as a solid, not a liquid). How was writing *Boom Baby* different from some of your more recent history-sleuthing plays like *Legislating Love* and—it's up next—*Area 33?* What was it like to finally write about Canada's tar sands, our Mordor?

NM: When I first came here, I was floored by the scope and scale of the environmental impact of the tar sands/oil sands (even in that slash, worlds abide). Growing up, as I did, in a resource economy, I could not really point fingers at workers who derived a living in mining or fishing; they were my family and resource extraction did, although I know this rhetoric can be abused, "put food on the table" literally. The systems and power structures that kept my Maritime family working for minimum wage in a subsistence fishery while large corporations destroyed the environment and made off with the profits were not unrelated to the ones making it unsafe for me to colour outside the lines, but I couldn't make all those links then; in fact, it's taken half a lifetime to do so, and the result is *Boom Baby*. This play links our problematic use of the land to the problematic use of a woman's reproductive capability in a monetized surrogacy situation. When I first got the idea for the play, some ten years ago, it came as an image: the green/blue arteries and tributaries of the Athabasca River, the watershed for the continent. Then came the picture of a pre-born child floating in the peaceful world of the womb. The river was the umbilical cord, all the rivers and streams the placenta. The images flickered, then became one. I tried it first as a poem, but gradually the characters (based in part on family, friends and loved ones) announced themselves and demanded to be voiced. As we mentioned, I grew up in a fishing town in Southwest Nova Scotia/the Mi'kma'ki, where in the space of two generations, small-scale sustainable single boat fishers have been displaced by huge ocean draggers that tear up the sea bottom. We lost family to the sea as they ventured ever offshore to make a living. My grandfather and uncles were long-liner fisherman lost in the great storm of 1966 aboard the *Polly* and *Robbie*. Much more recently, my cousin was one of the young men lost on the *Miss Ally* in 2013.

Many of us Maritimers went overland west or north in search of a living. As one of those economic refugees, I began to ask myself hard questions about extractive industries. Fish. Oil. How they connect through water. When I wrote the first notes for what became the play *Boom Baby*, I hadn't had children of my own yet. Now that I do brings the question of what we leave to the future even closer to home. The hard edges of this play, I hope, are balanced by warmth, laughter and human connection and in that I take my cue from my family and friends, many of whom work in these demanding environments and who have inspired this play.

DW: In what might seem like different terrain, I also hope to get you talking about your documentary and/or archival work on stage. Everyone with a streaming TV knows how often documentary stories are told with a camera; with your *Legislating Love* uncovering the very real story of Everett Klippert's decade-long incarceration for homosexuality and *A Child Like Me*, your play about African-Canadian sprinter Marjorie Turner Bailey, once the fastest woman in the world, some of your plays have documentary and/or archival impulses as well. What can you say about your shining a light like this? Was the documentary impulse a later-career maturation for you? Now that I am, in a word I rarely admit to, clearly middle-aged, I'm suddenly writing more creative nonfiction than fiction. Did so-called "real" stories become similarly more compelling to you as you and/or your career matured or have you always been interested in what *Creative Nonfiction* magazine defines as "True stories, well told"?

NM: Working with the real is both exciting and terrifying. I think I have always felt that the raw material of my own life and that of other queer folx, racialized folx and those outside the mainstream, deserved telling. But culture tells you that your stories are not worthy. It has been a journey in a way of bringing the story of others to light that has helped me find the courage to share my own. Being gifted, by his family, with the opportunity to be the first creative team to read the diaries and letters of Mr. Klippert during the time he was incarcerated was an amazing and heart-opening opportunity. I tried to balance the weight of this gift and the impulse to valourize. I considered Derrida's notions of archive fever and tried to build into the structure of the play structures for interrogating big-T truth. In the play, we meet a historian who is grappling with queer history. Maxine stages for us and exposes the apparatus of history making, striving to be truthful or at least operating in a place of fidelity to the facts as we know them, while admitting the gaps and silences in the queer archive. The result was a play that Stephen Hunt, of *The Globe and Mail* called "a new brand of historical drama" and this kind of balance of writing with fidelity and admitting what I don't know has been a guiding light since then.

DW: On a teaching note, are our students, who are usually some version of 20-years-old, interested in and/or ready for writing that is archivally informed (as with your access to Everett Klippert's letters) or unearthing repressed history? Crosstown playwright Clem Martini, at the University of Calgary, is rare here in this book for also teaching playwrights and encouraging them to write from observed dialogue. If you do teach any documentary gestures, do you think playwriting is more welcoming to documentary work than, say, undergraduate assignments in poetry or fiction?

NM: Yes, I think students in this age are very interested in "true stories, well told." They are also deeply sceptical (with good reason) of the authoritative version or what Walter Benjamin calls monumental history. It just hasn't served them and they know it. For this reason, theatre is the perfect polyvocal format to touch the real without tipping the balance towards any one character, or any one person's version of events that transpired. Poetry, I think, is open to this too, to a certain degree. It often occurs to me that the "I" of the poet and the "I" of the playwright are both provisional, open about their constructed nature and constantly under question. Likely the reason why these two genres feel like "home" to me more than the novel or fiction.

DW: How, if at all, has your teaching of Creative Writing changed over your, what is it, 20 years? You mention "neurodiverse" above, a word and, probably (maybe?), teaching condition none of us would have mentioned 20 years ago in what we almost certainly would have thought was the enlightened beginning of a new century. Have you been doing more of A and less of B over your decades in the CW workshop?

NM: I had no aspirations of teaching as a young writer. Coming as I did from a rural/working class background, I was drawn to any flow of innovation, ideas and culture that would feed and enrich my practice, so the university was a natural home. When I was offered my first class to teach, I wasn't much older than my students and so I strove to make each class a temporary community of practice, as rich and challenging as it could be for everyone there. I don't think much has changed, other than I have been able to add to my facilitation skills, knowledge base and skill set. Some of the terms have changed for sure, and it behoves us to shift our lexicon when they do, but from the first moment I got my foot in the door at the uni, I have been working to democratize writing and shake up the canon.

DW: What's the burning Natalie-Meisner question that Natalie Meisner has not yet been asked in a theatre talk, panel discussion or at a literary festival?

NM: The burning question I always want to be asked is "Why live?" Why live theatre, or the reading and performance of live poetry? Why is live performance the benchmark or kind of true test, for me, of when a piece of writing truly works?

The answer is that there is some other kind of creative "gear" that I can shift into when I know that a piece is about to be lifted from page to stage. It has to do, I think, with theatre's roots in the formation of social ties and the mitigation of the social contract. It is in live public gatherings that we get along in the most civil and honest fashion. The solutions to a lot of the very real problems facing us at the moment are going to require social solutions, and yet our ability to convene and share intellectual life is what is the most under threat right now. Finally, there is an element of live theatre and performance that has always been connected to the sacred. In a sense when I offer my writing, or am given the gift of others' writing in a live setting … it holds an element of non-denominational worship: of nature, of my fellow humans, for the writing itself.

Works Cited

Beaton, Kate. *Ducks: Two Years in the Oil Sands*. Drawn & Quarterly, 2022.

Harris, Kathleen. "'Our Collective Shame': Trudeau Delivers Historic Apology to LGBT Canadians." *CBC News*, 28 Nov. 2017, *Canadian Broadcasting Corporation*, https://www.cbc.ca/news/politics/homosexual-offences-exunge-records-1.4422546.

Hunt, Stephen. "Review: *Legislating Love* Reveals a New Brand of Historical Drama." *The Globe and Mail*, 23 Mar. 2018, https://www.theglobeandmail.com/arts/theatre-and-performance/reviews/article-review-legislating-love-reveals-a-new-brand-of-historical-drama/.

Lamott, Anne. *Almost Everything: Notes on Hope*. Riverhead, 2018.

Meisner, Natalie. *Baddie One Shoe: Poems*. Frontenac, 2023.

———. *Double Pregnant: Two Lesbians Make a Family*. Fernwood, 2014.

———. *Growing Up Salty (and Other Plays)*. Fernwood, 1997.

———. *It Begins in Salt*. Frontenac House, 2019.

———. *Legislating Love: The Everett Klippert Story*. U Calgary P, 2019.

———. *My Mommy, My Mama, My Brother, and Me: These Are the Things We Found by the Sea*. Nimbus, 2019.

———. *Speed Dating for Sperm Donors*. Playwrights Canada Press, 2020.

Whetter, Darryl. *Our Sands: A Novel*. Penguin Random House, 2020.

Prof. Meisner's Recurrent Comments on Student Writing

I find myself often asking students (both undergrads and also the group of Immigrant Seniors that I also work with): "Have you taken the hand of the reader?"

By this, I do not mean take their hand and lead them safely through. Rather, grasp it in the most exciting handshake deal you can make. This is likely owed to my artistic sensibilities that formed in theatre. In the first moments, as the audience sits in the dark and as the lights fade up (or the reader's eyes light upon the page), you have them unconditionally. They have come to you, especially in poetry and live theatre, for an uncommon experience. They want to be taken by the lapels: surprised and delighted, shocked and awed by the power of language. In these delicious few seconds, they are *with* you, they are rooting for you. It is a crime against literature to waste this. I tell my students to make the best, most honest and interesting bargain or proposal they can with their readers, in these moments. It might not always be comfortable for them or for you, but the rest of the piece is about making good the best way you know how.

Index

Note: **Bold** page numbers refer to tables.

Printed in the United States
by Baker & Taylor Publisher Services